ActionScript Developer's Guide to
PureMVC

Cliff Hall

O'REILLY®

Beijing · Cambridge · Farnham · Köln · Sebastopol · Tokyo

ActionScript Developer's Guide to PureMVC

by Cliff Hall

Published by O'Reilly Media, Inc., 1005 Gravenstein Highway North, Sebastopol, CA 95472.

O'Reilly books may be purchased for educational, business, or sales promotional use. Online editions are also available for most titles (*http://my.safaribooksonline.com*). For more information, contact our corporate/institutional sales department: (800) 998-9938 or *corporate@oreilly.com*.

Editors: Mike Hendrickson and Mary Treseler
Production Editor: Melanie Yarbrough

Cover Designer: Karen Montgomery
Interior Designer: David Futato
Illustrator: Robert Romano

Revision History for the First Edition:
    2011-12-19   First release
See *http://oreilly.com/catalog/errata.csp?isbn=9781449314569* for release details.

ISBN: 978-1-449-31456-9

[LSI]

1323727581

Adobe
Developer
Library

Adobe Developer Library, a copublishing partnership between O'Reilly Media Inc., and Adobe Systems, Inc., is the authoritative resource for developers using Adobe technologies. These comprehensive resources offer learning solutions to help developers create cutting-edge interactive web applications that can reach virtually anyone on any platform.

With top-quality books and innovative online resources covering the latest tools for rich-Internet application development, the *Adobe Developer Library* delivers expert training straight from the source. Topics include ActionScript, Adobe Flex®, Adobe Flash®, and Adobe Acrobat®.

Get the latest news about books, online resources, and more at *http://adobedeveloper library.com*.

This book is dedicated to my wife Helen, whose patience, love, and support enabled every keystroke.

Table of Contents

Preface

Code at the Speed of Thought

Too often in the development of a large application, the developer must stop and think about where to find some class he needs, where some new class should go, and how to wire them up in such a way that gets data from wherever it lives to a display so the user can interact with it or vice-versa.

Regardless of the high level complexities in your application, you will never truly be doing anything more involved at the lower levels than moving data from point A to point B and occasionally doing some calculations on it. You should not have to keep inventing ways to do it; instead, your energy should be focused on the requirements of your current use case.

PureMVC is a simple framework that helps reduce the amount of time spent thinking about these low level issues by providing solutions for organizing your code and an expression of the well known Model-View-Controller concept based on several time proven design patterns.

Not only can it help a lone developer get her work done faster, but a team that is all on the same page about where things go and how they talk to each other within the application can move fluidly as they implement use cases in parallel. This is actually possible without creating the spaghetti code that often occurs during the heat of development. And since PureMVC is a mature, feature-frozen framework, legacy code written this way becomes much easier to maintain since the organization and implementation principles remain as valid as when the code was originally written.

The Purpose of This Book

As the author of the framework, I have had the good fortune to remain engaged more or less constantly from the time it came out, applying it to one challenging project after another. I have also had the pleasure of talking with a great many other developers around the world who have shared gems of wisdom or worked through their problems with me. I want to try and convey the most important bits, of course, but in a holistic manner and within the context of a non-trivial application.

There is a wealth of discussion about the details of development on the PureMVC website as well as documentation, demos, and utilities. There are plenty of community blog posts about building small demo apps, but up until now, nothing has taken a developer through the process of building a non-trivial PureMVC application, giving a sense of how all the pieces need to fit together and in what order to approach building them. From rough conceptualization of an application to the finished product and all the steps in between, you will gain the insight to know which responsibilities need to be handled by framework actors and, just as importantly, which do not.

 Engineering an application that exposes every problem you might run into is impossible, but still we will touch on all the moving parts of the framework. The code for the application (StoryArchitect) we will begin building in the book is packaged within com.futurescale.sa package. Where it is necessary to demonstrate something in code that is not present in the application that is the focus of the book, the text preceding the code will set forth a hypothetical situation, and the example code will be packaged within com.mycompany.myapp package.

Who Should Read This Book

ActionScript developers who are interested in, or are already working with, PureMVC will gain usable insights, although Adobe Flex and AIR developers will be best served, as the example application is written with AIR.

You should already have some experience with Adobe's ActionScript, Flex, and AIR, Object Oriented Programming (classes, interfaces, inheritance), and your IDE of choice. To fully understand the Value Objects and View Components of the application we will build, you should know at least a little about ActionScript's implicit accessors (getters/setters), XML handling, Flash's event bubbling, and Flex data binding.

Also, while this book speaks directly to an ActionScript/Flex/AIR audience, developers who are using or learning any of the PureMVC ports to other programming languages could certainly use this book as a basis for understanding the framework classes and how they should be used. The Flex and AIR specific sections are when we build View Components, talk to the filesystem or services, and handle XML. But the PureMVC framework roles, responsibilities, and collaborations are universal to all ports, and clarifying them is the real focus of this book. The platform and language are incidental.

Acknowledgements

At O'Reilly, I'd like to thank Dan Fauxsmith, Sarah Hake, Mike Hendrickson, Rachel James, Sarah Kim, Sarah Schneider, Karen Shaner, Mary Treseler, and Melanie Yarbrough, for excelling in their roles and making this book possible. For a developer who has been well-guided by O'Reilly books for years, it is an honor to be published by the best of the best!

PureMVC Contributors

The PureMVC project could never have made it without the community. It would be impossible to list them all here, but I would like to give a heartfelt personal thanks to the following folks who have lent a hand in one way or another:

Ahmed Nuaman, Ali Mills, Andy Adamczak, Andy Bulka, Anthony Quinault, Brendan Lee, Brian Knorr, Bruce Phillips, Chandima Cumaranatunge, Chris Pyle, Dan Pedersen, Daniel Garay, Daniel Swid, Daniele Ugoletti, Dave Keen, David Deraedt, David Foley, David Knape, Denis Sheremetov, Denis Volokh, Dmitry Kochetov, Don Stinchfield, Dragos Dascalita, Duncan Hall, Eric La Rocca, Frederic Saunier, Frederic Sullet, Gary Paluk, Greg Jastrab, Hasan Otuome, Jake Dempsey, James Knight, Jari Kemppinen, Jason MacDonald, Javier Julio, Jens Krause, Jhonghee Park, Jim Bachalo, Jim Robson, Jody Hall, Joshua Gottdenker, Justin Wilaby, Luke Bayes, Marcel Overdijk, Marco Secchi, Mark Bathie, Mark Geller, Matt Brailsford, Matthieu Mauny, Michael Oddis, Michael Ramirez, Milos Zikic, Nate Rock, Nathan Levesque, Neil Manuell, Nick Collins, Nicola Bortignon, Omar Gonzalez, Ondina D. F., Paddy Keane, Patrick Lemiuex, Pedr Browne, Philip Sexton, Phuong Tang, Richard Germuska, Roman Pavlenko, Rostislav Siryk, Samuel Asher Rivello, Sasa Tarbuk, Sean Carnell, Simon Bailey, Stefan Richter, Steve Hueners, Thomas Schuessler, Tim Will, Toby de Havilland, Tony DeFusco, Yee Peng Chia, Zhang Ze Yuan, Zhong Xiao Chuan, and Zjnue Brzavi.

Enneagram Personality System

Conventions Used in This Book

The following typographical conventions are used in this book:

Italic
> Indicates new terms, URLs, email addresses, filenames, and file extensions.

`Constant width`
> Used for program listings, as well as within paragraphs to refer to program elements such as variable or function names, databases, data types, environment variables, statements, and keywords.

`Constant width bold`
> Shows commands or other text that should be typed literally by the user.

Constant width italic

> Shows text that should be replaced with user-supplied values or by values determined by context.

This icon signifies a tip, suggestion, or general note.

This icon indicates a warning or caution.

Using Code Examples

This book is here to help you get your job done. In general, you may use the code in this book in your programs and documentation. You do not need to contact us for permission unless you're reproducing a significant portion of the code. For example, writing a program that uses several chunks of code from this book does not require permission. Selling or distributing a CD-ROM of examples from O'Reilly books does require permission. Answering a question by citing this book and quoting example code does not require permission. Incorporating a significant amount of example code from this book into your product's documentation does require permission.

We appreciate, but do not require, attribution. An attribution usually includes the title, author, publisher, and ISBN. For example: "*ActionScript Developer's Guide to PureMVC* by Cliff Hall (O'Reilly). Copyright 2012 Futurescale, Inc., 978-1-449-31456-9."

If you feel your use of code examples falls outside fair use or the permission given above, feel free to contact us at *permissions@oreilly.com*.

Safari® Books Online

 Safari Books Online is an on-demand digital library that lets you easily search over 7,500 technology and creative reference books and videos to find the answers you need quickly.

With a subscription, you can read any page and watch any video from our library online. Read books on your cell phone and mobile devices. Access new titles before they are available for print, and get exclusive access to manuscripts in development and post feedback for the authors. Copy and paste code samples, organize your favorites, download chapters, bookmark key sections, create notes, print out pages, and benefit from tons of other time-saving features.

O'Reilly Media has uploaded this book to the Safari Books Online service. To have full digital access to this book and others on similar topics from O'Reilly and other publishers, sign up for free at *http://my.safaribooksonline.com*.

How to Contact Us

Please address comments and questions concerning this book to the publisher:

O'Reilly Media, Inc.
1005 Gravenstein Highway North
Sebastopol, CA 95472
800-998-9938 (in the United States or Canada)
707-829-0515 (international or local)
707-829-0104 (fax)

We have a web page for this book, where we list errata, examples, and any additional information. You can access this page at:

http://www.oreilly.com/catalog/9781449314569

To comment or ask technical questions about this book, send email to:

bookquestions@oreilly.com

For more information about our books, courses, conferences, and news, see our website at *http://www.oreilly.com*.

Find us on Facebook: *http://facebook.com/oreilly*

Follow us on Twitter: *http://twitter.com/oreillymedia*

Watch us on YouTube: *http://www.youtube.com/oreillymedia*

CHAPTER 1

Introduction

As a software developer, you are charged not only with the task of creating applications, but also with battling complexity. In almost every case, the programs you write must also be maintainable; requests for new features, bug fixes, and enhancements should be easily accommodated. And in today's fast-paced business environment, there is a common imperative to release software early and often, so there is little time to fully design a system before the development begins. Rapid shifts in technology are driving the need to support or migrate to new hardware platforms; desktop, web, tablet, and mobile versions of an app—all with different form factors, use cases, and user interfaces —are quickly becoming standard requirements.

With all of these pressures, how are developers and teams supposed to consistently meet deadlines while delivering robust, maintainable code? Design patterns have long been seen as a way of solving specific problems within an application. However, overall application architecture, even when composed of known patterns, can suffer and become unmaintainable if not well planned. This is the problem that the Model-View-Controller (MVC) concept (see Figure 1-1), and specifically PureMVC, is meant to address.

Classic MVC Architecture

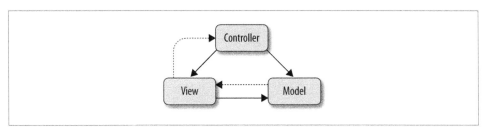

Figure 1-1. MVC Diagram: dashed lines indicate notification, solid lines are direct associations

This book is no place for a history lesson; suffice it to say that when MVC was first conceived in the 1970s, the world was a far simpler place. What computers could do —and by extension, the software that ran on them—was relatively limited. Yet the war against complexity was already being waged. MVC emerged as a major weapon in the arsenal because it targeted a simple but deadly problem at the heart of nearly all programs that present an interface to the user and let them manipulate data.

To appreciate the elegance of the solution that MVC offers, you must fully grasp the nature of the problem. That requires generalization; stepping back from the myriad details of your application's moving parts and seeing it in a much simpler form. Despite all that has changed in the 20+ years since MVC was first described, the basic problem it solves remains as prevalent as ever.

For a moment, picture your application as a huge pile of laundry that has accumulated in your closet for weeks and must be washed or you will have to go to work naked. You could just stuff random loads into the washer, toss in some detergent, and be done with it. Of course you might find that the towels have rubbed against your soft bedsheets and roughened them. And the hot water required to make your socks not stand up on their own anymore has caused your favorite t-shirts to shrink and your colors to run, staining your whites. Even the most carefree members of our profession would likely concede that separating your laundry according to some methodology is a worthwhile undertaking. So you sort it into piles according to some unspoken best practices of the laundry room.

The "piles" we are interested in making with MVC are:

- Code that deals with the data (Model)
- Code that deals with the user interface (View)
- Code that deals with business logic (Controller)

The power of the MVC concept is that this extreme generalization applies to any application with a user interface and a domain model. By separating your code according to this simple principle, you can mitigate one of the biggest threats to your project, slay the complexity beast, and be assured that on shipping day you will not have to go to work naked!

Dispensing with the laundry metaphor for now, we will refer to these piles as the "tiers" of our application: distinct levels through which data and control flow passes at runtime. MVC gives us not only the tiers for separating these key interests, but also a few simple rules governing how the actors (classes) in each tier should communicate with those in the other tiers:

- The Model tier may notify the View or Controller tiers
- The View tier may update the Model tier and notify the Controller tier
- The Controller tier may update the View tier or the Model tier

Three simple tiers, three simple rules. Easy to follow, easy to remember.

Strict "Three-tier Design" distinguishes itself from MVC with the requirement that all View interaction with the Model tier must pass through the Controller tier. With MVC, the View can update the Model and the Model can notify the View, skipping the Controller tier altogether. You may choose to impose a strict Three-tier Design limitation on your code if you wish, but it is not required. We will continue to use the word *tiers* when referring to the Model, View, and Controller regions of the application (as opposed to the actual classes, which will always appear as `Model`, `View`, and `Controller`).

The PureMVC AS3 Reference Implementation

A core goal of PureMVC is to be language-independent. So while most languages have powerful native features that set them apart, PureMVC chooses to use common conventions that can be found in most every language. The chief influences in PureMVC's original implementation stemmed from client-side concerns in a web-based, client-server environment: specifically Rich Internet Applications (RIAs) based upon Adobe's Flash Platform. While the author specialized in Flex development, there was a huge community of Flash developers that could also benefit from the framework if it did not rely on any classes specific to the Flex API. And at the time, an ActionScript engine called Tamarin was poised to fuel the next generation of JavaScript in browsers. So an even larger crowd could possibly benefit from the framework if it did not rely on any of the classes specific to the Flash API either.

Taking all that into account, the first decision after choosing the MVC approach was that the framework would rely solely upon elements of the ActionScript language itself; no references to `flash.events.Event` or Flex data binding. It would not inhibit best practice use of those features, but it would not rely upon them internally. Consequently, PureMVC has its own built-in mechanism for communication between framework actors called Notifications. Since ActionScript is much like any other OOP language in use these days, the framework's potential portability would be greatly enhanced if it stuck to the simplest language constructs and refrained from leveraging powerful but exotic features such as AS3 Namespaces and XML as a native datatype.

All of this shocks many ActionScript developers at first. Some have gone so far as to say that a framework that eschews these powerful features of Flex, Flash, and ActionScript cannot be optimal. Of course that is easy to say but hard to quantify or defend. Like art, the implementation may please you or it may not. But its effectiveness has been demonstrated repeatedly in fields as diverse as protein modeling, DNA sequencing, high availability video, virtualization hypervisors, and UAV communication systems testing. Chances are it will prove adequate for the amazing things you are doing as well.

And in truth, you do not have to give up all the rich features of the Flash Platform in order to use PureMVC; that is a common misconception. Just because the framework is self-contained does not mean you cannot communicate with it using events or use binding to move data around inside an MXML View Component. And it would be crazy to give up language features like Namespaces and XML as a datatype for the sake of some purist dogma. The key is understanding how and where they are best used in conjunction with the framework.

Many Open Source Software (OSS) projects begin with a few ideas, a little code, and an open ended future where developers throw in feature after feature. Refactoring and deprecation of old features in favor of new ones improve the project but keep dependent developers on a constant treadmill trying to keep up, in turn refactoring their own code in order to take advantage of the latest and greatest goodies.

In contrast (and partly in response), the goal for the AS3 implementation of PureMVC was to be feature-frozen, bug-fixed, and fully mature in as short a time as possible. MVC is fairly straightforward and not difficult to figure out. The scope was determined before coding began, and in the hands of the community, its shortcomings were quickly isolated and addressed. To keep the creepy feature creature at bay, it was decided that extension would happen through add-on utilities, not core framework changes.

Today, the AS3 implementation is referred to as the reference implementation because in addition to being a fully functional framework for the Flash Platform, it provides a class-by-class, method-by-method template for porting to other languages. At the time of this writing, there have been twelve other major ports including AS2, C#, C++, ColdFusion, Haxe, Java, JavaScript, Objective-C, Perl, PHP, Python, and Ruby, so you can easily apply your PureMVC core knowledge across all these languages. Strategies for carrying out the responsibilities of each actor may vary slightly, but their roles and collaboration patterns will remain the same.

The Role of PureMVC in Your Application

MVC is not really a design pattern, as it does not offer specific actors with definite roles, responsibilities, and collaborations. It is a sort of meta-pattern: good advice regarding the general separation of interests within an app. If followed, it can lead to Model tier classes that can be reused in a number of different applications, View tier classes that can be reused or refactored without major impact to the rest of the app, and business logic that can be triggered from multiple places within the app in a decoupled fashion.

We could simply write our applications informed by that advice and be done with it. Many developers do just that and report great success with no framework at all. Using a popular framework like PureMVC should and does offer benefits over just coding according MVC's advice alone. Some of those are:

- Reduced need for high-level architecture design, implementation, and documentation
- No indoctrination on the homegrown approach needed for developers joining your team

- Clear roles and collaboration patterns for actors, leading to less confusing code

PureMVC is not just a library, it is also a central organizing principle. Again, the advice of MVC is to separate the code into three specific tiers. One way this happens is in the packaging of your application: the folder arrangement you choose to store the class files in. Packaging OOP classes is an art learned with time and practice. Team members with varying skills often have different ideas about how it should be done.

Not only should your classes have clear collaboration patterns, they should also be easy to find if you are new to a project. When creating new classes, it should be obvious where to put them. Returning to the laundry metaphor for a moment, if you had separate bins to use when disrobing each night, then you would not need to waste time sorting your clothes on wash day. You would simply put articles into the proper bin to begin with.

While your packaging will probably vary slightly from the basic recommended structure, you will reap the first two of the above mentioned benefits by adhering to it: you do not need to figure it out yourself, and others working with your code will know where to find and put things if they have experience with PureMVC.

Pay No Attention to the Man Behind the Curtain

If you really want the nitty gritty on everything going on behind the scenes, the documentation on the PureMVC website (*http://puremvc.org*) covers all the actors in depth. The framework was built with the notion of complete, in-the-field replacement of any of its parts just in case there were actors you wanted to implement differently without extension. This is why every class has an associated interface. Also, the use of `public` or `protected` over `private` on everything you can safely override gives you a lot of flexibility to customize without modifying the framework itself.

Since almost all of the time you will use the same few actors in the standard, proscribed ways, we will briefly describe those classes first. You may notice that this approach is essentially the opposite of the online documentation. The intention there is to give a full technical rundown of the framework suitable for architects who may want to evaluate, port, or modify PureMVC at a very deep level. That same documentation has also had to serve developers who just want to use the framework to get on with their jobs. The result has been that the latter (and much larger) crowd tends to see the framework as overly complicated at first, when in fact, it is incredibly simple to use. Much effort has been invested in its design to make proper MVC separation the path of least resistance, hiding as much complexity as possible from the developer.

The focus of this book then, will be to present PureMVC in the most hands-on way possible, skipping or minimizing discussion of the abstractions. By no means does that mean you will be less prepared to enact ninja-like PureMVC skills than someone who knows every class and method inside and out. On the contrary, by focusing intently on what actually matters, you can safely treat the internals as a "black box."

Meet the Workhorses

The PureMVC framework is composed of actors from well-known design patterns, further increasing the likelihood that developers will already understand or at least be familiar with them. Furthermore, the framework has been written in such a way that of the 11 classes (each with a corresponding interface) of which it is composed, you only need to work directly with about five. But that tiny handful you will use are workhorses that in practice can easily account for all of your application aside from View Components, Value Objects, and constants classes.

Of those five classes you will typically work with, one will be written only once in your app to initialize and manage the system, three will represent actors operating inside each of the three MVC tiers, and one will be used to pass information between the tiers and does not even require instantiation thanks to a convenience method shared by the classes who need it. So in day-to-day development, there are only three classes of real consequence. You will extend these three classes all the time, so you will want to be sure you know their roles, responsibilities, and collaborations well.

They are `Proxy`, `Mediator`, and `SimpleCommand`.

Actors at the Boundaries

The so-called "boundaries" of your application are the places where it interfaces with the outside world: user-facing View Components and external data sources like filesystems or web services. Managing I/O at these boundaries is the responsibility of the `Mediator` and `Proxy` respectively.

Use a Proxy as a Data Source for the Application

The unique cloud of relevant terms surrounding your application's real-world problem domain is generally referred to as the *domain model*. The domain model of your application will likely be implemented as simple data carrier classes (commonly referred to as Value Objects), that represent data with strong types. There is no framework class for representing data because there are just too many ways to do it; it is not PureMVC's intent to represent data, but rather to retrieve, persist, and expose it to the user for viewing and manipulation. Retrieving and persisting the data—in whatever form it may take—is the primary role of the `Proxy`.

`Proxy` subclasses are long-lived actors that act as data sources within the application. Whether they handle access to the filesystem, remote servers, or hardware like the camera and microphone, `Proxy`s are typically created at startup and available throughout the runtime of the application, though we will explore transient usage patterns as well.

A simple proxy example

In Adobe AIR, there is a nice feature called the Encrypted Local Store (ELS). It allows you to store key / value pairs in an encrypted database on the local disk. In this example, we will see how to use a `Proxy` subclass to read and write a Value Object to the ELS. For the purposes of demonstration, we will store sensitive information about the location of the user's mail server and her credentials.

Our approach will be to have the `EmailConfigProxy` allow the getting and setting of a single Value Object called `EmailConfigVO`, which has the necessary properties. When the Value Object is set on the `EmailConfigProxy`, we will take the values off and store them in the ELS as key / value pairs with the key being a private constant defined on the `EmailConfigProxy`, and the value being the value of the corresponding property on the `EmailConfigVO`. When getting the Value Object from the `EmailConfigProxy`, the getter will simply return a new instance of the `EmailConfigVO` type created from the currently stored values in the ELS. Private setters and getters for the individual ELS key / value pairs are used by the setter and getter for the `EmailConfigVO` itself.

 This example also shows an ActionScript feature used often throughout the book called implicit accessors. As in most any language, you could always have `getUser()` and `setUser()` methods for manipulating a private variable called `user`. But using ActionScript's implicit accessors, you can have two methods that combine to look like a single property. Although this is a fairly exotic ActionScript feature, when porting your code to a platform without implicit accessors it is straightforward to transform property references into method calls, so portability is not impaired by their use in practice.

EmailConfigProxy

```
package com.mycompany.myapp.model.proxy
{
    import flash.data.EncryptedLocalStore;
    import flash.utils.ByteArray;

    import com.mycompany.myapp.model.vo.EmailConfigVO;

    import org.puremvc.as3.multicore.patterns.proxy.Proxy;

    /**
     * This is an example Proxy for persisting
     * email configuration items in the AIR
     * Encrypted Local Store (ELS) for MyApp.
     */
    public class EmailConfigProxy extends Proxy
    {
        public  static const NAME:String       = "EmailConfigProxy";
        private static const EMAIL_HOST:String  = NAME+"/email/config/host";
        private static const EMAIL_PORT:String  = NAME+"/email/config/port";
        private static const EMAIL_USER:String  = NAME+"/email/config/user";
```

```
        private static const EMAIL_PASS:String  = NAME+"/email/config/pass";

        // Constructor. Pass the Proxy constructor the
        // name of this subclass.
        public function EmailConfigProxy( )
        {
            super ( NAME );
        }

        // get the email configuration Value Object
        public function get emailConfigVO():EmailConfigVO
        {
            return new EmailConfigVO ( host, port, user, password );
        }

        // set the email configuration Value Object
        public function set emailConfig( config:EmailConfigVO ):void
        {
            host     = config.host;
            port     = config.port;
            user     = String(config.user);
            password = String(config.pass);
        }

        private function get host( ):String
        {
            return retrieve( EMAIL_HOST );
        }

        private function set host( host:String ):void
        {
            store( EMAIL_HOST, host );
        }

        private function get port( ):Number
        {
            return Number( retrieve( EMAIL_PORT ) );
        }

        private function set port( port:Number ):void
        {
            store( EMAIL_PORT, port.toString() );
        }

        private function get user( ):String
        {
            return retrieve( EMAIL_USER );
        }

        private function set user( user:String ):void
        {
            store( EMAIL_USER, user );
        }

        private function get password( ):String
```

```
    {
        return retrieve( EMAIL_PASS );
    }

    private function set password( pass:String ):void
    {
        store( EMAIL_PASS, pass );
    }

    // store a key /value pair in the ELS
    private function store( key:String, value:String ):void
    {
        if (key && value) {
            var bytes:ByteArray = new ByteArray();
            bytes.writeUTFBytes(value);
            EncryptedLocalStore.setItem(key,bytes);
        }
    }

    // retrieve a key /value pair from the ELS
    private function retrieve( key:String ):String
    {
        var bytes:ByteArray = EncryptedLocalStore.getItem( key );
        return (bytes)?bytes.readUTFBytes(bytes.length):null;
    }
    }
}
```

Use a Mediator as a Secretary for a View Component

The user interface of your application will be implemented as a hierarchy of View
Components. In Flash, those components could be placed on the stage at design time.
In Flex and AIR, the components will mostly be declared in MXML and created at
startup, and in either case they may also be dynamically instantiated and inserted into
the display list later. Some components will be custom and some out-of-box. Plugging
your View Components into the rest of the application is the role of the Mediator.

Mediator subclasses are long-lived actors whose primary function is to isolate the application's knowledge of a given component in the display list to a single framework
subclass. It will provide that component with the data it needs, pass data from the View
Component back into the system for processing by business logic, or update the Model
tier directly. It should not act as a so-called "code-behind" class that keeps state for the
View Component or manages its internals. Though the Mediator may *affect* the state
of a View Component indirectly via interaction with explicitly exposed properties and
methods, View Components should encapsulate their own internal implementation.
The Mediator should merely pass information between the View Component and the
rest of the application with a minimum amount of translation, much as an executive's
personal secretary handles his communication with the outside world, freeing him to
focus on his work.

A simple mediator example

Carrying on with the previous example, there must be—somewhere—a View Component for editing the email configuration information that we are saving with the EmailConfigProxy. We will call it EmailConfig and the EmailConfigMediator will tend it.

This EmailConfig View Component has a property called vo where a reference to the EmailConfigVO can be accessed as needed by the EmailConfigMediator. We will also exercise the alternative for the View Component to pass the data to the EmailConfigMe diator in a property of a custom Event. The properties of that Value Object will be used by the View Component to populate its form. When the user has entered or edited the data, he will be able to test the configuration and if the test passes, he will then be able to save the configuration. We will leave it to the View Component to encapsulate all of the necessary supporting behavior such as not enabling the "Save" button until a test has been done, and not enabling the "Test" button until all the information has been entered, and so on. All that we need to know to build the EmailConfigMediator is the relevant properties, methods, and Events that make up the API of the View Component. Treating the View Component as a "black box" can help companies outsource UI development or leverage strong internal UI developers who may not know PureMVC.

The EmailConfigMediator will listen to the EmailConfig View Component for certain Events that indicate the user's intent to save or test the current configuration. It will also be interested in Notifications (more about them later) from other parts of the system and handle those Notifications by interacting with the View Component. Finally, the EmailConfigMediator will also collaborate directly with the EmailConfig Proxy to retrieve or persist the EmailConfigVO.

EmailConfigMediator

```
package com.mycompany.myapp.view.mediator
{
    import com.mycompany.myapp.controller.constant.MyAppConstants;
    import com.mycompany.myapp.model.proxy.EmailConfigProxy;
    import com.mycompany.myapp.model.proxy.EmailProxy;
    import com.mycompany.myapp.model.vo.EmailConfigVO;
    import com.mycompany.myapp.view.components.EmailConfig;
    import com.mycompany.myapp.view.event.MyAppEvent;

    import org.puremvc.as3.interfaces.INotification;
    import org.puremvc.as3.patterns.mediator.Mediator;

    public class EmailConfigMediator extends Mediator
    {
        public static const NAME:String = "EmailConfigMediator";

        private var emailConfigProxy:EmailConfigProxy;

        // Pass Mediator constructor this mediator's name and component
        public function EmailConfigMediator( viewComponent:EmailConfig )
```

```
{
    super( NAME, viewComponent );
}

// get the View Component cast to the appropriate type
private function get emailConfig():EmailConfig
{
    return viewComponent as EmailConfig;
}

// Called at registration time. Form direct collaborations.
override public function onRegister():void
{
    // set listeners on View Components
    emailConfig.addEventListener( MyAppEvent.SAVE_EMAIL_CONFIG,
                                  saveEmailConfig );
    emailConfig.addEventListener( MyAppEvent.TEST_EMAIL_CONFIG,
                                  testEmailConfig );

    // retrieve needed proxies
    emailConfigProxy = facade.retrieveProxy(EmailConfigProxy.NAME)
                                            as EmailConfigProxy;
}

// We can get the config from the event if the component sends it this way.
// Here we save it immediately to the ELS via the EmailConfigProxy
private function saveEmailConfig( event:MyAppEvent ):void
{
    emailConfigProxy.emailConfigVO = event.data as EmailConfigVO;
}

// We can also get the data from the View Component.
// Here, we'll send it off in a notification to be processed by a Command
private function testEmailConfig( event:MyAppEvent ):void
{
    sendNotification( MyAppConstants.PERFORM_EMAIL_TEST, emailConfig.vo );
}

// Called at regisistration time, we should list the
// notifications we want to hear about
override public function listNotificationInterests():Array
{
    return [ MyAppConstants.SHOW_CONFIG,
             EmailProxy.TEST_RESULT
           ];
}

// Respond to notifications this mediator is interested in
override public function handleNotification( note:INotification ):void
{
    switch ( note.getName() )
    {
        // set the email configuration on the View Component
        case MyAppConstants.SHOW_CONFIG:
            emailConfig.vo = emailConfigProxy.emailConfigVO;
```

```
                            break;

                    // set the result of the email test on the View Component
                    case MyAppConstants.TEST_RESULT:
                        emailConfig.testResult = note.getBody as Boolean;
                        break;
                }
            }
        }
    }
```

Actors Between the Boundaries

Often in an application that does not follow strong OOP design principles, a class that communicates with the server will also perform lots of calculations on the data being received or transmitted, or even create and interact with the View Components that display it. Or a class that is used to display data will also load it, perform lots of calculations on it, and store it. By separating the responsibilities of the classes at those boundaries, you have already taken a giant step toward keeping your code from becoming a messy plate of spaghetti. Still, the boundary actors could use a little help to keep their responsibilities light and focused.

Isolated from the hustle and bustle of I/O going on at the external boundaries is where the thinking takes place in your application. Whether unique to a given application or shared amongst a suite of apps, business logic is the responsibility of the SimpleCommand and MacroCommand (collectively referred to as simply Commands throughout the book).

Let SimpleCommands Do Most of the Thinking

Besides handling I/O, your application will likely have a number of purely logical operations to perform throughout runtime. Activities like preparing the application for use at startup or performing a search-and-replace on a chunk of text fall outside the logical realm of responsibility for either the View tier's Mediator or the Model tier's Proxy.

SimpleCommand subclasses are short-lived actors that are created when needed, execute their function, and exit to be garbage-collected thereafter. The benefit of using a SimpleCommand for this sort of thing, as opposed to a class with static methods, is that the latter approach promotes the kind of spaghetti code that MVC is intended to avoid. It couples the calling actors to it, making them difficult to reuse separately. Such classes tend to become so-called "god objects," growing larger and taking on a more ill-defined role over time since they seem to be a handy place to put various odds and ends. By placing logic in discrete classes and triggering them in a decoupled fashion, you get code that is easier to understand, refactor, and reuse.

In our previous example of the EmailConfigMediator, we had a testEmailConfig() method that was called when the user pressed a "Test" button in the EmailConfig View Component. That component dispatched a custom Event carrying the EmailConfigVO to be tested. The EmailConfigMediator sent the EmailConfigVO off in a Notification named MyAppConstants.PERFORM_EMAIL_TEST. Here we will assume that a SimpleCom mand called PerformEmailTestCommand has been registered to handle this Notification (more on how that happens later). Though we will see much more involved logic happening in Commands later on in the book, here is an example of what that SimpleCom mand might look like:

PerformEmailTestCommand

```
package com.mycompany.myapp.controller.command
{
    import com.mycompany.myapp.model.proxy.EmailProxy;
    import com.mycompany.myapp.model.vo.EmailConfigVO;

    import org.puremvc.as3.interfaces.INotification;
    import org.puremvc.as3.patterns.command.SimpleCommand;

    public class PerformEmailTestCommand extends SimpleCommand
    {
        override public function execute( note:INotification ):void
        {
            // Get the email configuration from the notification body
            var config:EmailConfigVO = EmailConfigVO( note.getBody() );

            // Get the EmailProxy
            var emailProxy:EmailProxy;
            emailProxy = EmailProxy( facade.retrieveProxy(EmailProxy.NAME) );

            // Invoke the email configuration test.
            // The EmailProxy will send the result as
            // a Boolean in the body of an EmailProxy.TEST_RESULT note,
            // which will be handled by the EmailConfigMediator
            emailProxy.testConfiguration( config );
        }
    }
}
```

Use a MacroCommand to Execute Several SimpleCommands

For more complex operations, there is the MacroCommand, which simply groups any number of SimpleCommands (referred to as its subcommands), and executes them in First In First Out (FIFO) order. It is rarely sighted in the wild, but we will explore a reasonable usage later in this book.

The Rest of the Gang

You have been briefly introduced to the workhorse classes you will be writing every day: Mediator, Proxy, and SimpleCommand. Learning what goes into those classes (and just as importantly, what does not) and how to set up the collaborations between them that eventually bring your application to life will be the major focus of this book.

As promised, esoteric discussion of the PureMVC internals will be kept to a minimum. Nevertheless, there are a few other classes you will come into contact with or should at least know about, so we will cover those briefly here and more deeply as the need arises in the following chapters.

Notifications

Notifications provide the mechanism by which those workhorse classes communicate with each other. While a Proxy may listen to a service component for Events, it will broadcast its own status to the rest of the PureMVC actors using Notifications. Likewise, a Mediator may place event listeners on a View Component, but it will usually translate those Events into outbound Notifications in order to communicate user intent to other parts of the application.

A Notification has a name, an optional body (which can be any Object), and an optional type (a String). Mediator, Proxy, and SimpleCommand are all Notifier subclasses, meaning they all inherit a convenience method called sendNotification(), which takes the three properties just mentioned as arguments, constructs a new Notification, and broadcasts it.

Who will receive these Notifications? Take another look back at Figure 1-1, the MVC diagram.

Notice that the View and Controller tiers are potential recipients of notification, but the Model tier is not. The reason for that is to keep the Model tier portable. It is the combined duty of the View and Controller tiers to ensure that the user is able to interact with the data. Those tiers are both able to directly update the Model tier. The Model tier is only responsible for making the data available. For an actor of the Model tier to become interested in the business of presentation would be overstepping its role and potentially coupling it to one particular application implementation.

What this means is that Proxy, Mediator, and SimpleCommand can each send a Notification, but only Mediator and SimpleCommand may receive them.

 Notifications are commonly referred to as "notes" for short.

The Core Actors

Representing each of the three MVC tiers (and referred to as the Core actors) are three Singletons called Model, View, and Controller. They take care of registering and making available your Proxy, Mediator, SimpleCommand, and MacroCommand subclasses.

The Model and View act as registries of Proxy and Mediator instances (remember they are long-lived actors), respectively. The View also manages notifying all of the interested actors when a Notification is sent.

The Controller handles the mapping between SimpleCommand or MacroCommand class names and Notification names. It also creates and executes the appropriate class instances when a mapped Notification is broadcast by any actor.

Although these classes are the engine of PureMVC, you will never have to work with them directly or even care what they do. Why?

The Facade

This design pattern is very handy for providing an interface to an arbitrarily complex system so that clients of the system do not ever have to interact directly with the system's actors.

In the case of PureMVC, the Facade gives the developer the impression that we simply rolled the Model, View, and Controller classes up into one Singleton. All the necessary methods from each of the three Core actors are present on it. Since they are separate classes, you can replace or modify any of them individually if need be (which is almost never).

Imagine the Facade as the receptionist at a hotel. When a guest comes in, he does not just get on the elevator and go find a room. Instead, the receptionist gets him checked in, gets him his keys, and tells him where his room is. When he comes back an hour later, she also tells him where the ice machine is and gets him a bucket, or fetches a concierge if he needs to find a place to eat, or the maintenance guy if the lights in his room are not working.

Singletons: Good or Evil?

In PureMVC, four classes are made Singletons for the purpose of ensuring that there is only one instance of each. However, Singleton usage is commonly considered an anti-pattern in the OOP world. Its static factory method means you can reach the one allowed instance of the class from anywhere in your application. Inappropriate usage can turn your code into spaghetti as every class couples itself to the Singleton rather than get what it needs through a more appropriate actor. Due to the Facade, there is never a reason to access the other Singletons directly, allowing you to replace any or all of them with your own implementation. As for the Facade itself, all of the actors who need it already have a reference to it by design. Only the main application will call the Facade's getInstance() method, to pass in the initial display list. Thus, the undesired coupling that gives Singletons a bad reputation does not arise with normal use of the PureMVC framework.

Packaging Your Classes

Now that you are acquainted with the classes you will be writing, let us consider how they are packaged in a typical project.

First, a quick review of the most common actors:

Ordinary Classes

View Components
    The building blocks of your user interface
Events
    Dispatched by your View Components
Value Objects
    Data entities in your domain model
Enums
    Enumerations of valid values for multiple choice fields
Constants
    Classes with static constant values

Framework Classes

- Facade
- Mediator
- SimpleCommand / MacroCommand

Typical Package Structure

As mentioned earlier, there is a suggested package structure associated with PureMVC projects. Figure 1-2 shows those common classes packaged within a structure whose first division ensures everything in the system is conceptually sorted according to MVC.

Despite being simple enough to build quickly by hand, this structure is extremely extensible. For instance, if your application has a lot of View Components, you can subdivide the `view.components` package to any depth you like to cordon off the user interface elements of your various subsystems. If you have a very large domain model, you may enforce the same discipline with the `model.vo` package. Maintaining the MVC separation as your central organizing principle also helps you to separate your code into libraries (or combine multiple libraries) with confidence that your packaging

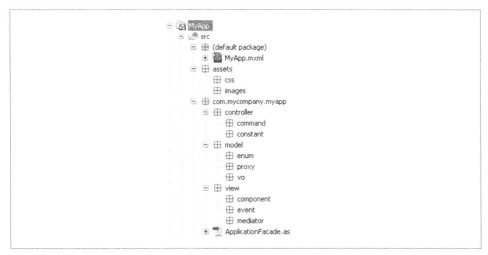

Figure 1-2. Typical package structure for a PureMVC-based application

schemes will mesh. You may find that you want to extract your entire Model tier into a library for reuse across applications. You might also want to build your Model tier in a separate library even if you do not have multiple apps planned. If that library is not allowed to reference the View tier and Controller tier code in the app, then you will have ensured that the most important separation of MVC has been maintained—isolation of the Model tier.

Of course, your codebase can be structured any way you please; the framework itself is not sensitive to your package structure. But the point of MVC is separation of interests, so that as the application's complexity increases, maintainability remains constant. Packaging is a powerful tool for that very purpose. If you are using PureMVC, you'll do current and future team members a favor by adhering to some common standards for packaging. Consider how implementation of the Dewey Decimal System helps a reader familiar with it go into any library, locate the card catalog, and find the book they need. Of course a local library could create their own internally self-consistent system for locating books, that is a given. But for anyone who is familiar with how most libraries organize their books, the seeker of knowledge in this home-brew library would encounter unnecessary mental friction until they had learned the local filing system. Remember the "Code at the Speed of Thought" goal stated in the Preface? Great strides toward that goal can be made by eliminating points of mental friction wherever possible.

Standard and MultiCore Versions

Shortly after PureMVC's release, the largest requested change that had not been originally scoped was implemented: the MultiCore version.

Since there can be only one instance of each of the `Facade` and Core actors, a powerful feature of the Flash Platform was difficult to work with: Flex Modules or loaded Flash SWF files that were themselves using PureMVC.

Imagine a truly modular design decoupled enough that it could accommodate third party PureMVC-based modules running together in a PureMVC-based host application. Unless the module writer has access to the host code, `Notification` naming collisions could occur, thereby causing unstable behavior.

The solution to the problem was to allow for separate sets of the `Facade` and Core MVC Singletons for the host and each module. They become Multitons now: registries of named instances rather than holders of a single instance. Each core could then run as a whole separate program.

How do you communicate between cores? Be it host-to-module, module-to-module, or module-to-host, you can always use interfaces and direct references to expose a communication API for your cores. Alternatively, you could use a utility called Pipes that was released along with the MultiCore version. Pipes was inspired by the Unix command line interface where you can chain programs together in pipelines and pass data through them for processing. You can plumb your inter-core communication paths by combining "pipes" and "pipe-fittings" such as splitting and joining tees, filters, etc., then send typed messages between cores, optionally carrying data or View Component references.

Some applications are just naturally good candidates for modular system design. Music production programs that allow virtual instruments to be combined with sequencing and mixing are a perfect example. Each virtual instrument could be implemented as a module, the sequencer as a module, and the mixing suite as a module. One nice benefit of a modular architecture like this is that it opens the door to third party plugin development. In a notional music production app, third parties could develop effects and instruments that could be plugged into your app to make it even more powerful. You could simply release an API library containing the interfaces, Value Objects, and message classes that are needed by all modules, and then developers could begin adding value to your app. If the app were not modular, then third parties would not be able to enhance it without access to the source code of the entire application, which you may not wish to give away.

MultiCore is a whole level of separation beyond MVC, and while it is extremely powerful, not everybody needs it. There is a small but unavoidable overhead in complexity for the developer that was deemed best implemented in an alternate version of the framework. MultiCore was created, and the existing version was dubbed Standard.

In this book, we are using the Standard version. The differences are not that great, so do not be worried when you find yourself needing a modular solution. See Chapter 10 for some resources to get you started with MultiCore.

If your team is blessed with the time for unit testing, then you should choose the MultiCore version instead of Standard, even if you are not writing a modular application. The reason is that MultiCore allows you to have an isolated core for each test method in a test class and/or each test class in a test suite. Otherwise, in Standard, each test is happening inside the same core for the duration of the test run, allowing the outcome of previous tests to conceivably affect the current test unless elaborate setup and teardown is performed. It is not necessary to use Flex Modules in order to use MultiCore, you can write your application the same way, the only real difference you will see is that your `Application Facade.getInstance()` method will need to take a `String` argument for a key.

Writing Portable Code

A few simple decisions made before PureMVC was implemented led to its high portability. Limited scope and use of only the most common OOP constructs ensured it would be easy to recreate in other languages. Since the framework is available in many popular programming languages, your application has numerous potential porting targets to choose from, should the need arise.

If you only write applications exclusively for the Flash Platform, PureMVC's portability may not seem that important to you. Fortunately, Adobe AIR is available on many hardware platforms today, increasing the Flash Platform developer's cozy feeling of safety. Just like rock and roll, AIR will never die—insert blazing air guitar solo here (pun only slightly intended). As I happen to love it and make a living using it, I certainly hope that will be the case.

Fortunes can change, however. The platform that you build and improve your applications on could easily go the way of the dinosaurs, and not because it was technically inferior.

Consider how Apple destroyed Flash's previous ubiquity by not allowing it on their popular iPhone and iPad products. For a time, they refused to let AIR apps onto those products as well. The only option for access to that huge market was to learn Objective C or to write your app in HTML, CSS, and JavaScript.

Less than a week before the delivery of this book's manuscript, Adobe announced its intention to donate Flex to the Apache Software Foundation, and the future of Flex now hangs in the balance. Will enterprise customers walk away from it now that it is no longer supported directly by Adobe, or will the community keep it alive and relevant? Only time will tell, but it is very likely that a large number of apps written in Flex will now be migrated to some other platform. Will the overall architecture of those applications be portable, helping to make the unavoidably tough migration straightforward, or will they have to be redesigned from scratch at great expense?

The point here is that the rule of "Survival of the Fittest" does not fully determine the fate of a major software platform. Industry hardware and software giants do. If your code is to survive long-term, it needs to be portable.

Not only might your chosen platform disappear, but plenty of agencies and independent software vendors develop for multiple platforms because no one language and toolset covers all the markets they want to reach. Can you imagine the hassle of having to maintain multiple versions of your application in different languages with completely different architectures?

Wait, you say, *Objective C is totally different from ActionScript!* Of course implementations of the same application are going to be different on each platform, right?

Right. The question is: what will be different because it must, and what will be different because you simply chose a different approach? That is what needs to be sorted out when considering the portability of your code. There will certainly be platform-specific differences. However, by consciously choosing PureMVC for each platform, you and your team can build your experiences on a single architecture and communicate more effectively on each project with less confusion.

One of the benefits of the PureMVC approach is that you can port what really matters: the architecture. The packaging, as well as the actors and their roles, responsibilities, and collaborations are all portable.

Other than the syntactic differences in the languages, the things that are likely to be different because they must are View Components, services, and the way you communicate with them; in other words, the boundaries of the app, which, conveniently, is the stuff that `Mediator` and `Proxy` isolate each other and the business logic from.

While you would certainly have to write the app again in its entirety on the target platform, you would not have to completely redesign the architecture.

You would write mostly the same classes with the same methods and properties, just accounting for the differences at the boundaries and preserving the logic and notification patterns. The business of adding new use cases to both applications would then largely amount to implementing the same actors in both places. The refactoring of existing use cases would not be complicated by differences in architecture.

It may sound odd, but the time to think about the portability of your code is before and while you write it, not when you are eventually forced to port it and have not yet mastered the new platform.

CHAPTER 2

Building an Application with PureMVC

Welcome to PureMVC Dojo.

There is a Way here. Not just a library and a packaging scheme, but also a set of conventions and wisdom pondered and accrued by the community in forums and workplaces over the last several years. This book will advise on process just about as often as framework usage. But remember, rules are meant to be broken. Like the framework itself, you can take or leave any piece of this holistic view, but it is all relevant to the goal of mastering PureMVC. The Way is not a dogma, nor is it a penultimate guide on how to do everything; just a few axioms that the advice on framework usage takes as given. If PureMVC developers are at least familiar with these concepts, then joining a new project is much easier for the new developer and the team since expectations are aligned about the basics. More time to focus discussion and effort on your actual use cases and less on ordinary plumbing.

Note that this book assumes no specification has been written and you have been charged with interviewing the client, determining what he needs from you, modeling his domain, and creating a suitable application for him. It assumes no particular development methodology is being used, other than iterative. With the approach described here, it is easy to build a limited functionality prototype and evolve it into the full working application.

Choosing the Platform

In this book we will build a PureMVC-based desktop application using Adobe AIR. However, any Flash Platform developer should be able to gain usable insight from the ideas and examples here.

The difference between Flex and AIR is merely one of a few libraries and where the compiled target runs; they are, for our intents and purposes, the same. The major rift is between Flex/AIR and Flash/Pure ActionScript, and that is mostly one of how the view is created. Flex and AIR have MXML, a declarative language for describing a view hierarchy. Flash offers creation of the initial view in an IDE, and with ActionScript alone, you have to create all of the View Components programmatically. In all cases, you may create and add components to the view dynamically. A couple of other features on the Flex and AIR side of the platform are data binding and services.

This means that how you create your view and connect it to PureMVC is slightly different, as are how you move data around inside of a View Component and how you store and fetch it. Aside from syntax, these are really the key differences between any two OOP platforms. The approach used to create a PureMVC application should be roughly the same, whatever language or platform you work with.

There were several reasons for choosing Adobe AIR as the platform for this book's application. Being declarative, MXML component definitions are far easier to work with in book form than Flash IDE screenshots. Also, AIR is rising in popularity since it has expanded from its cross-platform desktop roots onto many mobile devices including iOS and Android tablets and phones.

Today, there are a number of good options out there for building Flex and AIR applications. While the application is being authored in Adobe FlashBuilder 4.5, discussing details of the interaction with the IDE will be minimized. There are plenty of good books on using your given IDE. Our focus will be on building the application and taking advantage of ActionScript and AIR features while keeping the architecture essentially portable.

We have chosen our platform, now we need an application.

It Was a Dark and Stormy Night

I have been thinking of taking up fiction as a hobby. I may not turn out to be very good at it, but at least it will take advantage of my typing skills.

After some study on the subject, I could see numerous parallels between the construction of a good work of fiction and a robust software application. Common to both is the need for planning and structure. In both endeavors, defining clear roles, responsibilities, and collaborations for the actors is paramount to success. And like programming, there are as many approaches to knocking out the pages as there are authors.

An easy way to analyze or plan the actors of an object-oriented system is to create CRC (Classes, Responsibilities, Collaborations) cards. Using index cards and a pencil, write the name for a proposed class or interface on the top of the card. On the lines below, write the responsibilities of the actor. On the back, write a list of its collaborators (i.e. the actors it knows or who will know it). This process is good because you can quickly move responsibilities around: change collaboration patterns, and understand who needs what and how they will get it.

The same process can be used for planning fiction. All the characters get a card where you can describe their story goal, the things that will get in the way of their attainment of that goal, what their personality type is, and what they look like. The so-called "milieu" of your story is where it takes place. Cards describing each of the settings making up the milieu can be used to build a richness of place in the imagination before drafting the associated scenes. And successful scenes have structure that stems from good planning. The viewpoint character, their scene goal, the opposition (a character, natural forces, etc.), the setback that will befall them at the end of the scene are all things that can be jotted down quickly on a card.

So, I began jotting down cards for an idea that turned into a large, possibly novel-length story. I wanted a fairly detailed plan in order to make sure the story was something I wanted to embark upon, even as a hobby. I want to know how things would progress; at what points I will introduce or resolve subplots, raise the stakes, and heighten tension by alternating action with suspense. Where will I slow down to reflect and how will I gain sympathy for the hero while making the villain as despicable and resourceful as possible? These are questions that can be answered quickly and extended as they are thought out over time with this process. The nice thing about index cards is they are just as easy to toss as they are to jot on. It keeps your thinking fluid, since you do not feel that invested in them. Once you begin to type—be it code or prose—it is easy to feel like you are already building, so it's easy to go off on a tangent when you really just need to keep things at the simple planning level.

It did not take long to realize that the number of index cards was going to be insane even when I introduced an advanced grouping tool, the paper clip. To plan things to the level I wanted but still feel fluid (and be mobile so I could do it away from my desk), I started creating files in a word processor on my BlackBerry PlayBook tablet. I might draft some scenes I have planned in order to get a better feel for my cast and milieu, or jot down some notes about a character's personality and motivations, which I find a challenge. I did find a helpful site describing personality types and their related "emotional centers" and "development levels" which can inform a more believable character.

A bit later, I have a bunch of folders filled with all of these bits of story stuff. I can create a new draft of a scene by copying the file and tweaking it. I do all the writing at the scene level, so it's best to keep them in separate files, since I'm not sure where all the chapter boundaries are yet, and I may move them around. Sometimes I stitch the current drafts of several scenes together into an intermediate document using cut-and-paste, just to see how they flow. But I do not edit those; instead, I make any changes in the original documents (or new drafts of them). Sometimes, I find that drafting later scenes can tell me a lot about what needs to happen earlier in the plot.

I am feeling my way toward a process for intertwined plotting, researching, imagining, and drafting that can move forward with the same fluid way that modern software development does.

Of course, as any coder can see, this is a problem that could use a program. And coincidentally, so could this book.

StoryArchitect, A Tool for Writing Fiction

The AIR application that will be the focus of this book is called StoryArchitect.

What will it do? What features of AIR will it use? How will it store data? Will it run on a tablet? It would be easy to simply dictate the feature set and implementation without preamble or explanation. But the choices we make at the code level are influenced by what we know or do not know about the domain, in this case, writing fiction.

In the previous section, we were provided two of the most important inputs into a new software project that a developer could know: what the user is trying to do and how they are doing it now.

Unless it is to be a copy of a competitor's application or a variation on a product class, the developer will usually be working from what the client says they want, and most companies who wisely pay to have software written for them by professionals have core competencies in areas other than software design.

Those vague if well-meaning ideas are often filtered through a requirement writer's interpretation where they are expanded, twisted, and stretched, then passed on to designers to be generously belled and whistled. The result is presented to you, the developer, as your next challenge. And developers do love a challenge. The next thing you know, the small cookie bakery who just wanted to sell cookies online has rocketship games to play while you wait for your order to be processed. Attaining levels gives you discounts on your next purchase, and of course tweeting that you just bought yummy cookies will get you more coupons.

That all sounds good, but in my experience, the result of this process is almost never The Right Thing. A feature list in a requirements document rarely tells you much about the pain points in the current process. But if you can find a way to understand the user's domain data and current processes from their perspective, you have a better chance of seeing the places where your craft can actually benefit their existence on a daily basis.

Now we will follow the process of transforming the thoughts of our would-be client into a working application. Your requirements, design, and development processes will probably differ, even from job to job depending on who you work for, but I hope to convey a general sense of how to confidently approach a new project using PureMVC.

Statement of Purpose

To keep the whole team, including users, on the same page about the spirit of the software's purpose, we need something even shorter than an elevator pitch: a meaningful, summarizing one-liner.

StoryArchitect will allow the fiction writer to...what?

Let's go back to the ruminations of the user in the discovery phase. There was a summation of an evolving process:

> I am feeling my way toward a process for intertwined plotting, researching, imagining, and drafting…

Alright, then. That was clear enough without sounding like a feature list. It should inform all our decisions about features and implementation. Our Purpose Statement then:

StoryArchitect is a fiction writer's tool for intertwined plotting, researching, imagining, and drafting.

Determining Scope

As a user of this potentially awesome app, I have all sorts of ideas about what it should eventually do.

But what I really need it to do is to replace the laborious file management process I use now to keep scene drafts, character and setting studies, etc. I also some need way to work from drafts of individual scenes, while being able to dynamically generate a chapter, part, or book made from the current draft of every scene. I should be able to write a draft of a scene, then back out to the chapter level in a read-only mode and see how that chapter reads with my new scene in it. And since the process of writing a short story, novella, novel, or series are all essentially the same (a matter of scale and increasing levels of scene grouping), I would like to be able to do any of those with this one tool. Essentially a simple word processor that understands the hierarchy of a story, and the equivalent of index cards for jotting down notes about any level of the story hierarchy, character, or setting.

Grand ideas for the future include generating an outline from the descriptions and notes from each level of the story hierarchy, and plot arcs for each character or story that show how events affect a character or the storyline over time and in multiple dimensions. For instance, a car crash could have a terrible effect on the character's health, but positive implications for her wealth after the subsequent lawsuit. Imagining and plotting the cause and effect behind the multifaceted fortunes of a character or twists in a story plot could benefit from a visualization tool, I am convinced. But we will leave that for the sequel; it is the seductive whisper of the creepy feature creature we are hearing now.

An important discipline in maintaining scope is to plan only the essential features for the current version of the application that you are working on. Be sure to capture ideas for advanced features in a list. They will be a start on your next version's planning if they are still relevant after building and working with this version.

Now we have a very rough idea of what we are going to try and build. Let's first think about the things that our application will manage, and then look at the user interface that will help us create and edit those things.

Describing the Domain

When planning a project you may need to research a bit more about your domain. Learn about the basics—in this case, writing fiction—before proceeding. Fortunately, our discovery phase in the previous section has provided us with valuable clues about the domain model for StoryArchitect. Reflecting on the various forms that fiction comes packaged in, we can easily arrive at some proposed entities.

No matter what the length—from a six scene fable about three pigs and a wolf to a sweeping, multi-episode saga of galactic empire and rebellion—a *Story* is made of *Scenes*.

Scenes would seem to be the atomic Story unit, but remember that a Scene may have multiple *Drafts*, only one of which will be considered the current Draft. Ultimately, a Story is made of all the current Drafts of all its Scenes.

As Stories grow larger, their Scenes are normally grouped into *Chapters*.

Sometimes a more complex fiction Story will have its Chapters further grouped into *Parts*.

Nonfiction and references such as this book often subdivide a Chapter into *Sections*, but we can safely omit those in our fiction-focused app.

A *Series* has Stories (usually referred to as episodes, but Stories nonetheless), and those are sometimes grouped into *Seasons* if it is a TV show.

Both Stories and Series have an associated *Cast* of Characters, and a *Milieu* made up of various *Settings*, and generally, all the Stories of a Series share a common Cast and Milieu.

For the first iteration, this will be more than enough territory to cover. Some items may be pushed to a future iteration as development proceeds, which is a natural part of the iterative development process. At a bare minimum, we require the ability to persist all these items and a user interface that allows us to create and navigate a story. When we design our Value Objects, we will decide what details to track for each of these domain model entities.

Imagining the User Interface

In the old days, you rolled a new sheet of paper into the typewriter and typed. The pages piled up and soon you had a book. Simple. Of course, getting a quick and accurate word count or randomly hopping around from scene to scene, drafting a bit here, a bit there was not so simple.

As for the look of the application, I imagine it to be very clean. It should have that simple, old-school "paper meets platen, go!" feel to it that an old Underwood typewriter has. Drafting scenes will not require advanced text decoration or formatting; we do not need Microsoft Word. However, we will need control of font size and margin while editing. And the most important thing is the ability to create and extend the structure at any level of the story easily and to be able to navigate that structure quickly to support the nonlinear drafting approach. We will need a timeline of some sort that allows us to drill down into any point in the Story, but it should easily be hidden when we do not need it. When we create or open a Story, it should take us to the end of the Story, ready to add new prose immediately. Also, we want a handy way of being able to access the name, description, and notes of the currently selected item (Story, Part, Chapter, etc.). Like the timeline navigation, those details should be hidden but easily accessible. Also it would be nice if they could both be visible at the same time, so that you could navigate and edit the metadata about the currently selected item and then easily move to the next item to edit. We should be able to delete or reorder the items with their siblings (easily swap Chapter 3 with Chapters 2 or 4). We will save the actual deleting and reordering functionality until the next iteration, but the interface should be present.

One of the things about the current process of writing on a tablet is that I can break free of the confines of the office to do it (as I am doing with much of the book you are reading). So eventually this application will have to be mobile. However, this is not a book about mobile development, and you may not have a tablet to try this out on. But I am sure you have a laptop or desktop computer, so we will target the desktop in this first iteration. By building on AIR, we are sure that an easy path to mobile devices is available. Knowing this to begin with helps us to design in such a way that will make it easier when that time comes. For instance, avoiding components that are difficult to use on a tablet like hidden context menus and tree controls in favor of big, friendly buttons and interface components that can be revealed as needed.

Persistence Strategy

Another reason for choosing AIR and not Flex for this application was that we can store data on the local filesystem; we do not need to also concoct a server-side component in order to persist data.

However, since there will eventually be a tablet version of the app, it is not unreasonable to expect that we will eventually want to be able to access the same data on the desktop or tablet. That would mean that we need an optional server-side component at some point, probably a service that exposes cloud storage functionality through a simple API like Amazon S3 or Dropbox, or both. If we build with that in mind, then we can add those online storage options in a later iteration without massive refactoring of the app.

As for how the data will be stored, there are many approaches we could take. It is a given that we will want to work with strongly typed objects throughout the application, and from our understanding of the domain model so far, we can see that it is very hierarchical. *Series*, *Season*, *Story*, *Part*, *Chapter*, *Scene*, *Draft*. Some levels are optional, but still, it is a tree.

AIR provides a relational database called SQLite that allows us to index, store, and retrieve data in tables using a variant of the Structured Query Language (SQL). This can be a real pain for hierarchical data, involving lots of table joins and code to be sure everything is escaped properly when the actual query is created. It does not mesh so well with the idea of simple filesystem storage that could be extended to work from the cloud, but could still conceivably allow collaboration since SQLite works with a database in a single file. Finally, all the code to parse the SQL query results into Value Objects (or objects into queries) can be pretty tedious stuff.

ActionScript offers XML as a native datatype, and hierarchical data is XML's specialty. Plus, the language has built-in features for traversing the XML data and pulling out just what you need. It is hard to imagine a better choice for working with hierarchical data. The great thing is, the data is always ready to be worked with or stored as a simple file.

But we want strongly typed objects. XML data is just a bunch of elements and attributes containing strings, and we do not want to litter the tiers of our application with code that is doing all sorts of XML manipulation when working with our data structure. Is there not an easy way to use XML without these problems?

Fortunately, ActionScript also provides us with a feature called implicit accessors: a pair of `get` and `set` methods that combine to look like a property on an instance of the class. We can write our Value Objects in such a way as to hide the fact that their data is in XML form. Accessors can expose typed properties to the application while storing the actual data in the XML structure. All of the business of serializing the data to and from XML is encapsulated inside the Value Object itself.

XML as a native datatype and implicit accessors are two powerful features of Action-Script that are not so common to other OOP languages, but combined they can be used in a very portable way. Porting the app to another language without XML as a type, the application still deals with objects. The `Proxy` responsible for persistence might have to take on a little more responsibility, or a `SimpleCommand` might be used to serialize or deserialize the data. Or it could work in the same way, allowing the Value Objects to encapsulate the XML manipulation themselves, but for the most part it would be business as usual with regard to handling the Value Objects.

So we will store and retrieve XML files for the structural information. We will implement storage on the local filesystem with an eye toward storing those files online in a later iteration.

Erecting the Startup Scaffolding

As with any project, there is a one time bit of setup work to be done. Once you are familiar with the structure and the standard startup flow (see Figure 2-1), this phase should really take no more than 10 minutes to complete.

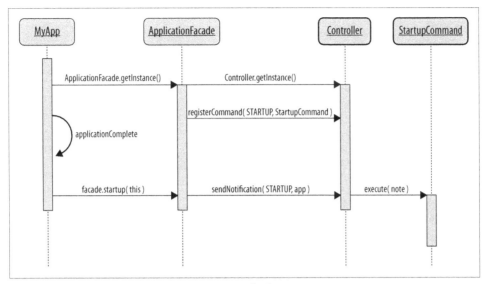

Figure 2-1. Typical PureMVC startup sequence with Flex

Prepare the Project and Initial Package Structure

Using your favorite IDE, create a new Flex Desktop (AIR) project. Out of the box, your Flex/AIR project should have a `lib` or `libs` folder where you can place libraries in SWC format to be compiled into your application. In this folder, you will place a copy of `PureMVC_AS3_2_0_4.swc`, which can be found in the downloadable archive for the PureMVC AS3 Standard Version (*http://trac.puremvc.org/PureMVC_AS3/wiki/Down loads*). With the library in place, your classes may use the PureMVC framework classes. Refer back to the Typical Package Structure in Chapter 1 for creating a basic packaging arrangement.

Create an Application Constants Class

In the `controller/constant` package, create an ActionScript class called `AppConstants` to hold static constants for `Notification` names that will be sent and received by the View and Controller tiers of your application. `STARTUP` is usually the first one you will define and use. Throughout the development phases to come, you will revisit this class often to add new note names.

 Together, the View and Controller tiers are commonly referred to as the *App* because the Model tier should be easily extracted to a library and reused in another App.

The Model tier should never accept dependencies on the App, but the App will be dependent on the Model, and that is perfectly OK. The App's sole purpose is to expose the details of the domain model to the user and allow them to interact with it, so it is understandable that the View and Controller tiers will know the actors of the Model tier well. Thus, the note names that Proxys send are either defined on the Proxys themselves or in a separate ModelConstants file.

Class

AppConstants.as

Code

```
package com.futurescale.sa.controller.constant
{
  /**
   * Notification Constants for the 'App' (View and Controller tiers)
   */
  public class AppConstants
  {
      public static const STARTUP:String = "Startup"
  }
}
```

Create a Startup Command

Create a StartupCommand to prepare your Model and View tiers for use. It will receive a reference to the main application in the note body and will mostly just register Proxys and Mediators. When your initial view hierarchy has been created, this first bit of business logic will create the PureMVC apparatus you define and attach the application to it. For now, you will not know your Proxys and Mediators yet, so you will create a startup command and go so far as to pluck the application reference from the note body.

You should generally register Proxys before registering Mediators in your StartupCommand, because most Mediators will form a long-term collaboration with one or more Proxys. They will do so by retrieving the given Proxy(s) when they are registered. Thus, a Proxy should already be registered by the time the Mediators that collaborate with it are registered.

Class

StartupCommand.as

Code

```
com.futurescale.sa.controller.command
{
  import org.puremvc.as3.interfaces.INotification;
```

```
import org.puremvc.as3.patterns.command.SimpleCommand;

/**
 * Startup the PureMVC apparatus, preparing the app for use.
 */
public class StartupCommand extends SimpleCommand
{
  override public function execute( note:INotification ):void
  {
    // Get the application instance from the note
    var app:StoryArchitect = StoryArchitect( note.getBody() );

    // That is it for the scaffolding phase.
    // The following will be added incrementally later...

    // Register the Proxys
    // .
    // .
    // .

    // Register the Mediators
    // .
    // .
    // .
  }
}
}
```

Create the Application Facade

Create a `Facade` subclass called `ApplicationFacade`. Here is what it should do:

- Implement a `getInstance()` method, so that the subclass is used for the Singleton instance.
- Override the `initializeController()` method, calling the superclass method first, then registering your `StartupCommand` to respond to the STARTUP note.
- Add a public convenience method called `startup()` for the application to call, taking an instance of the app as an argument. That method will simply send off the app in the body of the STARTUP note.

Class

`ApplicationFacade.as`

Code

```
package com.futurescale.sa
{
  import com.futurescale.sa.controller.command.StartupCommand;
  import com.futurescale.sa.controller.constant.AppConstants;

  import org.puremvc.as3.patterns.facade.Facade;
```

```
public class ApplicationFacade extends Facade
{
 /**
  * The Singleton instance factory method.
  */
  public static function getInstance( ) : ApplicationFacade
  {
    if ( instance == null ) instance  = new ApplicationFacade( );
    return instance as ApplicationFacade;
  }

  /**
   * Initialize the Controller and Register the Commands.
   */
  override protected function initializeController():void
  {
    super.initializeController();
    registerCommand( AppConstants.STARTUP, StartupCommand );

    // Register the rest of the Commands incrementally later...
    // .
    // .
    // .

  }

  /**
   * A convenience method for starting up the PureMVC
   * apparatus from the application.
   */
  public function startup( app:MyApp ):void
  {
    sendNotification( AppConstants.STARTUP, app );
  }
 }
}
```

Initialize the Application Facade and call startup()

In your main AIR Application (or WindowedApplication, or ViewNavigatorApplica
tion) do the following:

- Create a private variable called facade of type ApplicationFacade and initialize it
  from the Singleton instance factory method
- In the handler for applicationComplete, call facade.startup(this)

Class

StoryArchitect.mxml

Code

```xml
<?xml version="1.0" encoding="utf-8"?>
<s:WindowedApplication
  applicationComplete="facade.startup(this)"
  xmlns:fx="http://ns.adobe.com/mxml/2009"
  xmlns:s="library://ns.adobe.com/flex/spark"
  xmlns:mx="library://ns.adobe.com/flex/mx">

  <fx:Script>
      <![CDATA[
          import com.futurescale.sa.ApplicationFacade;

          // Initialize the ApplicationFacade during MXML application construction
          private var facade:ApplicationFacade = ApplicationFacade.getInstance();
      ]]>
  </fx:Script>

</s:WindowedApplication>
```

Building from the Outside In

At this point we can publish our application and see a blank screen, running error free. Putting a trace statement or setting a breakpoint in our StartupCommand confirms all is well. Our startup scaffolding is complete. So, what is next?

Irrespective of the framework you use (or whether you use one at all), every application will have a domain model and View Components to expose it to the user. A generally sensible approach is to define the Value Objects first then the View Components that expose them to the user for interaction. These are the classes *outside* of the boundaries of your application. Imagine them existing in an inky black void: separate, but meant for one another like hand and glove. When written, your application will bring them together. It makes sense to create and tailor Value Objects and View Components to each other before you even begin writing the code that is meant to connect them.

This approach allows you to prototype very quickly since you do not need to worry about loading the data and shuttling it to the view. Value objects should require no other classes to do their job. View components can be readily instantiated in MXML and may provide themselves Value Objects populated with dummy data for the purpose of getting the component wired to display and interact with the VO. One benefit of this approach is that someone who does not even know the framework can create the Value Objects and View Components. It ensures that these classes do not take on dependencies on the framework itself, keeping them reusable.

Once your Value Objects and View Components are created, you can create a PureMVC apparatus that uses them to meet your requirements. Begin building inward from the boundaries. First, you need Proxys to act as data sources for the application. Once they are in place, you can go back to the view and build the Mediators that will feed that data to the View Components.

You will notice that the following steps describe a thread of attention bouncing from the Model tier to the View tier and back. This weaving approach is effective from the start, and will continue throughout phases of iterative development and legacy maintenance. Once the MVC tiers are in place, adding and modifying use cases always breaks down to simply moving some data from the Model tier to the View tier or vice-versa. And sometimes a little chatter between the View and Controller tiers for reorganizing the user interface in response to user input.

Step 1: Value Objects

After setting up your project's startup scaffolding, the first order of business is creating the Value Objects. Consider the domain and create Value Objects for each entity you come up with. You might also define enumerations or constants for valid values of properties if you know them.

Write the classes and formal or informal tests using them in whatever way you like. Having a suite of tests for your Value Objects is a great way to get a feel for how your code that manipulates them will work while you are still building them, and later helps you to guard against changes breaking the application. The tests provide a reference for how the entities should be used and should be kept up-to-date, reflecting current usage in the application.

 It is customary to add VO to the end of the entity name in order to make the role of the class clear when it is used in code. For instance, Invoice HeaderVO. This convention will also help avoid name collision with View Components, which are often named for the domain model entity they display. See the example for View Components in "Step 2: View Components" on page 34.

Step 2: View Components

Next, design and build View Components adequate for your use cases against the domain model. At this stage, you will be able to mock up View Components quickly, populating them with dummy data in the form of your typed Value Objects. You will also get a feel for what each View Component needs, whether from its parent in the display list or from its Mediator. You will expose public properties for the Mediator or parent to set, but keep private or protected those needed for encapsulation of the View Component's responsibilities.

Do not design thin View Components that you expect the Mediator or parent component to puppeteer the internals of. Instead, expose a custom API of methods, properties, and events so that the component has a clear communication protocol and can be given just what it needs to work. Encapsulate the behavior of the component so that it can function without the Mediator. Above all, do not plan for the View Component to know anything about the framework actors.

Test your View Components in the quickest way possible by embedding them in the MXML application, populating them with dummy data, and interacting with them. From this process, you may discover that you need to make adjustments to your Value Objects. At the opening stages of the project, you can go back and forth between "Step 1: Value Objects" on page 34 and "Step 2: View Components" on page 34, tweaking Value Objects and View Components until they are roughly what you want them to look like in the first iteration.

Finally, do yourself a favor by scoping View Component responsibilities very tightly. Break large component groups into smaller custom components in their own classes. View Components should encapsulate their own logic for meeting their responsibilities, so keep them as simple as you can so that the internal workings are easy to understand and modify.

 View Components should be named in such a way as to describe their function, not necessarily their implementation. For example, a component for displaying an invoice header form might be implemented as a Halo `Panel` but later reimplemented as a Spark `Group`. So naming the component according to its role is better: `InvoiceHeader` rather than `InvoiceHeaderPanel`.

Step 3: Proxys

Decide how you will store and access the Value Objects and this will lead you to think about the `Proxys` you may need and what responsibilities they will take on in order to manage their data. To start, you can have them use dummy methods to mock up and accept or send data. If you already have services or are using local storage, you may go ahead and write some of the methods for dealing with that. But just getting the main `Proxys` into place with a sense of how they will work is fine for the first pass.

There are many uses for the `Proxy` subclass. You can use them to access your FlashVars and URL Parameters, Local Shared Object (LSO), Encrypted Local Storage (ELS), the filesystem, web services, Real Time Messaging Protocol (RTMP or "server push") channels—pretty much any data source the application can access (even transient data about the application's state, although this information is not considered part of the domain model proper).

Regardless of where the data comes from, the `Proxy` class has a data property that you will use implicit accessors to cast to the proper type. `Proxy` subclasses usually expose either a Value Object or a collection of the same type of Value Objects. They can be more complex than that if necessary, but that is the common usage. It is also possible for one `Proxy` to collaborate with another to maintain the integrity of separately managed but related data, thus reducing the complexity of the individual `Proxys`.

Consider an `InvoiceProxy` that talks to a remote service for storing, retrieving, and updating `InvoiceVO` objects in the database on the server. The Proxy exposes methods such as `createInvoice`, `saveInvoice`, `deleteInvoice`, `findInvoiceByID`, that are called by Commands, Mediators, and other Proxys as need be. Since they talk to services, these are all asynchronous in nature. After the method call, the service is invoked (and the result is later handled) by the `InvoiceProxy`. When the result comes back, such as from a `findInvoiceByID` call, the `InvoiceProxy` might set its data property to the `InvoiceVO` from the result and send out an `InvoiceProxy.INVOICE_LOADED` note with the `InvoiceVO` in the note body.

 Typically you will name the Proxys after the data entity they provide such as `InvoiceProxy` for managing the `InvoiceVO`s.

Step 4: Mediators

You should have a good idea about the needs of your View Components, since most of them are already written to some extent. Now is the time to decide where along the view hierarchy you need mediation. Every component does not need a `Mediator`; some can receive data from the parent View Component in the Flash display list. Providing that data then becomes the responsibility of the parent component. But data (and new View Components) must be injected and taken away from the view hierarchy somewhere, and these are the points where you want mediation.

Your first Mediator should be for the top-level application, usually called `Application Mediator` (in a Flash or ActionScript-only project, you will instead mediate the `Stage` with a `StageMediator`). In a relatively uncomplicated user interface, this may be the only `Mediator` you need. However, most applications will have a number of the application's children also be mediated.

Let's say you have an `Invoice` View Component with `InvoiceHeader` and `InvoiceDe tails` components as children. You could mediate the `Invoice` component and allow it to tend to its children such that only an `InvoiceMediator` is needed. The `InvoiceMe diator` could get an `InvoiceVO` from the `InvoiceProxy` and set it on the `Invoice` View Component. That component could then distribute a reference to the `InvoiceVO` (perhaps using Flex binding) down to its children the `InvoiceHeader` and `InvoiceDetails` components where the appropriate data from the `InvoiceVO` would be displayed. When the user interacts with the `InvoiceHeader` or `InvoiceDetails` components, causing, for instance a request to save changes, those components could dispatch a bubbling event which passes up through the `Invoice` component. The `InvoiceMediator` could listen for those events and respond by passing data to a `Proxy`, or perhaps sending the data off in a note to be validated and submitted by a `Command`.

From this example you can see that every View Component in the hierarchy does not need its own `Mediator`. So, begin by writing as few `Mediators` as possible. But remember that a Mediator should not break the encapsulation of a View Component by reaching down many levels into its implementation to set or get data. Nor should a parent View Component. The relationship between Invoice, InvoiceHeader, and InvoiceDetails components is simple. But for either the Invoice component or the InvoiceMediator to access invoiceDetails.detailsGrid.selectedItem.id would be considered bad OOP form and should guide you in the consideration of component design and the granularity of its mediation.

But communication is a two-way street. The Mediator is not only concerned with the View Component it tends and the events that component generates, but also with Notifications from other parts of the system that may be relevant to its View Component. To follow the thread left dangling in "Step 3: Proxys" on page 35, imagine the InvoiceProxy has sent out an InvoiceProxy.INVOICE_LOADED note with the InvoiceVO in the note body. The InvoiceMediator will have expressed an interest in this note when it was registered, so it will be notified, and respond by taking the InvoiceVO from the note body and setting it on its View Component, where it will be displayed.

Name Mediators after the View Components they tend, such as Invoi ceMediator for the Invoice View Component.

Sometimes Flex will defer the instantiation of child components that are defined in MXML but not shown until the user navigates to them, such as children of the ViewStack component. These components require special handling when it comes to mediation. The same goes for popups and dynamically created View Components. We will talk more about these issues in Chapter 9.

Step 5: Commands

By the time you get to implementing some Commands, most of your initial actors will be in place aside from the StartupCommand created in the scaffolding phase. There are many roles for Commands, but generally they respond to notifications from other Commands, Proxys, or Mediators and in turn perform some sort of logic, often making Proxy calls, or sending notifications to be handled by another Command or some number of interested Mediators.

To carry forward the example from "Step 4: Mediators" on page 36, let's say the user changed the terms property of the InvoiceVO in the InvoiceHeader component and clicked a button in that component to save the changes. It dispatched a bubbling custom event that InvoiceMediator was listening to the Invoice component for. The Invoi ceMediator handles the event by sending an AppConstants.VALIDATE_AND_SUB MIT_INVOICE note with the InvoiceVO from the event in the note body. This note is registered to the ValidateAndSubmitInvoiceCommand, which does just what its name implies.

Name Commands after the processes they implement, such as ValidateAnd SubmitInvoiceCommand for a Command that takes invoice data generated or modified in the View tier, validates the contents, and submits it to a service (via collaboration with a Proxy).

CHAPTER 3

Modelling the Domain

You must have some way of representing the basic data that your app will manage and, in the OOP world, that usually takes the form of some class with typed properties. There are lots of pressures that guide the ultimate implementation of your domain model entities in a client application. For instance, if you are using LCDS, BlazeDS, or WebORB, you can create classes on the server that map property for property to corresponding classes in the client. When a Java service sends one of these classes in a result, the ActionScript version of that class shows up already populated in the client and there is no need to parse the result onto an object yourself. Or you might receive JSON or XML from a REST service and programmatically convert it to typed Action-Script objects in the client when you receive the result. And using Flex and AIR, you might want those objects to have bindable properties so that View Components that use them as data providers can be updated when they change. A key thing to remember is that these classes should not know the architecture framework classes (PureMVC) or the View Component framework (Flex). These classes should stick to representing data. They might use collection types defined by Flash or Flex (such as `Vector` or `ArrayCollection`), but never `Buttons`, `DataGrids`, or other display list objects.

Designing the Schema

Earlier, we thought through the entities that the StoryArchitect application will concern itself with managing. We also decided how we plan to store the data: XML files. At first, they will be stored on the local machine and in the future, perhaps in an online storage service such as Amazon S3. Finally, that guided us to the approach of encapsulating the XML handling inside the Value Objects. So our logical starting point is designing the XML schema.

If we were persisting to a database, we would design the database schema first, defining all the tables and indices. It is no different if you plan to store your data as XML. It is dangerous to allow your XML entities to be defined loosely on the fly as you build your app. By using a an XML Schema creation and visualization tool such as Altova's XMLSpy (which was used to create the diagrams in this section), you can do this in a visual interface and come out of the process not only with a concise understanding of how your XML structures will work, but an underlying ruleset that can be used to validate an XML entity purporting to adhere to the schema. While schema-based validation is outside the scope of this book, it is certainly a bonus to creating the schema first.

 Do you always need to use Value Objects wrapping XML for PureMVC to work properly? No, not at all. However, this is a good pattern to use in conjunction with PureMVC that helps take the pressure off the Proxy for knowing everything about the VOs, and keeps you from feeling the need to create amorphous utility/helper classes with loose roles that increase dependencies and complexity. Since so much data is in XML form already, this pattern can help you get going quickly with handling the result of many existing server APIs as well as those you design from scratch.

Reviewing the Entities

Here, in relative order of complexity, are StoryArchitect's domain model entities:

Note
> A URL and/or free form text about any entity

Setting
> A location where part of a Story takes place

Milieu
> A collection of Settings associated with a Story or Series

Character
> An individual within a Story or Series

Cast
> A collection of Characters associated with a Story or Series

Draft
> A version of the raw text of a Scene

Scene
> The atomic unit of a Story, may have multiple Drafts

Chapter
> A grouping of Scenes within a Part or a Story

Part
> A grouping of Chapters within a Story

Story
> A collection of Scenes, possibly grouped into Chapters and Parts

Season
> An optional grouping for Stories in a Series

Series
    A collection of Stories with a common Cast and Milieu

Creating the Schema

In the following diagrams, you will see the XML structure for the various domain entities represented graphically. Generally speaking, we are looking at elements that have attributes and/or other elements or text for content. The more complicated entities may take a number of possible forms, such as a Story having different collections (Parts, Chapters, or Scenes) based on its type, for instance. We will work up from the simpler structures to the more complex. Along with each diagram will be a snippet of somewhat representative XML for comparison.

ValueObject

The VO requires a unique id, but everything else is optional, including a name, description, Note collection, ordinal for sorting, and a flag to indicate if the object is a stub (a placeholder that needs to be loaded from storage). In the other diagrams, these attributes and elements will be collapsed. The dashed lines in the diagrams indicate an element or attribute that is optional. This is an element that is never created by itself, but other elements will inherit its attributes and child element definitions. Therefore, Figure 3-1 will be the one diagram without an accompanying XML snippet.

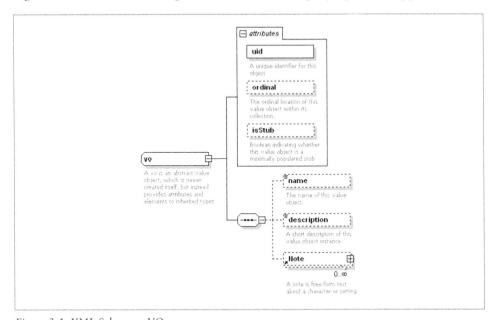

Figure 3-1. XML Schema—VO

Note

Unlike all the other Value Objects discussed below, `Note` does not extend VO since it is contained within a VO and does not require any of the properties of the VO. It simply gives us the a way to attach some free-form text and/or a URL to any of the other entities. Nothing more complicated than an index card. See Figure 3-2.

```
<Note url="http://bit.ly/0gz7Q">Interesting article about filaments of Dark Matter
pulling in gas and funneling it across the galaxy.</Note>
```

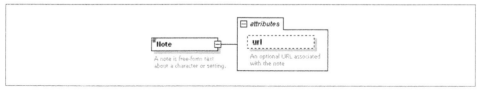

Figure 3-2. XML Schema—Note

Setting

A Setting inherits all of the properties it needs from VO, except an element name. We can give it a name, a description, and add any number of `Notes`. See Figure 3-3.

```
<Setting uid="Setting-434514-1">
  <name>Captain Froop's Cabin</name>
  <description>Utilitarian room with a viewscreen filling one wall.</description>
  <Note url="http://bit.ly/qYeGZi">Here is an illustration with the general look.</
Note>
</Setting>
```

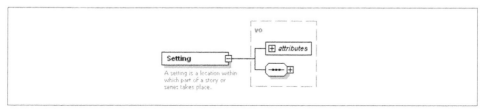

Figure 3-3. XML Schema—Setting

Milieu

A Milieu is a simple wrapper for a collection of Settings that we can give a unique ID, save in a separate file, and share between Stories in a Series. See Figure 3-4.

```
<Milieu uid="Milieu-3454553-34">
  <Setting uid="Setting-434514-1">
    <name>Captain Froop's Cabin</name>
    <description>Utilitarian room with a viewscreen filling one wall.</description>
  </Setting>
</Milieu>
```

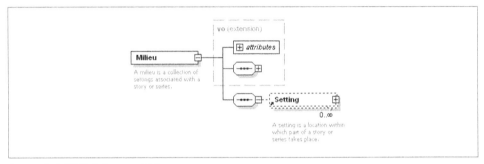

Figure 3-4. XML Schema—Milieu

Character

A Character adds to the VO a few attributes to describe personality according to the popular Enneagram (*http://www.enneagraminstitute.com/*) system. That system basically has a gradient of nine personality archetypes, three "emotional centers," and nine "levels of development." This is an incredibly powerful way of exploring and understanding the personalities and motivations of your fictional characters and determining how they will behave in various situations. See Figure 3-5.

```
<Character uid="Character-56432464-1" egramType="8" egramCenter="1" egramLevel="4">
  <name>Captain Froop</name>
  <description>Green, slithery, has tentacles. Captain of the Vroomfastian
intergalactic transport ship.</description>
</Character>
```

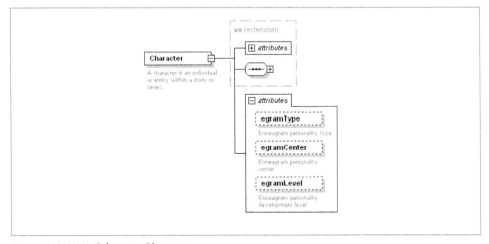

Figure 3-5. XML Schema—Character

Cast

A Cast inherits from VO and is a simple wrapper for a collection of Characters. Again, a unique ID allows us to save the collection separately from the Story(s) or Series that it is associated with. See Figure 3-6.

```
<Cast uid="Cast-2345213-1">
  <Character uid="Character-56432464-1" egramType="8" egramCenter="1" egramLevel="5">
    <name>Captain Froop</name>
    <description>Green, slithery, has tentacles. Captain of the Vroomfastian
intergalactic transport ship.</description>
  </Character>
  <Character uid="Character-33454645-24" egramType="1" egramCenter="0" egramLevel="4">
    <name>Jerry</name>
    <description>Twelve year old kid. Red hair, freckles.</description>
  </Character>
</Cast>
```

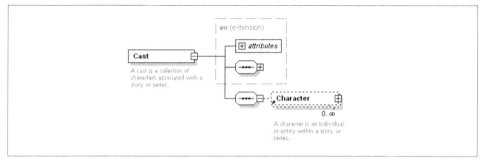

Figure 3-6. XML Schema—Cast

Draft

Although it will inherit from VO, we will not use any elements within the Draft; its content will be text only. It has a flag indicating if it is the current Draft for the Scene. See Figure 3-7.

```
<Draft uid="Draft-5443523-22" isCurrent="true">Dawn hit him in the face like a sack of
frozen turnips.</Draft>
```

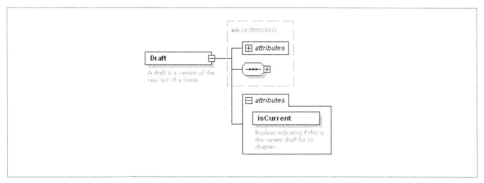

Figure 3-7. XML Schema—Draft

Scene

Scene inherits from VO and has a collection of Drafts, only one of which can be considered the current Draft.

Scenes are generally written from one particular *viewpoint*. These include First Person (such as eyewitness accounts), Second Person (not very popular since the book is telling the reader what they are experiencing, using the word "you"), Third Person (limited to a specific Character's *point of view* or omniscient; seeing into any character at will). The viewpoint will be tracked in an attribute, and in the application we will define a special class to track the valid settings.

Also, if the Scene is from the point of view of a Character in the Story, we will associate the Scene with the Character by storing the unique ID of the Character as an attribute of the Scene. See Figure 3-8.

```
<Scene uid="Scene-89543346-3" ordinal="1">
  <Draft uid="Draft-9678546-34" ordinal="1" isCurrent="true">A harsh klaxon echoed
through the ship as the autopilot disengaged from hyperspace.</Draft>
</Scene>
```

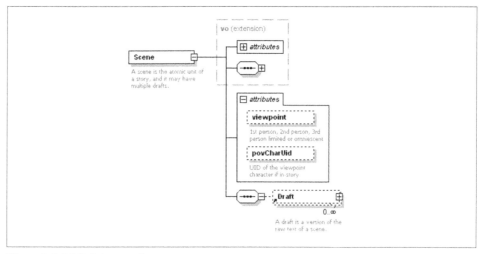

Figure 3-8. XML Schema—Scene

Chapter

Chapter is a pretty simple entity. It inherits from VO and has a collection of Scenes. With regard to numbering, Chapters are either relative to the Story or the Part they happen to be in. See Figure 3-9.

```
<Chapter uid="Chapter-54435453-6" ordinal="12">
  <Scene uid="Scene-89543346-3" ordinal="1">
    <Draft uid="Draft-5465344-43" ordinal="1" isCurrent="true">It was a dark and stormy
night.</Draft>
  </Scene>
  <Scene uid="Scene-56562546-2"  ordinal="1" />
  <Scene uid="Scene-78678346-12" ordinal="2" />
</Chapter>
```

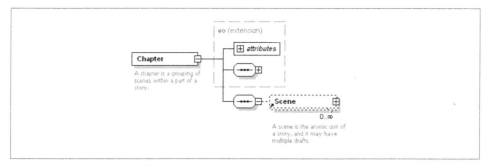

Figure 3-9. XML Schema—Chapter

Part

Just another grouping mechanism, Part is predictably similar to Chapter. It inherits the properties of a VO and has a collection of Chapters. Parts do not make a book any larger, just more complex. Usually Parts are used to group Chapters that happen in different periods of time, or to allocate large chunks of the Story to the viewpoint of a single character.

Parts are optional in a story, but if a Story uses Parts then the Story's Chapters will reside inside the Part elements themselves. Ordinals will be assigned based on the next available Part for the Story. See Figure 3-10.

```
<Part uid="Part-12345678-5" ordinal="1">
  <name>The Early Years</name>
  <Chapter uid="Chapter-3454656-32" ordinal="1">
    <Scene uid="Scene-56562546-2" ordinal="1" />
    <Scene uid="Scene-78678346-12" ordinal="2" />
  </Chapter>
  <Chapter uid="Chapter-7867834-45" ordinal="2" />
</Part>
```

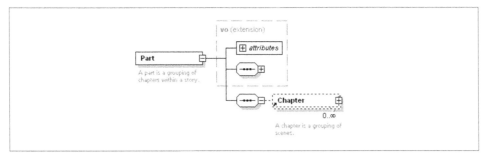

Figure 3-10. XML Schema—Part

Story

A Story will inherit the attributes and elements of the VO. It has an optional collection of Notes. It will also be capable of representing several different types that tell us how the Scenes are arranged.

In a simple short story, we will just have a collection of Scenes. In a normal novella or novel-length Story, we will have a collection of Chapters, which will of course contain Scenes. In a more complex work, we may have Parts, which will contain Chapters that contain Scenes. In the diagram, this selection is indicated by the "switch" showing us that we will have either a collection of Parts, Chapters, or Scenes, but not a mix.

Also, the Story element will contain optional Cast and Milieu elements. This is a place where the isStub attribute of the VO comes into play. Cast and Milieu elements will be saved to separate files (since a Series may share them between multiple Stories). This means that when we store a Story, we will need to replace the Cast and Milieu with stubs, and when we load a Story, we will load the Cast and Milieu (by their unique id) and replace the stubs before sending to the View tier. See Figure 3-11.

```xml
<Story uid="Story-12345678-1" ordinal="1" isStub="false" type="0">
  <name>Untitled Scifi Story</name>
  <description>The Vroomfastians have been traveling the Dark Matter Highway for quite awhile. They've just pulled off at our exit, and Man are they hungry!</description>
  <Note url="http://bit.ly/Ogz7Q">Interesting article about filaments of Dark Matter pulling in gas and funneling it across the galaxy.</Note>
  <Note>How about "Once, Upon the Dark Matter Highway" for a title?</Note>
  <Cast/>
  <Milieu/>
  <Scene uid="Scene-89543346-3" ordinal="1">
    <Draft uid="Draft-5465344-43" ordinal="1" isCurrent="false">It was a dark and stormy night.</Draft>
    <Draft uid="Draft-5443523-22" ordinal="2" isCurrent="false">Dawn hit him in the face like a sack of frozen turnips.</Draft>
    <Draft uid="Draft-9678546-34" ordinal="3" isCurrent="true">A harsh klaxon echoed through the ship as the autopilot disengaged from hyperspace.</Draft>
  </Scene>
  <Scene uid="Scene-56562546-2" ordinal="2" />
  <Scene uid="Scene-78678346-12" ordinal="3" />
</Story>
```

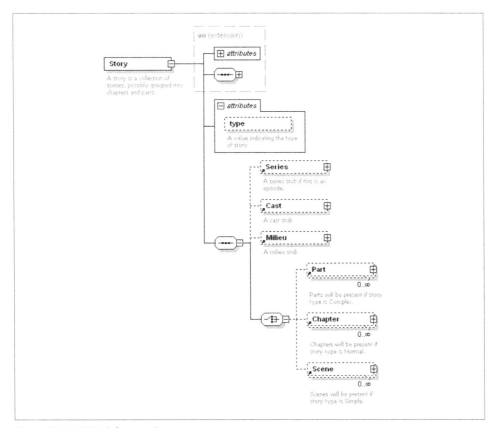

Figure 3-11. XML Schema—Story

Season

A Season is a simple wrapper around a collection of Story elements. Seasons are optional in a Series, but if a Series uses Seasons, then the Story elements will be stored within the Season elements. See Figure 3-12.

```
<Season uid="Season-43534573-1" ordinal="1">
  <Story uid="Story-56562546-41" ordinal="1" />
  <Story uid="Story-78678346-24" ordinal="2" />
</Story>
```

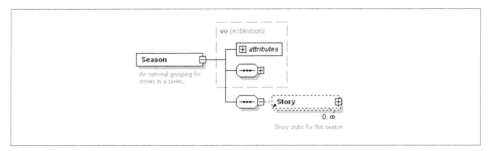

Figure 3-12. XML Schema—Season

Series

A Series will inherit the attributes and elements of the VO. It has an optional collection of Notes. Also, the Series element will contain optional Cast and Milieu elements, which are shared with all the Stories in a Series. See Figure 3-13.

```
<Series uid="Story-12345678-1" ordinal="1" isStub="false" useSeasons="false">
  <name>Untitled Scifi Series</name>
  <description>A young boy becomes a central figure in a saga of galactic intrigue when
he and his father are abducted by aliens and given a powerful secret to keep.</
description>
  <Note url="http://bit.ly/Ogz7Q">Interesting article about filaments of Dark Matter
pulling in gas and funneling it across the galaxy.</Note>
  <Cast/>
  <Milieu/>
  <Story uid="Story-56562546-2" ordinal="1">
    <name>Once, Upon the Dark Matter Highway</name>
    <description>The Vroomfastians have been traveling the Dark Matter Highway for
quite awhile. They've just pulled off at our exit, and Man are they hungry!</
description>
  </Story>
  <Story uid="Scene-78678346-12" ordinal="2" />
</Series>
```

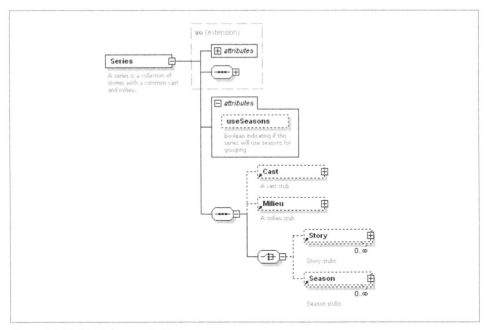

Figure 3-13. XML Schema—Series

Creating the Value Objects

Based on the work designing the XML schema, we have a good understanding of what properties the Value Object classes will have to expose. These Value Objects will be self-serializing, so they will use *implicit accessors*—pairs of functions for getting and setting a typed value that appear, to callers, to be a single property. This will allow us to take a typed property and store it in an XML structure or vice-versa. Clearly, we will not include the source of all the VOs here, but it is important to understand how such classes will work. We will examine three important ones in order of complexity.

 It is important to build your VOs in such a way that they not reference any PureMVC classes. They should be independently testable and usable outside of your PureMVC application.

A Simple Case

Let's start with a simple but important data carrier: the NoteVO. A collection of them are available to any other VO in the system via inheritance from ValueObject.

Notice the NoteVO has a [Bindable] tag prior to the beginning of the class declaration. We will do this on all the VOs. It is a given that View Components will collaborate with

Value Objects to represent and expose data. The [Bindable] tag allows a View Component in possession of a NoteVO instance to be updated when the NoteVO's properties change. Like our use of XML as a native data type, this is another positive leveraging of the platform functionality while retaining MVC separation in our architecture.

Also, the constructor for this class takes an optional XML argument. When we pull raw XML from the filesystem and create corresponding Value Objects, we do so by passing that XML into the constructors of the appropriate Value Object class. But if we do not pass in any XML, a valid default element must be created, since all further interaction with the object will be through its accessors, which in turn manage bits of the XML structure.

Notice how the accessors do the job of serializing and deserializing the values so that the data is always stored in the XML structure, ready to be saved by simply writing out the xml property. The url accessors store and retrieve a String on an attribute of the XML element, while the text accessors manage the text content of the element itself.

NoteVO

```
package com.futurescale.sa.model.vo
{
    /**
     * A Note is a URL and/or freeform text about any other entity
     */
    [Bindable] public class NoteVO
    {
        /**
         * The XML element name.
         */
        public static const ELEMENT:String = "Note";

        /**
         * Construct a NoteVO.
         */
        public function NoteVO( xml:XML=null )
        {
            this.xml = (xml)?xml:<{ELEMENT}/>;
        }

        /**
         * The text of this Note.
         */
        public function set text( t:String ):void
        {
            x.setChildren(t);
        }
        public function get text():String
        {
            return xml.toString();
        }

        /**
```

```
      * An optional URL.
      */
     public function set url( u:String ):void
     {
         xml.@url = u;
     }
     public function get url():String
     {
         return xml.@url;
     }

     /**
      * XML representation of the Note.
      */
     public function set xml( x:XML ):void
     {
         this.x = x;
     }
     public function get xml():XML
     {
         return x;
     }
     protected var x:XML;
   }
 }
```

A Slightly More Complex Case

As the base class for all the other VOs (except NoteVO), the ValueObject class provides some valuable inherited functionality.

Note the way that the name getter works. If there is no <name/> element, then a name is generated based on the XML element name and the ordinal number. This will allow, for instance, for Chapters to have unique names if we set them, or logical generated names like *Chapter 52* otherwise.

Another important feature of the ValueObject is the getNextOrdinal method, which is used to derive a next available ordinal for a child object. When a new ChapterVO is added to a StoryVO, we need to know what chapter number should be assigned. This is determined by the getNextOrdinal method. A method for sorting ValueObjects by ordinal allows us to ensure that regardless of how SceneVOs are added to a ChapterVO, they can be sorted in the correct order for display. There is also a method for sorting ValueObjects by name, so that CharacterVOs and SettingVOs can be presented in a sensible ordering by the CastVO and MilieuVO.

The getStub() method returns an XML element representation of the ValueObject that only contains the properties defined on the ValueObject. This may seem like a straightforward clone operation at first, but remember the other VOs in the system will extend ValueObject, and they are the ones that getStub() will be called on. There are a few places in the app where we do not want the entire VO. When we save StoryVOs, for instance, they will go into a folder by themselves, but in order to get a list of available

StoryVOs without having to open each one and read it completely, we will need an index of some sort. That index will be composed of the StoryVO stubs, which will have isStub set to true and will have only the basic ValueObject properties. Another place where a stub is needed is in the list of StoryVOs in a SeriesVO. When we load a SeriesVO, we will want to be able to see some basic information about its episodes, but we do not want the entire contents of every Story to be saved as part of a Series. Instead, we want to save a SeriesVO with StoryVO stubs, and then load the Stories on demand later.

Perhaps the most important inherited functionality is the ability to provide a default element for any subclass with a unique identifier. As you probably noticed in the XML snippets of "ValueObject" on page 41, the uid properties all followed a similar pattern that is created in the validateOrProvideDefault() method, which is called by the constructor. In a remote database scenario, new objects created at the view typically do not have an ID until they have been added to the database. But here, we can easily generate our own on the fly as the object is created. The procedure being used for generating a unique ID is to prepend the name of the element, e.g., *Story* or *Character*, to a value representing the number of seconds since the epoch plus the number of ValueObject subclasses created this runtime.

ValueObject

```
package com.futurescale.sa.model.vo
{
    import mx.formatters.DateFormatter;

    /**
     * A base class for Value Object
     */
    [Bindable] public class ValueObject
    {
        /**
         * Constants for separation of concatenated text.
         */
        public static const DOUBLE_SPACE:String = "\n\n";
        public static const DASH:String = "-";
        public static const SPACE:String = " ";

        /**
         * Construct a ValueObject. The element name must be passed
         * in, but the XML is optional. The XML will be validated to
         * be of the element type defined, or replaced with a default
         * XML element of the given type.
         */
        public function ValueObject( element:String, xml:XML=null )
        {
            this.xml = validateOrProvideDefault( element, xml );
        }

        /**
         * Get a stub of this Value Object.
```

```
 *
 * Certain objects need to be stubbed in the parent XML
 * structure before the parent can be saved. For instance,
 * all the Story elements in a Series or the Cast and Milieu
 * in both the Story and Series.
 */
public function getStub( ):XML
{
    var stub:XML = validateOrProvideDefault( xml.localName() );
    var vo:ValueObject = new ValueObject( xml.localName(), stub );
    vo.isStub = true;
    vo.uid = this.uid;
    vo.name = this.name;
    vo.ordinal = this.ordinal;
    vo.description = this.description;
    return stub;
}

/**
 * The name of the Value Object. If no name is set,
 * element and ordinal attribute are concatenated.
 */
public function set name( n:String ):void
{
    xml.name = n;
}
public function get name():String
{
    return (String(xml.name)!="") ?
            String(xml.name) : String(xml.localName()+SPACE+ordinal);
}

/**
 * Ordinal location of this Value Object within the collection.
 */
public function set ordinal( o:Number ):void
{
    xml.@ordinal = o;
}
public function get ordinal():Number
{
    return Number(xml.@ordinal);
}

/**
 * Unique identifier for this ValueObject
 */
public function set uid( u:String ):void
{
    xml.@uid = u;
}
public function get uid():String
{
    return String(xml.@uid);
}
```

```
/**
 * Is this ValueObject an unpopulated stub?
 */
public function set isStub( s:Boolean ):void
{
    xml.@isStub = s;
}
public function get isStub():Boolean
{
    return (x.@isStub=="true");
}

/**
 * A short description of this ValueObject
 */
public function set description( d:String ):void
{
    xml.description = d;
}
public function get description():String
{
    return String(xml.description);
}

/**
 * An Vector of a ValueObject's NoteVOs.
 */
public function get notes():Vector.<NoteVO>
{
    var v:Vector.<NoteVO> = new Vector.<NoteVO>();
    var xl:XMLList = xml.child(NoteVO.ELEMENT);
    for each ( var nx:XML in xl ) {
        var note:NoteVO = new NoteVO(nx);
        v.push(note);
    }
    return v;
}
public function set notes( v:Vector.<NoteVO> ):void
{} // read-only but bindable

/**
 * Add a Note to the ValueObject
 */
public function addNote( note:NoteVO ):void
{
    xml.appendChild( note.xml );
}

/**
 * XML representation of Value Object. Override
 * accessors to provide default.
 */
public function set xml( x:XML ):void
{
```

```
        this.x = x;
    }
    public function get xml():XML
    {
        return x;
    }
    protected var x:XML;

    /**
     * A function for sorting ValueObjects by ordinal.
     */
    public static function ordinalSort( v1:ValueObject, v2:ValueObject ):Number
    {
        var retval:Number = 0;                              // equality
        if (v1.ordinal < v2.ordinal) { retval = -1; }       // less
        else if (v1.ordinal > v2.ordinal) { retval = 1; }   // greater
        return retval;
    }

    /**
     * A function for sorting ValueObjects by name.
     */
    public static function nameSort( v1:ValueObject, v2:ValueObject ):Number
    {
        var retval:Number = 0;                              // equality
        if (v1.name < v2.name) { retval = -1; }             // less
        else if (v1.name > v2.name) { retval = 1; }         // greater
        return retval;
    }

    /**
     * Get the next ordinal for a child element.
     */
    protected function getNextOrdinal( xl:XMLList ):Number
    {
        var n:Number = 0;
        var x:XML;
        for each ( x in xl ) {
            var o:Number = Number(x.@ordinal);
            if (o > n) n = o;
        }
        return ++n;
    }

    /**
     * Validate that the XML element passed in is not null and that
     * its element name is correct. Otherwise provide a default with a
     * unique identifier.
     */
    protected function validateOrProvideDefault( elementName:String, xml:XML ):XML
    {
        if (xml == null || xml.localName() != elementName) {
            var u:String = elementName + DASH + new Date().time +
                        DASH + uidRuntimeUniquifier++;
            xml = <{elementName} uid={u}/>
```

```
            }
            return xml;
        }

        /**
         * Number of unique Value Objects created this runtime.
         * Used to ensure two objects of the same type created
         * within the same millisecond will have a unique uid.
         */
        protected static var uidRuntimeUniquifier:Number = 0;
    }
}
```

An Advanced Case

The most complex example in this application is the StoryVO. Recall from its XML schema design that it sports three different story types that determine whether it contains a collection of PartVOs, ChapterVOs, or SceneVOs.

Since it is the data carrier in possession of these collections, and it inherits the getNextOrdinal() method from ValueObject, StoryVO can easily pass in the XMLList of child elements and get the next available one. Also, its accessors for the collections are somewhat more involved. Rather than managing a simple value from an attribute or element, it must construct a collection of Value Objects created from a list of XML elements. In this implementation, we will use ActionScript's Vector class. This allows us to have a collection and specify the type of objects it can contain. Also, in this particular implementation, the collection accessors are asymmetrical. For instance, you may retrieve the list of PartVOs but you may not set it; it is read-only. New PartVOs are added via getNewPart() or addPart(). The getNewPart() method will create a new PartVO, automatically assign the next available uid for a Part and call addPart() to actually add the XML element to the StoryVO's XML structure. Calling addPart() directly is done when we want to add an existing PartVO from somewhere else, such as another StoryVO. Note that the addPart() method goes to the length of reordering the PartVOs in the collection if the incoming PartVO already has an ordinal that falls in the existing range, otherwise it assigns the next highest value.

As mentioned earlier, we have three story types: simple, normal, and complex. In the XML schema, this is implemented as a type attribute on the <Story/> element. We will store a simple value of 0, 1, or 2 to represent the types. However, in code that is difficult to remember. Note the type accessors on the StoryVO work with something called a StoryTypeEnum. That class enumerates the valid values for the field and gives them constant names. So in order to set the value of the type field directly, the calling code would have to also know the StoryTypeEnum class. In order to encapsulate the handling of the type property, you will notice some accessors for three Boolean properties called useScenes, useChapters, and useParts. Now with an instance of StoryVO, you can say storyVO.useParts=true, and the type setter will be called with StoryTypeEnum.COMPLEX, which will in turn set the type attribute of storyVO.xml to a value of 2.

Another important feature of StoryVO is the getText() method for obtaining the read-only text of the entire Story, composed of the raw text of the current Drafts of all the Scenes, however they are grouped. The same method is implemented in PartVO, Chap terVO, and SceneVO. In each case, the method goes through the direct children and invokes their getText() methods, or simply gets the text property in the case of Sce neVO, concatenating them, adding double spaces between Scenes, and if there is more than one Chapter, it adds headings for each Chapter, and likewise for Parts.

If you are of the school that says Value Objects should be dumb data carriers, this may seem like a lot of logic to be putting into a VO. But all this code has to go somewhere, and it is needed everywhere in the application that may handle a VO. Some folks build so-called helper or utility classes to place all this logic in, reasoning that they are separating the logic from the data and that must be good. Then they proceed to make the methods that deal with these objects static and access them from everywhere in the app, creating dependencies on not just the Value Object, but now the helper.

StoryVO

```
package com.futurescale.sa.model.vo
{
    import com.futurescale.sa.model.enum.StoryTypeEnum;

    import mx.utils.StringUtil;

    /**
     * A Story could be a standalone work or an Episode of a
     * Series. Its Chapters may optionally be grouped by
     * Parts, and it has a Cast, a Milieu, and one or
     * more Plots. This Value Object represents a single
     * Story.
     */
    [Bindable] public class StoryVO extends ValueObject
    {
        /**
         * The XML element name.
         */
        public static const ELEMENT:String = "Story";

        /**
         * Construct a StoryVO.
         */
        public function StoryVO( xml:XML=null )
        {
            super( ELEMENT, xml );
        }

        /**
         * The Cast stub.
         */
        public function get cast():CastVO
        {
            return ( x.Cast[0] )?new CastVO( x.Cast[0] ):null;
```

```
}
public function set cast( c:CastVO ):void
{
    x.Cast = c.xml;
}

/**
 * The Milieu stub.
 */
public function get milieu():MilieuVO
{
    return ( x.Milieu[0] )?new MilieuVO( x.Milieu[0] ):null;
}
public function set milieu( m:MilieuVO ):void
{
    x.Milieu = m.xml;
}

/**
 * The Series stub, if this is an Episode.
 */
public function get series():SeriesVO
{
    return ( x.Series[0] )?new SeriesVO( x.Series[0] ):null;
}
public function set series( s:SeriesVO ):void
{
    x.Series = s.xml;
}

/**
 * Is this an Episode of a Series?
 */
public function get isEpisode():Boolean
{
    return ( x.Series[0] );
}
public function set isEpisode( e:Boolean ):void
{} // read only but bindable

/**
 * What type of Story is this?
 * StoryTypeEnum.SIMPLE  = Scenes only
 * StoryTypeEnum.NORMAL  = Chapters, and Scenes
 * StoryTypeEnum.COMPLEX = Parts, Chapters, and Scenes
 */
public function get type():StoryTypeEnum
{
    return (x.@type!=undefined)?StoryTypeEnum.list[ Number( x.@type ) ]:null;
}
public function set type( t:StoryTypeEnum ):void
{
    x.@type = t.ordinal;
}
```

```
/**
 * Use Scenes only for this Story?
 */
public function get useScenes():Boolean
{
    return ( this.type == StoryTypeEnum.SIMPLE );
}
public function set useScenes(u:Boolean):void
{
    this.type = StoryTypeEnum.SIMPLE;
}

/**
 * Use Chapters for this Story?
 */
public function get useChapters():Boolean
{
    return ( this.type == StoryTypeEnum.NORMAL );
}
public function set useChapters(u:Boolean):void
{
    this.type = StoryTypeEnum.NORMAL;
}

/**
 * Use Parts for this Story?
 */
public function get useParts():Boolean
{
    return ( this.type == StoryTypeEnum.COMPLEX );
}
public function set useParts(u:Boolean):void
{
    this.type = StoryTypeEnum.COMPLEX;
}

/**
 * An ordinal-sorted Vector of a SIMPLE Story's Scenes.
 */
public function get scenes():Vector.<SceneVO>
{
    var v:Vector.<SceneVO> = new Vector.<SceneVO>();
    var xl:XMLList = xml..Scene;
    for each ( var sx:XML in xl ) {
        var scene:SceneVO = new SceneVO(sx);
        v.push(scene);
    }
    v.sort(ValueObject.ordinalSort);
    return v;
}
public function set scenes( v:Vector.<SceneVO> ):void
{} // read-only but bindable

/**
 * An ordinal-sorted Vector of a NORMAL Story's Chapters.
```

```
    */
    public function get chapters():Vector.<ChapterVO>
    {
        var v:Vector.<ChapterVO> = new Vector.<ChapterVO>();
        var xl:XMLList = xml..Chapter;
        for each ( var cx:XML in xl ) {
            var chapter:ChapterVO = new ChapterVO(cx);
            v.push(chapter);
        }
        v.sort(ValueObject.ordinalSort);
        return v;
    }
    public function set chapters( v:Vector.<ChapterVO> ):void
    {} // read-only but bindable

    /**
     * An ordinal-sorted Vector of a COMPLEX Story's Parts.
     */
    public function get parts():Vector.<PartVO>
    {
        var v:Vector.<PartVO> = new Vector.<PartVO>();
        if (useParts) {
            var xl:XMLList = xml.child(PartVO.ELEMENT);
            for each ( var px:XML in xl ) {
                var part:PartVO = new PartVO(px);
                v.push(part);
            }
            v.sort(ValueObject.ordinalSort);
        }
        return v;
    }
    public function set parts( v:Vector.<PartVO> ):void
    {} // read-only but bindable

    /**
     * Get a new Scene for the Story.
     */
    public function getNewScene():SceneVO
    {
        var scene:SceneVO = new SceneVO();
        addScene( scene );
        return scene;
    }

    /**
     * Get a new Chapter for the Story.
     */
    public function getNewChapter(   ):ChapterVO
    {
        var chapter:ChapterVO = new ChapterVO();
        addChapter( chapter );
        return chapter;
    }

    /**
```

```
 * Get a new Part for the Story.
 */
public function getNewPart():PartVO
{
    var part:PartVO = new PartVO();
    addPart( part );
    return part;
}



/**
 * Add a Scene to the Story, renumbering the existing
 * Scenes if the added Scene already has an ordinal less
 * than the next Scene ordinal. Otherwise next Scene
 * ordinal is assigned.
 *
 * Forces the story type to NORMAL if no part argument
 */
public function addScene( scene:SceneVO ):void
{
    if ( scene.ordinal > 0 && scene.ordinal < nextPartOrdinal ) {
        var scenes:Vector.<SceneVO> = this.scenes;
        for each (var svo:SceneVO in scenes ){
            if (svo.ordinal >= scene.ordinal) svo.ordinal++;
        }
    } else {
        scene.ordinal = nextSceneOrdinal;
    }
    xml.appendChild( scene.xml );
    useScenes=true;
}

/**
 * Add a Chapter to the Story.
 * Renumbers the existing Chapters if the added Chapter
 * already has an ordinal less than the next Chapter
 * ordinal. Otherwise next Chapter ordinal is assigned.
 *
 * Forces the story type to NORMAL if no part argument
 */
public function addChapter( chapter:ChapterVO ):void
{
    // renumber chapters if inserting
    if ( chapter.ordinal > 0 && chapter.ordinal < nextChapterOrdinal ) {
        var chapters:Vector.<ChapterVO> = this.chapters;
        for each ( var cvo:ChapterVO in chapters ){
            if ( cvo.ordinal >= chapter.ordinal ) cvo.ordinal++;
        }
    } else {
        chapter.ordinal = nextChapterOrdinal;
    }
    xml.appendChild( chapter.xml );
    useChapters=true;
}
```

```
/**
 * Add a Part to the Story, renumbering the existing
 * Parts if the added Part already has an ordinal less
 * than the next Part ordinal. Otherwise Part is assigned
 * next Part ordinal.
 *
 * Forces the story type to COMPLEX
 */
public function addPart( part:PartVO ):void
{
    if ( part.ordinal > 0 && part.ordinal < nextPartOrdinal ) {
        var parts:Vector.<PartVO> = this.parts;
        for each (var pvo:PartVO in parts ){
            if (pvo.ordinal >= part.ordinal) pvo.ordinal++;
        }
    } else {
        part.ordinal = nextPartOrdinal
    }
    xml.appendChild( part.xml );
    useParts=true;
}


/**
 * Get the text of the current Draft of each Scene
 * in the Story. Story title is optionally included
 * at the beginning of the text.
 *
 * If using Parts and there is more than one, Part
 * headings are included.
 *
 * If using Chapters and there is more than one, Chapter
 * headings are included.
 */
public function getText( includeHeading:Boolean=false ):String
{
    var text:String = includeHeading ? name + DOUBLE_SPACE : "";
    if (useParts) {
        var partList:Vector.<PartVO> = parts;
        if (partList.length > 1) {
            // multiple parts with headings
            for each ( var pvo:PartVO in partList) {
                text += pvo.getText(true) + DOUBLE_SPACE;
            }
        } else if (partList.length == 1){
            // single part sans heading
            text += PartVO(partList[0]).getText(false);
        }
    } else if (useChapters) {
        var chapterList:Vector.<ChapterVO> = chapters;
        if (chapterList.length > 1) {
            // multiple chapters with headings
            for each ( var cvo:ChapterVO in chapterList) {
                text += cvo.getText(true) + DOUBLE_SPACE;
            }
        } else if (chapterList.length == 1){
```

```
                // single chapter sans heading
                text += ChapterVO(chapterList[0]).getText(false);
            }
        } else if (useScenes) {
            var sceneList:Vector.<SceneVO> = scenes;
            if (sceneList.length > 1) {
                // multiple scene with headings
                for each ( var svo:SceneVO in sceneList) {
                    text += svo.getText(true) + DOUBLE_SPACE;
                }
            } else if (sceneList.length == 1){
                // single scene sans heading
                text += SceneVO(sceneList[0]).getText(false);
            }
        }

        // read-only text of story
        return StringUtil.trim( text );
    }

    /**
     * The word count for the full text of the Story.
     */
    public function get wordCount():Number
    {
        var wc:Number = 0;
        var storyText:String = getText(false);
        if ( storyText.length > 0 ) {
            wc = storyText.split(/\s+/g).length;
        }
        return wc;
    }

    public function set wordCount( c:Number ):void
    {} // read only but bindable

    /**
     * Get the next Part ordinal for this Story.
     * For COMPLEX stories with Parts, Chapters, and Scenes.
     */
    private function get nextPartOrdinal():Number
    {
        return getNextOrdinal( xml..Part );
    }

    /**
     * Get the next Chapter ordinal for this Story.
     * For NORMAL stories with Scenes and Chapters.
     */
    private function get nextChapterOrdinal():Number
    {
        return getNextOrdinal( xml..Chapter );
    }

    /**
```

```
        * Get the next Scene ordinal for this Story.
        * For SIMPLE stories with Scenes only.
        */
        private function get nextSceneOrdinal():Number
        {
            return getNextOrdinal( xml..Scene );
        }
    }
}
```

Creating the Enums

Some other languages, like Java, have a facility built into the language for *Enums*. But alas, ActionScript does not. So, what are Enums, exactly, and why do we care?

Enums are a way of enumerating all the possible values for a data field as static members of a class. As an example, let's look at the simplest way to handle enumerating the valid values for the `type` property of the `StoryVO`.

What would be wrong with something like this?

```
package com.futurescale.sa.model.constant
{
    public class StoryConstants
    {
        public static const SIMPLE:String  = "0";
        public static const NORMAL:String  = "1";
        public static const COMPLEX:String = "2";
    }
}
```

Nothing would be wrong with it at all, but there are a few things that would be nice to have.

First, a list of the possible values that could be used to populate a visual control for selecting the Story type. What else? Well, it would be good to have a name of the valid values and not just the values themselves. A combo box with 0, 1, and 2 as options for Story type would not be very user-friendly. It would be nice if it actually said "Simple," "Normal," and "Complex." It might be nicer if there was a description of those names shown beside combo: "Scenes Only," "Chapters and Scenes," and "Parts, Chapters, and Scenes." If there is no selection in the combo box, it would be nice if there was another version of the list that had an option that said "No Selection," but had a negative value so that the View Component could determine if a selection had been made. That way, business logic that iterates through the valid values, would not have to take the "No Selection" entry into account. Also, sometimes we want to have control over the order of items in a list, separate from the value. Finally, we need a way to determine equality of two Enums based on their complex content.

Now, all these nice frills could be hardcoded into the View Components that are meant to collect or display the Story type, but often there are multiple places in the app that need to interpret the Story type, so the Enum gives us a way of concentrating all these related things into the actual valid values we are interested in. They are just as easy to use as a simple constant, as shown above. Implementation is a bit more complex, but again, all of these responsibilities have to go somewhere, and the Enum role is a good fit.

 Do you always need to use Enums, and are they in some way necessary for PureMVC? No, absolutely not. However, they are a common pattern used in conjunction with PureMVC that take the pressure off other actors for knowing everything about the VOs and the valid values for their fields. The Enum is another kind of domain model entity, one where the values of all the properties are predetermined and not intended to be created dynamically from user input. Like VOs, they are not framework actors; they help keep the framework actors from taking on more responsibilities than fit their roles.

Enumerating the Enums

So we are beginning to understand the role of Enums, but what, specifically, do we need them for in our application?

- StoryTypeEnum: Valid values for the type property of StoryVO
- ViewPointEnum: Valid values for the viewpoint property of SceneVO
- EgramTypeEnum: Valid values for the egramType property of CharacterVO
- EgramCenterEnum: Valid values for the egramCenter property of CharacterVO
- EgramLevelEnum: Valid values for the egramLevel property of CharacterVO

The Base Class

Now let's have a look at the Enum class, which will provide some basic functionality to the subclasses in the same way ValueObject did for the VOs. It provides an ordinal, a name, and a description. It also has an equals method that will compare the properties of the current instance to another Enum instance.

Enum

```
package com.futurescale.sa.model.enum
{
    /**
     * A base class for enumerations
     */
    [Bindable] public class Enum
    {
        public var name:String;
        public var ordinal:Number;
        public var description:String;
```

```
        public function Enum( ordinal:Number, name:String, description:String )
        {
            this.name = name;
            this.ordinal = ordinal;
            this.description = description;
        }

        /**
         * Compare to another enum instance
         */
        public function equals( enum:Enum ):Boolean
        {
            return ( ( this.name        == enum.name )     &&
                     ( this.ordinal     == enum.ordinal ) &&
                     ( this.description == enum.description )
                   );
        }
    }
}
```

An Enum Subclass

The responsibilities of the Enum subclasses include defining static constants for some
data field's valid values that are actually static instances of the class. They provide these
constants in a list getter that returns an array. Also, there is a comboList getter, which
returns an ArrayCollection containing the list with a "No Selection" option added to
the front. ArrayCollection implements IList, which is necessary for list-based Spark
controls. The base class provides an equals method that you can probably trust as-is,
since it compares the three basic inherited properties of any Enum subclass. However,
your subclass may contain more properties to compare, or you may want to ensure that
not only are the basic properties a match, but so is the class of the instance being
compared. You can lock all this down by overriding the equals method, checking the
instance type and extra properties, and running the superclass method to ensure the
basic properties match.

Next up, we will see how a simple Enum subclass, the StoryTypeEnum, is implemented.

StoryTypeEnum

```
package com.futurescale.sa.model.enum
{
    import mx.collections.ArrayCollection;

    /**
     * An enumeration of Story types.
     */
    public class StoryTypeEnum extends Enum
    {
        public static const NONE:StoryTypeEnum      =
                new StoryTypeEnum( -1, "--None Selected--", "Choose a Story Type" );
```

```
public static const SIMPLE:StoryTypeEnum   =
        new StoryTypeEnum(  0, "Simple",   "Scenes only" );

public static const NORMAL:StoryTypeEnum    =
        new StoryTypeEnum(  1, "Normal",   "Chapters and Scenes" );

public static const COMPLEX:StoryTypeEnum   =
        new StoryTypeEnum(  2, "Complex", "Chapters, Parts, and Scenes" );

public function StoryTypeEnum( ordinal:Number, name:String, description:String )
{
    super( ordinal, name, description );
}

public static function get list():Array
{
    return [ SIMPLE, NORMAL, COMPLEX ];
}

public static function get comboList():ArrayCollection
{
    return new ArrayCollection( [ NONE ].concat( list ) );
}

override public function equals( enum:Enum ):Boolean
{
    return ( enum is StoryTypeEnum && super.equals( enum ) );
}
    }
}
```

Testing the Entities

The classes we have just built are the foundation of the entire application. The purpose of all other code is merely to expose instances of these classes to the user for manipulation and persisting. Particularly because these entities encapsulate logic for performing on-the-fly serialization and deserialization, it is important to test them before moving on. If you are not certain that your domain model is solid, then troubleshooting code that uses the entities will always include an unacceptable level of uncertainty. Time saved skipping your tests will surely be lost later to debugging. You do not have to write formal tests using a testing framework, but using a common one is the fastest way to unit-testing joy.

A Flex Unit Test Class

FlashBuilder integrates the FlexUnit testing framework and makes it really easy to create and run tests, so I have chosen to use it for this application. Most popular testing frameworks operate on a similar principle, varying mostly in the metadata that decorates each method. How you create new test classes will vary by IDE, but essentially for each class to be tested you can have the IDE generate a skeleton class that has methods for exercising all the code of the class you wish to test. Most offer the ability to do some setup and teardown before and after the entire test class is evaluated as well as around each of the test class methods. We will look at a simple example: a FlexUnit test class for the NoteVO. In our test class, we will work our way through the NoteVO's methods, starting with the constructor, which we test with two separate test methods since the class provides its own default if there is no XML passed in, leading to two separate behaviors that need testing. Once we have an object created and populated, we simply make assertions about it, as many as we can think of. If any of our assertions are not true, then we have a corresponding message to report.

Of course, unit testing is no magic bullet; bugs will show up later from edge cases you did not think of, or someone will add code that breaks something and they'll fail to run the tests to make sure the code still passes. But if your tests are thorough when you run them, resulting in the *Big Green Bar*, as shown in Figure 3-14, that tells you everything passed, it instills a great amount of confidence in the code you are building upon.

Figure 3-14. Flex Unit Test Runner—NoteVOTest.as

NoteVOTest

```
package com.futurescale.sa.model.vo.test
{
    import com.futurescale.sa.model.vo.NoteVO;
    import flexunit.framework.Assert;
    public class NoteVOTest
    {
        [Test] public function testNoteVOWithXML():void
```

```
    {
        var url:String = "http://google.com";
        var text:String = "Some stuff I'm keeping in the cloud.";
        var xml:XML = <Note url={url}>{text}</Note>;
        var vo:NoteVO = new NoteVO( xml );
        if (! vo is NoteVO ) Assert.fail("Construction with xml failed");
        if ( vo.text != text ) Assert.fail("text match failed");
        if ( vo.url != url ) Assert.fail("url match failed");
    }

    [Test] public function testNoteVOWithoutXML():void
    {
        var vo:NoteVO = new NoteVO();
        if (! vo is NoteVO ) Assert.fail("Construction without xml failed");
        if ( vo.xml.localName() != NoteVO.ELEMENT )
                Assert.fail("default xml not provided");
    }

    [Test] public function testSet_text():void
    {
        var text:String = "Bunnies are nice!";
        var vo:NoteVO = new NoteVO();
        vo.text = text;
        if ( vo.text != text ) Assert.fail("text match failed");
    }

    [Test] public function testSet_url():void
    {
        var url:String = "http://puremvc.org";
        var vo:NoteVO = new NoteVO();
        vo.url = url;
        if ( vo.url != url ) Assert.fail("url match failed");
    }

    [Test] public function testSet_xml():void
    {
        var url:String = "http://puremvc.org";
        var text:String = "Code at the Speed of Thought!";
        var xml:XML = <Note url={url}>{text}</Note>;
        var vo:NoteVO = new NoteVO();
        vo.xml = xml;
        if ( vo.text != text ) Assert.fail("text match failed");
        if ( vo.url != url ) Assert.fail("url match failed");
    }
    }
}
```

CHAPTER 4

Implementing the User Interface

The classes making up your user interface should encapsulate their own behavior and appearance. View Components may require data or the occasional method invocation from the outside in order to have something to display or to know they need to change to another visual state. But they should be capable of making those visual transitions themselves once given the input and impetus. When they have something to communicate to the rest of the application, they should do this solely by dispatching events or setting properties and making method invocations on their child components. In the context of a PureMVC application, a View Component should never know anything about the PureMVC framework classes or their subclasses.

One reason it is a good idea to build the View Components after building the Value Objects, and before getting deeply into the PureMVC apparatus, is that you do not yet have the ability to access those `Mediator`, `Proxy`, and `Command` classes since they have not yet been created. Since we have already created our Value Objects and Enums, we can populate our View Components with dummy VOs as we build them without having to have all the rest of the system in place to feed them to us. In fact, you should be able to farm out the development of the View Components to a separate company, team, or team member that knows nothing at all about PureMVC and still be successful. If the team is at another company, you might want to repackage your Model classes into a separate library for their use while they build the View Components.

The main thing to remember in your implementation of the View Components is that they should expose an API of events, properties, and methods for interacting with them. This API should hide the internal implementation of the components. For example, it should not be expected that the caller will reach into the component and set the `data Provider` property of a `DataGrid` instance declared within. Instead a bindable, public property named something like `displayItems` should be exposed. The `DataGrid` instance's `dataProvider` property should then be bound to the `displayItems` property. This means that the `Mediator` subclass that will tend the component does not know or care how the component is implemented, it just knows that there is a `displayItems` property to be set for displaying the data. The View Component could later be refactored to use a drop-down list with a different ID and the `Mediator` would be completely unaffected by the change.

Also, as with any class in an OOP application, try not to heap too many responsibilities onto any given View Component. Once you see a great many nested structures declared in one place and lots of associated logic and variables, you should consider creating custom components to replace large chunks of MXML. While this can be argued to create complexity (in the form of more classes), it actually simplifies the View Components, clarifies their roles, and makes them more reusable as you will see in this chapter.

A Tale of Two Views

After much work at the whiteboard considering how our goals for the Story Architect application should be translated into a user interface, it was determined that there will be two primary views to the application: a Chooser and an Editor. When you open up the application, you have a number of options available with regard to creating and managing your Stories and Series. You could choose a Story and export it as a file, delete it, change its name, etc. Or you could choose to write, and that leads you to the Editor, where you will be able to do just that. The Editor will provide you with the functionality for attaching descriptions and notes to any part of the Story, as well as a timeline for navigating and extending the Story.

While the functionality for dealing with a Series is a big part of the application, it is far less important to the primary goal of writing a Story, as is management of Cast and Milieu. This book will focus discussion on the primary Story-related use cases and user interface elements. Remember, our major goal for the first iteration is to create and persist a Story, edit and extend its structure, name any part of the structure, and add descriptions and notes to it.

Now we will examine some of the more important pieces of the user interface. In addition to the main application and components, we will define one bubbling event called `AppEvent` that can carry data, and a class similar to a Value Object called `Selec tionContext` for sharing information about the current selection among the View Components.

With regard to collaborations, notice that all of these View Components basically know only their direct child components, the `AppEvent` class, the `SelectionContext` class, `Enum` and its subclasses, and `ValueObject` and its subclasses. There are no PureMVC `Facade`, `Mediator`, `Command`, `Proxy`, or `Notification` classes referenced anywhere within the View Components (with the exception of the main application itself, which must know the `Facade` to bootstrap the startup process). View Components expose properties to receive data, send events to communicate user intentions, observe and conform to the shared selection context, and interact only with their direct children and the data objects they are fed (either from a parent component or from a `Mediator`).

In the first view, upon opening the application, you can add or choose a Story or Series and access various functionalities associated with your selection. This is called the Chooser View and is shown in Figure 4-1. Functions like creating and managing the Story will open pop-ups to collect and apply the user input.

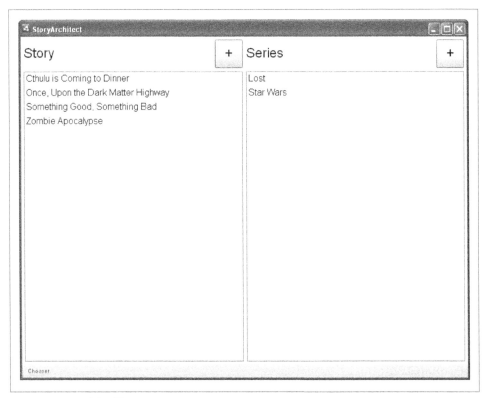

Figure 4-1. UI—The Chooser View

When you have created or chosen a Story from the list, then you are taken to the Editor View (see Figure 4-2), where you can immediately begin writing the current draft of the last scene in your Story, however the scenes happen to be grouped. You can also reveal the timeline and details components for navigating the Story and extending and annotating.

Figure 4-2. UI—The Editor View

The Application

Class

StoryArchitect.mxml

Responsibilities

- Declare and layout the Chooser and Editor components
- Initialize the PureMVC Facade
- Trigger PureMVC startup process, passing a reference to the app for mediation
- Define three display modes for Starting, Chooser, and Editor
- Expose a bindable public property for setting the word count
- Expose a bindable public property for setting the display mode
- Expose a bindable public property for setting the SelectionContext
- Provide the SelectionContext object to children that require it

- Control visibility and layout inclusion of subcomponents based on display mode
- Display mode in the status bar (and additionally word count when in Editor mode)
- Listen to the Editor component for `ReportWordCount` `AppEvents`, updating the word Count property when they occur

Collaborations

At runtime, Flash builds the main application (`StoryArchitect`) first, initializing its display list and variables. This makes it the perfect place to kick off the initialization of the PureMVC apparatus. Thus, `StoryArchitect` knows the `ApplicationFacade`, for the purpose of initializing it and triggering the startup process. The main application is the exception to the rule about View Components not knowing the PureMVC Facade. Interaction with the Facade by the application should be limited to fulfilling these two responsibilities. No other View Component ever has a reason to know about the Facade.

`StoryArchitect` also knows the `SelectionContext` class, a construct created specifically for this application that allows components to be informed about the current selection. When the `SelectionContext` is set on `StoryArchitect`, it is passed to its children via Flex binding. You will note that many of the View Components in our UI have this bindable property and pass it on to their children. It allows us to, for example, have the `Time line` component automatically open up to the current Draft of the last Scene in the last Chapter of the last part of a Story. We will describe this class in more detail shortly.

`StoryArchitect` knows and controls its direct children, the `Chooser` and `Editor` components.

`StoryArchitect` is known by the `ApplicationFacade`, which exposes a convenience method for passing the application to the `StartupCommand`, which references it briefly to register the `ApplicationMediator`, who will mediate communications between `Story Architect` and the rest of the system.

Code

```
<?xml version="1.0" encoding="utf-8"?>
<!-- STORY ARCHITECT APPLICATION -->
<s:WindowedApplication xmlns:editor="com.futurescale.sa.view.component.editor.*"
                       xmlns:chooser="com.futurescale.sa.view.component.chooser.*"
                       xmlns:s="library://ns.adobe.com/flex/spark"
                       xmlns:fx="http://ns.adobe.com/mxml/2009"
                       applicationComplete="facade.startup(this); // startup app"
                       minWidth="800" minHeight="600">
    <fx:Script>
        <![CDATA[
            import com.futurescale.sa.ApplicationFacade;
            import com.futurescale.sa.view.context.SelectionContext;

            public static const MODE_STARTING:String = "Starting...";
            public static const MODE_CHOOSER:String  = "Chooser";
```

```
            public static const MODE_EDITOR:String    = "Editor";

            // Selection context shared between View Components.
            [Bindable] public var context:SelectionContext;

            // Word Count (displayed on status bar in Editor mode)
            [Bindable] public var wordCount:String = "";

            // Display Mode (Chooser/Editor)
            [Bindable] private var mode:String = MODE_STARTING;

            // Initialize the PureMVC Facade
            private var facade:ApplicationFacade = ApplicationFacade.getInstance();

            /**
             * Set the application display mode, and if showing
             * the Editor, initialize the word count from the
             * selected Story.
             */
            public function setMode( mode:String ):void
            {
                this.mode=mode;
                if (mode == MODE_EDITOR && context.story) {
                    wordCount = context.story.wordCount.toString();
                } else {
                    wordCount = "";
                }
            }
        }

    </fx:Script>

    <!-- LAYOUT -->
    <s:layout>
        <s:VerticalLayout horizontalAlign="center"/>
    </s:layout>

    <!-- STATUS BAR -->
    <s:status>{mode}{(wordCount != "")?" | "+wordCount+" words":""}</s:status>

    <!-- CHOOSER -->
    <chooser:Chooser id="chooser" width="100%" height="100%"
                  includeInLayout="{mode == MODE_CHOOSER}"
                  visible="{mode == MODE_CHOOSER}"/>

    <!-- EDITOR -->
    <editor:Editor id="editor" width="100%" height="100%"
                  includeInLayout="{mode == MODE_EDITOR}"
                  visible="{mode == MODE_EDITOR}"
                  reportWordCount="wordCount=String(event.data)"
                  context="{context}"/>

</s:WindowedApplication>
```

The Chooser

Class

Chooser.mxml

Responsibilities

- Declare and layout the StoryChooser and SeriesChooser components
- Expose a bindable public property for setting the list of StoryVOs
- Expose a bindable public property for setting the list of SeriesVOs
- Provide the Story and Series lists to children

Collaborations

The Chooser only knows and controls its direct children, the StoryChooser and Serie sChooser components. Note that the Chooser *does not* require access to the Selection Context object, as its children only display simple lists and dispatch events to be processed when a selection is made and a button pressed.

The Chooser is known by its parent, the StoryArchitect application, and the Startup Command, which references it briefly to register the ChooserMediator. The ChooserMedia tor who knows and mediates communications between the rest of the system and the Chooser (and *indirectly* its StoryChooser and SeriesChooser child components). The Story and Series lists that populate the children will be set on the Chooser by the Choo serMediator. The *bubbling* events that are dispatched from the children will be handled by the ChooserMediator who will set listeners on the Chooser.

Code

```
<?xml version="1.0" encoding="utf-8"?>
<s:HGroup xmlns:s="library://ns.adobe.com/flex/spark"
          xmlns:fx="http://ns.adobe.com/mxml/2009"
          xmlns:chooser="com.futurescale.sa.view.component.chooser.*"
          verticalAlign="middle" horizontalAlign="center"
          paddingLeft="5" paddingRight="5" width="100%"
          paddingBottom="5" paddingTop="5" height="100%"
          >
    <fx:Script>
        <![CDATA[
            import mx.collections.ArrayCollection;

            // The list of stories
            [Bindable] public var storyList:ArrayCollection;

            // The list of series
            [Bindable] public var seriesList:ArrayCollection;

    </fx:Script>
```

```
<!-- STORY CHOOSER -->
<chooser:StoryChooser id="storyChooser" storyList="{storyList}"
                      width="50%" height="100%"/>

<!-- SERIES CHOOSER -->
<chooser:SeriesChooser id="seriesChooser" seriesList="{seriesList}"
                       width="50%" height="100%"/>

</s:HGroup>
```

The Story Chooser

Figure 4-3. UI - The Story Chooser

Class

StoryChooser.mxml

Responsibilities

• Declare a list for displaying the StoryVOs for selection

- Declare and layout the various buttons for acting on a selection
- Control visibility and layout inclusion for buttons based on selection
- Declare a prominent "Add" (+) button for adding a new Story
- Dispatch appropriate events when buttons are pressed

Collaborations

The StoryChooser knows and controls its direct children: Flex Button, Label, and List components. It also knows the AppEvent class, which it constructs and dispatches in response to certain button presses.

The StoryChooser is known only by its parent, the Chooser component.

Code

```
<?xml version="1.0" encoding="utf-8"?>
<s:VGroup xmlns:fx="http://ns.adobe.com/mxml/2009"
        xmlns:s="library://ns.adobe.com/flex/spark"
        minWidth="390" minHeight="290">

    <fx:Script>
        <![CDATA[
            import com.futurescale.sa.view.event.AppEvent;

            import mx.collections.ArrayCollection;

            // The list of StoryVOs
            [Bindable] public var storyList:ArrayCollection;

            // Create and dispatch an AppEvent
            private function sendEvent( type:String, data:Object=null ):void
            {
                dispatchEvent( new AppEvent(type,data ) );
            }

    </fx:Script>

    <!-- CHOOSER HEADER -->
    <s:HGroup fontSize="24" verticalAlign="middle"
            width="100%" height="50">

        <!-- TITLE -->
        <s:Label text="Story" width="100%"/>

        <!-- ADD BUTTON-->
        <s:Button label="+" width="50" height="100%"
                click="sendEvent( AppEvent.ADD_STORY )" />

    </s:HGroup>

    <!-- STORY LIST-->
    <s:List labelField="name" id="lstStories"
```

```
                    dataProvider="{storyList}" fontSize="16"
                    width="100%" height="100%"/>

        <!-- CONTROLS -->
        <s:HGroup fontSize="16" verticalAlign="middle"
                visible="{lstStories.selectedItem != null}"
                includeInLayout="{lstStories.selectedItem != null}"
                width="100%" height="100">

            <!-- CAST / MILIEU -->
            <s:VGroup height="100%" width="25%">
                <s:Button label="Cast"   height="50%" width="100%"/>
                <s:Button label="Milieu" height="50%" width="100%"/>
            </s:VGroup>

            <!-- NOTES / OUTLINE -->
            <s:VGroup height="100%" width="25%">
                <s:Button label="Notes"   height="50%" width="100%"/>
                <s:Button label="Outline" height="50%" width="100%"/>
            </s:VGroup>

            <!-- MANAGE / EXPORT -->
            <s:VGroup height="100%" width="25%">

                <!-- MANAGE -->
                <s:Button label="Manage" height="50%" width="100%"
                        click="sendEvent( AppEvent.MANAGE_STORY,
                                        lstStories.selectedItem )" />
                <!-- EXPORT-->
                <s:Button label="Export" height="50%" width="100%"/>
            </s:VGroup>

            <!-- WRITE -->
            <s:Button label="Write" fontSize="24"
                    click="sendEvent( AppEvent.EDIT_STORY,
                                    lstStories.selectedItem )"
                    height="100%" width="25%"/>

        </s:HGroup>

    </s:VGroup>
```

The Editor

Class

Editor.mxml

Responsibilities

- Declare and layout a TextArea for writing or displaying read-only, aggregated text
- Declare and layout the Controls subcomponent

- Expose a bindable public property for setting the SelectionContext
- Provide the SelectionContext object to children that require it
- Provide a public function for setting focus to the text editor
- Update the text of the selected DraftVO and when text is edited
- Dispatch an event reporting the current word count when text is edited
- Control the TextArea's font size and percentage width with values from the Controls component
- Declare Flex metadata indicating that the component will dispatch ReportWord Count AppEvents
- Listen to the Control instance for SelectScene and SelectDraft AppEvents and set focus to the TextArea when they occur (the AppEvents will still bubble and be handled by a Mediator)

Collaborations

The Editor knows and controls its direct children: the Flex TextArea and Controls custom component. It also knows the AppEvent class, which it constructs and dispatches in response to text editing. It also knows the SelectionContext class, which it references in methods and binding expressions.

The Editor is known by its parent the StoryArchitect application and by the Startup Command who references it briefly in order to register the EditorMediator. The EditorMe diator will mediate communications between the Editor and the rest of the system.

Code

```
<?xml version="1.0" encoding="utf-8"?>
<!-- EDITOR -->
<s:VGroup xmlns:fx="http://ns.adobe.com/mxml/2009"
          xmlns:s="library://ns.adobe.com/flex/spark"
          xmlns:mx="library://ns.adobe.com/flex/mx"
          xmlns:editor="com.futurescale.sa.view.component.editor.*"
          paddingBottom="5" paddingTop="5" horizontalAlign="center"
          paddingLeft="5" paddingRight="5"
          minWidth="400" minHeight="300" >

    <fx:Metadata>
        [Event(name="reportWordCount", type="com.futurescale.sa.view.event.AppEvent")]
    </fx:Metadata>

    <fx:Script>
        <![CDATA[
            import com.futurescale.sa.view.context.SelectionContext;
            import com.futurescale.sa.view.event.AppEvent;

            // Selection Context
            [Bindable] public var context:SelectionContext;
```

```
            // Called when the user types in the text editor
            private function textEdit():void
            {
                if (context.draft) {
                    // Update draft with latest text from the editor
                    context.draft.text = textEditor.text;

                    // Dispatch an event reporting the current wordcount of the story.
                    var event:AppEvent = new AppEvent( AppEvent.REPORT_WORDCOUNT,
                                                       context.story.wordCount );
                    dispatchEvent( event );
                }
            }

    </fx:Script>

    <!-- TEXT EDITOR -->
    <s:TextArea id="textEditor" borderVisible="{context.draft != null}"
                percentWidth="{100 - controls.editMarginPct}" height="100%"
                visible="true" editable="{context.draft != null}"
                text="{context.selectedText}" change="textEdit()"
                fontSize="{controls.editFontSize}" fontFamily="serif"
                paddingLeft="10" paddingRight="10"
                paddingTop="10" paddingBottom="10"/>

    <!-- CONTROLS-->
    <editor:Controls id="controls" width="100%"
                     selectDraft="textEditor.setFocus()"
                     selectScene="textEditor.setFocus()"
                     context="{context}"/>
</s:VGroup>
```

The Editor Controls

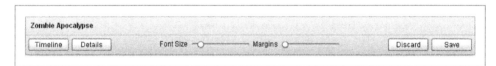

Figure 4-4. UI—The Editor Controls

Class

Controls.mxml

Responsibilities

- Base on Panel with vertical layout showing the name of the selected StoryVO for the title
- In the control bar, declare buttons for discarding or saving edits

---

- In the control bar, declare buttons for revealing the `Timeline` and `Details` components
- In the control bar, declare sliders for controlling font size and margins for the text editor
- Declare the `Timeline` and `Details` components and control their visibility and layout inclusion based on the buttons
- When the "Timeline" and "Details" buttons are not selected, only the `Panel` header and control bar should be visible
- Expose bindable public properties for the font size and margin percentage
- Expose a bindable public property for setting the `SelectionContext`
- Provide the `SelectionContext` object to children that require it
- Dispatch the appropriate `AppEvent` when the "Discard" or "Save" buttons are pressed
- Declare Flex metadata indicating that the component will dispatch `SelectScene` and `SelectDraft` `AppEvents`

Collaborations

The `Controls` component knows and controls its direct children: the `Timeline` and `Details` custom components as well as Flex `Panel`, `Button`, `Label`, and `HSlider` components declared in its control bar area. It also knows the `AppEvent` class, which it constructs and dispatches in response to text editing. It also knows the `SelectionContext` class, which it references in methods and binding expressions.

The `Controls` component is known only by its parent, the `Editor` component.

Code

```
<?xml version="1.0" encoding="utf-8"?>
<!-- CONTROLS -->
<s:Panel xmlns:fx="http://ns.adobe.com/mxml/2009"
         xmlns:s="library://ns.adobe.com/flex/spark"
         xmlns:timeline="com.futurescale.sa.view.component.timeline.*"
         xmlns:details="com.futurescale.sa.view.component.details.*"
         title="{(context.series) ? context.series.name : context.story.name }"
         width="100%" minHeight="0">

    <fx:Metadata>
        [Event(name="selectScene", type="com.futurescale.sa.view.event.AppEvent")]
        [Event(name="selectDraft", type="com.futurescale.sa.view.event.AppEvent")]
    </fx:Metadata>

    <fx:Script>
        <![CDATA[
            import com.futurescale.sa.view.context.SelectionContext;
            import com.futurescale.sa.view.event.AppEvent;
```

```
            [Bindable] public var editFontSize:Number=16;
            [Bindable] public var editMarginPct:Number=0;

            // Selection Context
            [Bindable] public var context:SelectionContext;

            private function discardChanges():void
            {
                var event:AppEvent;
                if ( context.story ) {
                    event = new AppEvent( AppEvent.DISCARD_STORY, context.story );
                } else if ( context.series ) {
                    event = new AppEvent( AppEvent.DISCARD_SERIES, context.series );
                }
                dispatchEvent( event );
            }

            private function saveChanges():void
            {
                var event:AppEvent;
                if ( context.story ) {
                    event = new AppEvent( AppEvent.SAVE_STORY, context.story );
                } else if ( context.series ) {
                    event = new AppEvent( AppEvent.SAVE_SERIES, context.series );
                }
                dispatchEvent( event );
            }

    </fx:Script>

    <!-- DETAILS -->
    <details:Details id="details"
                     context="{context}"
                     width="100%" height="100%"
                     visible="{detailsButton.selected}"
                     includeInLayout="{detailsButton.selected}"/>

    <!-- TIMELINE -->
    <timeline:Timeline id="timeline"
                       context="{context}"
                       story="{context.story}"
                       width="100%" height="100%"
                       visible="{timelineButton.selected}"
                       includeInLayout="{timelineButton.selected}"/>

    <!-- CONTROL BAR -->
    <s:controlBarContent>

        <!-- TOGGLE TIMELINE -->
        <s:ToggleButton id="timelineButton" label="Timeline"/>

        <!-- TOGGLE DETAILS -->
        <s:ToggleButton id="detailsButton" label="Details"/>

        <!-- SPACER -->
```

```
        <s:Spacer width="100%"/>

        <!-- FONT SIZE -->
        <s:Label text="Font Size"/>
        <s:HSlider id="fontSlider" change="editFontSize=fontSlider.value"
                   minimum="12" maximum="48" value="{editFontSize}"/>

        <!-- MARGIN SIZE -->
        <s:Label text="Margins"/>
        <s:HSlider id="marginSlider" change="editMarginPct=marginSlider.value"
                   minimum="0" maximum="75" value="{editMarginPct}"/>

        <!-- SPACER -->
        <s:Spacer width="100%"/>

        <!-- DISCARD OR SAVE CHANGES -->
        <s:Button label="Discard" click="discardChanges()"/>
        <s:Button label="Save" click="saveChanges()"/>

    </s:controlBarContent>

    <!-- PANEL LAYOUT -->
    <s:layout>
        <s:VerticalLayout gap="0"/>
    </s:layout>

    <!-- CONTROL BAR LAYOUT -->
    <s:controlBarLayout>
        <s:HorizontalLayout verticalAlign="middle"
                            paddingLeft="5" paddingRight="5"
                            paddingBottom="5" paddingTop="5"/>
    </s:controlBarLayout>

</s:Panel>
```

The Details Component

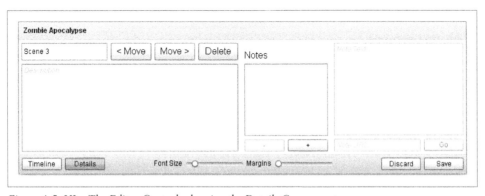

Figure 4-5. UI—The Editor Controls showing the Details Component

Class

Details.mxml

Responsibilities

- Declare the ItemInfo and Notes components
- Expose a bindable public property for setting the SelectionContext
- Provide the SelectionContext object to children that require it

Collaborations

The Details component knows and controls its direct children, the ItemInfo and Notes custom components. It also knows the SelectionContext class, which it references in methods and binding expressions.

The Details component is known only by its parent, the Controls component. In a future iteration, it will also be known by the Chooser component, which will allow modification of item info and the ability to add notes to the top-level VOs when selected without having to enter the Editor to do so.

Code

```
<?xml version="1.0" encoding="utf-8"?>
<!-- DETAILS -->
<s:HGroup xmlns:fx="http://ns.adobe.com/mxml/2009"
        xmlns:s="library://ns.adobe.com/flex/spark"
        xmlns:details="com.futurescale.sa.view.component.details.*"
        width="100%" height="100%">

    <fx:Script>
        <![CDATA[
            import com.futurescale.sa.view.context.SelectionContext;

            //Selection context
            [Bindable] public var context:SelectionContext;


    </fx:Script>

    <!-- ITEM INFO -->
    <details:ItemInfo context="{context}" width="50%" height="100%" />

    <!-- NOTES -->
    <details:Notes context="{context}" width="50%" height="100%" />

</s:HGroup>
```

The Item Info Component

Figure 4-6. UI—The Item Info Component

Class

`ItemInfo.mxml`

Responsibilities

- Declare a `TextInput` and `TextArea` for the `name` and `description` of the selected item (a `ValueObject`)
- Update the selected item's `name` and `description` in response to user edits
- Declare buttons for deleting and reordering the selected in the list of its siblings (functionality deferred to a later iteration)
- Only show the "Move" and "Delete" buttons when the selected item is not a top-level VO (`CastVO`, `MilieuVO`, `StoryVO`, or `SeriesVO`)
- Expose a bindable public property for setting the `SelectionContext`

Collaborations

The `ItemInfo` component knows and controls its direct children, the Flex `Button`, `TextInput`, and `TextArea` components. It also knows the `SelectionContext` class, which it references in methods and binding expressions. And it knows the top-level VOs (`CastVO`, `MilieuVO`, `StoryVO`, or `SeriesVO`), which it must hide the "Move" and "Delete" buttons for.

The `ItemInfo` component is known only by its parent, the `Details` component.

Code

```
<?xml version="1.0" encoding="utf-8"?>
<!-- ITEM INFO -->
<s:VGroup xmlns:fx="http://ns.adobe.com/mxml/2009"
          xmlns:s="library://ns.adobe.com/flex/spark"
          xmlns:details="com.futurescale.sa.view.component.details.*"
          width="100%" height="100%" paddingTop="5" paddingBottom="5"
```

```
                paddingLeft="5" paddingRight="5">
    <fx:Script>
        <![CDATA[
            import com.futurescale.sa.model.vo.CastVO;
            import com.futurescale.sa.model.vo.MilieuVO;
            import com.futurescale.sa.model.vo.SeriesVO;
            import com.futurescale.sa.model.vo.StoryVO;
            import com.futurescale.sa.model.vo.ValueObject;
            import com.futurescale.sa.view.context.SelectionContext;

            //Selection context
            [Bindable] public var context:SelectionContext;

            // Update the selected item's name when edited
            private function nameEdit():void
            {
                if (context.selectedItem) context.selectedItem.name = itemName.text;
            }

            // Update the selected item's description when edited
            private function descEdit():void
            {
                if (context.selectedItem) context.selectedItem.description =
itemDesc.text;
            }

            // Show or hide the move and delete buttons based the selection
            private function showButtons( vo:ValueObject ):Boolean
            {
                return (!(vo is StoryVO) &&
                        !(vo is SeriesVO) &&
                        !(vo is CastVO) &&
                        !(vo is MilieuVO) );
            }

    </fx:Script>

    <s:HGroup width="100%">

        <!-- ITEM NAME -->
        <s:TextInput id="itemName" width="100%" height="30" prompt="Name"
                    change="nameEdit()" text="{context.selectedItem.name}"/>

        <!-- MOVE ITEM LEFT -->
        <s:Button label="&lt; Move" fontSize="16" height="100%"
                    visible="{showButtons( context.selectedItem )}"
                    includeInLayout="{showButtons( context.selectedItem )}"/>

        <!-- MOVE ITEM RIGHT -->
        <s:Button label="Move &gt;" fontSize="16" height="100%"
                    visible="{showButtons( context.selectedItem )}"
                    includeInLayout="{showButtons( context.selectedItem )}"/>

        <!-- DELETE ITEM -->
        <s:Button label="Delete" fontSize="16" height="100%"
```

```
                        visible="{showButtons( context.selectedItem )}"
                        includeInLayout="{showButtons( context.selectedItem )}"/>


      </s:HGroup>

      <!-- ITEM DESCRIPTION -->
      <s:TextArea id="itemDesc" width="100%" height="100%"
                  change="descEdit()" prompt="Description"
                  text="{context.selectedItem.description}"/>

   </s:VGroup>
```

The Notes Component

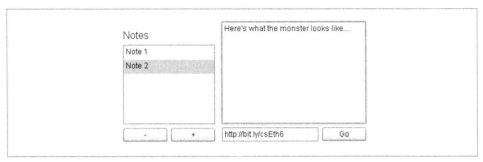

Figure 4-7. UI—The Notes Component

Class

Notes.mxml

Responsibilities

- Declare a Flex Label and List for displaying the selected item's Note list
- Declare Flex Buttons for adding and removing Notes
- Declare a Flex TextArea and TextInput for editing the selected Note
- Declare a Flex Button for launching a browser to view the selected Note's URL
- Provide a label function to supply names for the Notes in the List, since Notes do not have a name field
- Populate the form fields upon selection of a Note in the list
- Update the selected Note's text and url in response to user edits
- Dispatch appropriate events when the "Add Note" (+) button is pressed (remove function deferred to a later iteration)
- Expose a bindable public property for setting the SelectionContext

- Wrap the selected item's `Vector` of `NoteVO`s in an `ArrayCollection` for the `List` dataProvider

Collaborations

The `Notes` component knows and controls its direct children, the various Flex `Button`, `TextInput`, `List`, and `TextArea` components. It also knows the `SelectionContext` class, which it references in methods and binding expressions. And it knows the `NoteVO`, `ValueObject`, and `AppEvent` classes. It also dispatches AppEvents for adding and selecting a Note.

The `Notes` component is known only by its parent, the `Details` component.

Code

```
<?xml version="1.0" encoding="utf-8"?>
<!-- NOTES -->
<s:HGroup xmlns:fx="http://ns.adobe.com/mxml/2009"
          xmlns:s="library://ns.adobe.com/flex/spark"
          xmlns:details="com.futurescale.sa.view.component.details.*"
          width="100%" height="100%">
    <fx:Script>
        <![CDATA[
            import com.futurescale.sa.model.vo.NoteVO;
            import com.futurescale.sa.model.vo.ValueObject;
            import com.futurescale.sa.view.context.SelectionContext;
            import com.futurescale.sa.view.event.AppEvent;

            import mx.collections.ArrayCollection;

             // Selection context
            [Bindable] public var context:SelectionContext;

            // Wrap the vector in a collection for the list.
            public function wrapNotes( vo:ValueObject ):ArrayCollection
            {
                var notes:Array = new Array();
                for each (var note:NoteVO in vo.notes) {
                    notes.push(note);
                }
                return new ArrayCollection( notes );
            }

            // Add a note to the selected item
            private function addNote():void
            {
                var event:AppEvent = new AppEvent( AppEvent.ADD_NOTE );
                event.data = context.selectedItem;
                dispatchEvent( event );
            }

            // Select a note from the selected item's note list
            private function selectNote():void
```

```
        {
            var event:AppEvent = new AppEvent( AppEvent.SELECT_NOTE );
            event.data = noteList.selectedItem;
            dispatchEvent( event );
        }

        // Provide a label for notes in the list
        private function noteLabelFunction(item:Object):String
        {
            var label:String = "Note ";
            var notes:Vector.<NoteVO> = context.selectedItem.notes;
            for ( var i:int = 0; i<notes.length; i++ ) {
                if ( notes[i].xml === NoteVO(item).xml ) {
                    label += String(i+1);
                    break;
                }
            }
            return label;
        }

        // Update selected note text when edited
        private function textEdit():void
        {
            if (context.note) context.note.text = noteText.text;
        }

        // Update selected note URL when edited
        private function urlEdit():void
        {
            if (context.note) context.note.url = noteURL.text;
        }

        // Open a browser to view the selected note URL
        private function openURL():void
        {
            var urlRequest:URLRequest = new URLRequest(context.note.url);
            navigateToURL(urlRequest);
        }

</fx:Script>

<!-- NOTES LIST MANAGEMENT -->
<s:VGroup height="100%"
        paddingRight="0" paddingLeft="0"
        paddingBottom="5" paddingTop="5">

    <!-- LABEL -->
    <s:HGroup height="30" width="100%" verticalAlign="bottom" >
        <s:Label text="Notes" fontSize="16"/>
    </s:HGroup>

    <!-- NOTE LIST -->
    <s:List id="noteList" width="100%" height="100%"
            dataProvider="{ wrapNotes( context.selectedItem ) }"
            change="selectNote()"
```

```
                    labelFunction="noteLabelFunction"/>

        <!-- NOTE BUTTONS -->
        <s:HGroup width="100%">
            <s:Button label="-"  width="50%"
                    enabled="{noteList.selectedItem != null}"/>
            <s:Button label="+" width="50%" click="addNote()"/>
        </s:HGroup>

    </s:VGroup>

    <!-- NOTE FORM -->
    <s:VGroup height="100%" width="100%" enabled="{context.note != null}"
            paddingRight="5" paddingLeft="5"
            paddingBottom="5" paddingTop="5">

        <!-- NOTE TEXT -->
        <s:TextArea id="noteText" text="{context.note.text}"
                    prompt="Note Text..." change="textEdit()"
                    width="100%" height="100%"/>

        <!-- NOTE URL -->
        <s:HGroup width="100%"
                    paddingRight="0" paddingLeft="0"
                    paddingBottom="0" paddingTop="0">

            <!-- URL INPUT -->
            <s:TextInput id="noteURL" width="100%" prompt="Note URL..."
                        text="{context.note.url}" change="urlEdit()"  />

            <!-- GO BUTTON -->
            <s:Button label="Go" click="openURL()"
                        enabled="{context.note.url.length != 0}" />

        </s:HGroup>

    </s:VGroup>
```

The Timeline Component

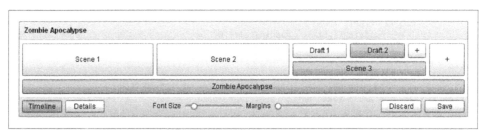

Figure 4-8. UI—The Editor Controls showing the Timeline Component

Class

Timeline.mxml

Responsibilities

- Base on Flex Scroller class
- Declare Flex HGroup for containing the scrollable content
- Expose a public property for setting the StoryVO to be displayed
- Create a StoryTile and replace any existing children of the HGroup with it when the StoryVO is set
- Provide a label function to supply names for the notes in the List, since Notes do not have a name field
- Expose a bindable public property for setting the SelectionContext
- Provide the displayed StoryTile with the SelectionContext object

Collaborations

The Timeline component knows and controls its direct children, the Flex HGroup and custom StoryTile components. It also knows the SelectionContext class, which it passes to the StoryTile, and the StoryVO, which it uses to create a StoryTile.

The Timeline component is known only by its parent, the Controls component.

Code

```xml
<?xml version="1.0" encoding="utf-8"?>
<!-- TIMELINE -->
<s:Scroller xmlns:fx="http://ns.adobe.com/mxml/2009"
        xmlns:s="library://ns.adobe.com/flex/spark">

    <fx:Script>
        <![CDATA[
            import com.futurescale.sa.model.vo.StoryVO;
            import com.futurescale.sa.view.context.SelectionContext;

            // Selection context
            [Bindable] public var context:SelectionContext;

            // The Story
            public function set story( storyVO:StoryVO ):void {
                _story = storyVO;
                storyGroup.removeAllElements();
                if (storyVO) {
                    var storyTile:StoryTile = new StoryTile();
                    storyTile.context    = context;
                    storyTile.story      = story;
                    storyGroup.addElement( storyTile );
                }
            }
```

```
        public function get story( ):StoryVO  {
            return _story;
        }
        private var _story:StoryVO;

    </fx:Script>

    <!-- STORY GROUP -->
    <s:HGroup id="storyGroup" width="100%" height="100%"
            paddingRight="5" paddingBottom="5"
            paddingLeft="5"/>

</s:Scroller>
```

The Story Tile

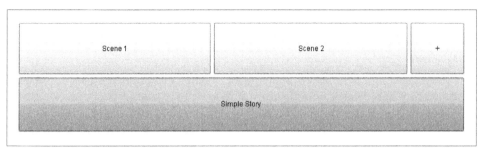

Figure 4-9. UI—The Story Tile (Simple Story)

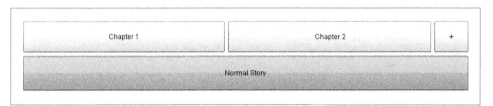

Figure 4-10. UI—The Story Tile (Normal Story)

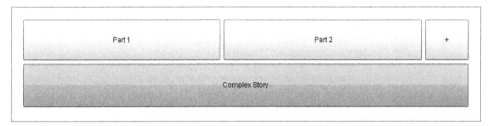

Figure 4-11. UI—The Story Tile (Complex Story)

Class

StoryTile.mxml

Responsibilities

- Base on Flex VGroup class
- Declare a Flex HGroup for containing PartTile, ChapterTile, or SceneTile instances
- Declare a Flex ToggleButton for selecting the StoryVO
- Expose a public property for setting the StoryVO to be displayed
- When StoryVO is selected, create appropriate PartTile, ChapterTile, or SceneTile instances, replacing any existing children of the HGroup
- When the appropriate tile components are added to the HGroup, add an AddTile to the end, set to dispatch the appropriate event for adding another child
- Removing and recreating all tiles when the StoryVO is selected or deselected will have the effect of expanding or collapsing those tiles
- Expose a bindable public property for setting the SelectionContext
- Provide the displayed PartTile, ChapterTile, or SceneTile instances with the SelectionContext object

Collaborations

The StoryTile component knows and controls its direct children, the Flex HGroup, and custom PartTile, ChapterTile, SceneTile, and AddTile components. It knows the SelectionContext class, which it passes to the tile components, and the StoryVO, PartVO, ChapterVO, and SceneVO, which it uses to create the appropriate tile components depending on the Story type.

The StoryTile component is known only by its parent, the Timeline component. In future iterations, it will also be known by the SeasonTile component when Series functionality is added to the Timeline component.

Code

```
<?xml version="1.0" encoding="utf-8"?>
<!-- STORY TILE -->
<s:VGroup xmlns:fx="http://ns.adobe.com/mxml/2009"
        xmlns:s="library://ns.adobe.com/flex/spark"
        height="100%" width="100%">

    <fx:Script>
        <![CDATA[
            import com.futurescale.sa.model.vo.ChapterVO;
            import com.futurescale.sa.model.vo.PartVO;
            import com.futurescale.sa.model.vo.SceneVO;
            import com.futurescale.sa.model.vo.StoryVO;
            import com.futurescale.sa.view.context.SelectionContext;
```

```
import com.futurescale.sa.view.event.AppEvent;

// Selection context
[Bindable] public var context:SelectionContext;

// The Story.
[Bindable] public function set story( storyVO:StoryVO ):void
{
    _story = storyVO;
}
public function get story():StoryVO
{
    return _story;
}
private var _story:StoryVO;

// Remove or add tiles according to the selected story
private function changeStorySelection( selection:Boolean ):Boolean
{
    if (!selection) {
        removeTiles();
    } else {
        createTiles();
    }
    return selection;
}

// Create Tiles
private function createTiles():void
{
    removeTiles();
    var addTile:AddTile = new AddTile();

    if ( story.useScenes )
    {
        // Create the SceneTiles
        var scenes:Vector.<SceneVO> = story.scenes;
        for (var s:int=0; s< scenes.length; s++ ) {
            var sceneTile:SceneTile = new SceneTile();
            sceneTile.context = context;
            sceneTile.scene   = scenes[s];
            tileGroup.addElement( sceneTile );
        }

        // Create the 'Add Scene' tile
        addTile.addType     = AppEvent.ADD_SCENE;
        addTile.addTarget   = story;
    }
    else if ( story.useChapters )
    {
        // Create the ChapterTiles
        var chapters:Vector.<ChapterVO> = story.chapters;
        for (var c:int=0; c<chapters.length; c++ ) {
            var chapterTile:ChapterTile = new ChapterTile();
            chapterTile.context = context;
```

```
                    chapterTile.chapter = chapters[c];
                    tileGroup.addElement( chapterTile );
                }

                // Create the 'Add Chapter' tile
                addTile.addType      = AppEvent.ADD_CHAPTER;
                addTile.addTarget    = story;

            }
            else if ( story.useParts )
            {
                // Create the PartTiles
                var parts:Vector.<PartVO> = story.parts;
                for (var p:int=0; p< parts.length; p++ ) {
                    var partTile:PartTile = new PartTile();
                    partTile.context = context;
                    partTile.part    = parts[p];
                    tileGroup.addElement( partTile );
                }

                // Create the 'Add Part' tile
                addTile.addType      = AppEvent.ADD_PART;
                addTile.addTarget    = story;
            }
            tileGroup.addElement( addTile );
            tileGroup.percentHeight=100;
        }

        // Remove any existing tiles
        private function removeTiles():void
        {
            tileGroup.removeAllElements();
            tileGroup.percentHeight=0;
        }

        // Select the story
        private function selectStory():void
        {
            var appEvent:AppEvent = new AppEvent(AppEvent.SELECT_STORY);
            appEvent.data         = story;
            dispatchEvent(appEvent);
        }


</fx:Script>

<!-- TILE GROUP -->
<s:HGroup id="tileGroup" width="100%"/>

<!-- STORY BUTTON -->
<s:ToggleButton id="storyButton" click="selectStory()"
               selected="{changeStorySelection(context.story.uid == story.uid)}"
               height="100%" width="100%" minWidth="150" minHeight="25"
               label="{story.name}"/>
```

```
    </s:VGroup>
```

The Part Tile

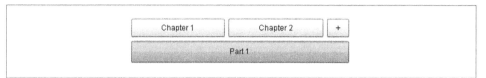

Figure 4-12. UI—The Part Tile

Class

PartTile.mxml

Responsibilities

- Base on Flex VGroup class
- Declare a Flex HGroup for containing ChapterTile instances
- Declare a Flex ToggleButton for selecting the PartVO
- Expose a public property for setting the PartVO to be displayed
- When PartVO is selected create ChapterTile instances, replacing any existing children of the HGroup
- When the appropriate tile components are added to the HGroup, add an AddTile to the end, set to dispatch the appropriate event for adding another child
- Removing or recreating all tiles when the PartVO is selected or deselected will have the effect of expanding or collapsing those tiles
- Expose a bindable public property for setting the SelectionContext
- Provide the displayed ChapterTile instances with the SelectionContext object

Collaborations

The PartTile component knows and controls its direct children, the Flex HGroup, and custom ChapterTile and AddTile components. It also knows the SelectionContext class, which it passes to the tile components, and the PartVO and ChapterVO, which it uses to create the appropriate tile components. Finally, it knows the AppEvent class, which it uses to inform the AddTile of the appropriate event to dispatch.

The PartTile component is known only by its parent, the StoryTile component.

Code

```
<?xml version="1.0" encoding="utf-8"?>
<!-- PART TILE -->
```

```
<s:VGroup xmlns:fx="http://ns.adobe.com/mxml/2009"
          xmlns:s="library://ns.adobe.com/flex/spark"
          xmlns:mx="library://ns.adobe.com/flex/mx"
          height="100%" width="100%">

    <fx:Script>
        <![CDATA[
            import com.futurescale.sa.model.vo.ChapterVO;
            import com.futurescale.sa.model.vo.PartVO;
            import com.futurescale.sa.view.context.SelectionContext;
            import com.futurescale.sa.view.event.AppEvent;

            // Selection context
            [Bindable] public var context:SelectionContext;

            // The Part
            [Bindable] public var part:PartVO;

            // Remove or add tiles according to the selected Part
            private function changePartSelection( selection:Boolean ):Boolean
            {
                if (!selection) {
                    removeTiles();
                } else {
                    createTiles();
                }
                return selection;
            }

            // Create Tiles
            private function createTiles():void
            {
                // Create the Chapter tiles
                removeTiles();
                var chapters:Vector.<ChapterVO> = part.chapters;
                for (var i:int=0; i<chapters.length; i++ ) {
                    var chapterTile:ChapterTile = new ChapterTile();
                    chapterTile.context = context;
                    chapterTile.chapter = chapters[i];
                    chapterGroup.addElement( chapterTile );
                }

                // Create the 'Add Chapter' tile
                var addTile:AddTile = new AddTile();
                addTile.addType    = AppEvent.ADD_CHAPTER;
                addTile.addTarget  = part;
                chapterGroup.addElement( addTile );
                chapterGroup.percentHeight=100;
            }

            // Remove Tiles
            private function removeTiles():void
            {
                chapterGroup.removeAllElements();
                chapterGroup.percentHeight=0;
```

```
        }

        // Toggle the Part selection
        private function selectPart():void
        {
            var event:AppEvent;
            if (partButton.selected) {
                event = new AppEvent(AppEvent.SELECT_PART);
            } else {
                event = new AppEvent(AppEvent.DESELECT_PART);
                removeTiles();
            }
            event.data    = part;
            event.related = context.story;
            dispatchEvent(event);
        }


    </fx:Script>

    <!-- CHAPTER GROUP -->
    <s:HGroup id="chapterGroup" width="100%"/>

    <!-- PART BUTTON -->
    <s:ToggleButton id="partButton" click="selectPart()"
                    selected="{changePartSelection(context.part.uid == part.uid)}"
                    height="100%" width="100%" minWidth="150" minHeight="25"
                    label="{part.name}"/>

</s:VGroup>
```

The Chapter Tile

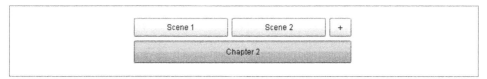

Figure 4-13. UI—The Chapter Tile

Class

ChapterTile.mxml

Responsibilities

- Base on Flex VGroup class
- Declare a Flex HGroup for containing SceneTile instances
- Declare a Flex ToggleButton for selecting the ChapterVO
- Expose a public property for setting the ChapterVO to be displayed

- When `ChapterVO` is selected, create `SceneTile` instances, replacing any existing children of the `HGroup`
- When the appropriate tile components are added to the `HGroup`, add an `AddTile` to the end, set to dispatch the appropriate event for adding another child
- Removing or recreating all tiles when the `ChapterVO` is selected or deselected will have the effect of expanding or collapsing those tiles
- Expose a bindable public property for setting the `SelectionContext`
- Provide the displayed `SceneTile` instances with the `SelectionContext` object

Collaborations

The `ChapterTile` component knows and controls its direct children, the Flex `HGroup`, and custom `SceneTile` and `AddTile` components. It also knows the `SelectionContext` class, which it passes to the tile components, and the `SceneVO` and `ChapterVO`, which it uses to create the appropriate tile components. Finally, it knows the `AppEvent` class, which it uses to inform the `AddTile` of the appropriate event to dispatch.

The `ChapterTile` component is known only by its two possible parents, the `StoryTile` and `PartTile` components.

Code

```
<?xml version="1.0" encoding="utf-8"?>
<!-- CHAPTER TILE -->
<s:VGroup xmlns:fx="http://ns.adobe.com/mxml/2009"
          xmlns:s="library://ns.adobe.com/flex/spark"
          xmlns:mx="library://ns.adobe.com/flex/mx"
          height="100%" width="100%">

    <fx:Script>
        <![CDATA[
            import com.futurescale.sa.model.vo.ChapterVO;
            import com.futurescale.sa.model.vo.SceneVO;
            import com.futurescale.sa.view.context.SelectionContext;
            import com.futurescale.sa.view.event.AppEvent;

            // Selection context
            [Bindable] public var context:SelectionContext;

            // The Chapter
            [Bindable] public var chapter:ChapterVO;

            // Remove or add tiles according to the selected Chapter
            private function changeChapterSelection( selection:Boolean ):Boolean
            {
                if (!selection) {
                    removeTiles();
                } else {
                    createTiles();
                }
```

```
            return selection;
        }

        // Create Tiles
        private function createTiles():void
        {
            // Create SceneTiles
            removeTiles();
            var scenes:Vector.<SceneVO> = chapter.scenes;
            for (var i:int=0; i<scenes.length; i++ ) {
                var sceneTile:SceneTile = new SceneTile();
                sceneTile.context = context;
                sceneTile.scene   = scenes[i];
                sceneGroup.addElement( sceneTile );
            }

            // Create 'Add Scene' Tile
            var addTile:AddTile = new AddTile();
            addTile.addType     = AppEvent.ADD_SCENE;
            addTile.addTarget   = chapter;
            addTile.addArgument = (context.part)?context.part:context.story;
            sceneGroup.addElement( addTile );
            sceneGroup.percentHeight=100;
        }

        // Remove tiles
        private function removeTiles():void
        {
            sceneGroup.removeAllElements();
            sceneGroup.percentHeight=0;
        }

        // Toggle the Chapter selection
        private function selectChapter():void
        {
            var event:AppEvent;
            if (chapterButton.selected) {
                event = new AppEvent(AppEvent.SELECT_CHAPTER);
            } else {
                event = new AppEvent(AppEvent.DESELECT_CHAPTER);
                removeTiles();
            }
            event.data    = chapter;
            event.related = (context.part)?context.part:context.story;
            dispatchEvent(event);
        }

    </fx:Script>

    <!-- SCENE GROUP -->
    <s:HGroup id="sceneGroup" width="100%"/>

    <!-- CHAPTER BUTTON -->
    <s:ToggleButton id="chapterButton" click="selectChapter()"
```

```
                    selected="{changeChapterSelection(context.chapter.uid ==
    chapter.uid)}"

                    height="100%" width="100%" minWidth="150" minHeight="25"
                    label="{chapter.name}"/>

    </s:VGroup>
```

The Scene Tile

Figure 4-14. UI—The Scene Tile

Class

SceneTile.mxml

Responsibilities

- Base on Flex VGroup class
- Declare a Flex HGroup for containing DraftTile instances
- Declare a Flex ToggleButton for selecting the SceneVO
- Expose a public property for setting the SceneVO to be displayed
- When SceneVO is selected, create DraftTile instances, replacing any existing children of the HGroup
- When the appropriate tile components are added to the HGroup, add an AddTile to the end, set to dispatch the appropriate event for adding another child
- Removing or recreating all tiles when the SceneVO is selected or deselected will have the effect of expanding or collapsing those tiles
- Expose a bindable public property for setting the SelectionContext
- Provide the displayed DraftTile instances with the SelectionContext object

Collaborations

The SceneTile component knows and controls its direct children, the Flex HGroup, and custom DraftTile and AddTile components. It also knows the SelectionContext class, which it passes to the tile components, and the SceneVO and DraftVO, which it uses to create the appropriate tile components. Finally, it knows the AppEvent class, which it uses to inform the AddTile of the appropriate event to dispatch.

The SceneTile component is known only by its three possible parents: the StoryTile, PartTile, and ChaperTile components.

Code

```
<?xml version="1.0" encoding="utf-8"?>
<!-- SCENE TILE -->
<s:VGroup xmlns:fx="http://ns.adobe.com/mxml/2009"
          xmlns:s="library://ns.adobe.com/flex/spark"
          height="100%" width="100%">

    <fx:Script>
        <![CDATA[
            import com.futurescale.sa.model.vo.DraftVO;
            import com.futurescale.sa.model.vo.SceneVO;
            import com.futurescale.sa.view.context.SelectionContext;
            import com.futurescale.sa.view.event.AppEvent;

            //Selection context
            [Bindable] public var context:SelectionContext;

            // The Scene
            [Bindable] public var scene:SceneVO;

            // Remove or add tiles according to the selected Scene
            private function changeSceneSelection( selection:Boolean ):Boolean
            {
                if (!selection) {
                    removeTiles();
                } else {
                    createTiles();
                }
                return selection;
            }

            // Create Tiles
            private function createTiles():void
            {
                // Create the Draft tiles
                removeTiles();
                var drafts:Vector.<DraftVO> = scene.drafts;
                for (var i:int=0; i<drafts.length; i++ ) {
                    var draftTile:DraftTile = new DraftTile();
                    draftTile.context = context;
                    draftTile.draft   = drafts[i];
                    draftGroup.addElement( draftTile );
                }

                // Create the 'Add Draft' tile
                var addTile:AddTile = new AddTile();
                addTile.addType     = AppEvent.ADD_DRAFT;
                addTile.addTarget    = scene;
                draftGroup.addElement( addTile );
                draftGroup.percentHeight=100;
            }

            // Remove tiles
            private function removeTiles():void
            {
```

```
            draftGroup.removeAllElements();
            draftGroup.percentHeight=0;
        }

        // Toggle the Scene selection
        private function selectScene():void
        {
            var event:AppEvent;
            if (sceneButton.selected) {
                event = new AppEvent(AppEvent.SELECT_SCENE);
            } else {
                event = new AppEvent(AppEvent.DESELECT_SCENE);
                removeTiles();
            }
            event.data    = scene;
            event.related = (context.chapter)?context.chapter:context.story;
            dispatchEvent(event);
        }

    </fx:Script>

    <!-- DRAFT GROUP -->
    <s:HGroup id="draftGroup" width="100%"/>

    <!-- SCENE BUTTON -->
    <s:ToggleButton id="sceneButton" click="selectScene()"
                    selected="{changeSceneSelection(context.scene.uid == scene.uid)}"
                    height="100%" width="100%" minWidth="150" minHeight="25"
                    label="{scene.name}"/>

</s:VGroup>
```

The Draft Tile

Figure 4-15. UI—The Draft Tile

Class

DraftTile.mxml

Responsibilities

- Base on Flex VGroup class
- Declare a Flex HGroup for padding to exact height of other tiles, since this tile has no children
- Declare a Flex ToggleButton for selecting the DraftVO

- Expose a public property for setting the `DraftVO` to be displayed
- Clicking the `ToggleButton` should set the selected `SceneVO`'s `currentDraft` and dispatch the appropriate event to select the `DraftVO`
- Expose a bindable public property for setting the `SelectionContext`
- Provide the displayed `DraftTile` instances with the `SelectionContext` object

Collaborations

The `DraftTile` component knows and controls its direct children: the Flex `HGroup` and `Button` components. It also knows the `SelectionContext` class, the `DraftVO` class, and the `AppEvent` class.

The `DraftTile` component is known only by its parent, the `SceneTile` component.

Code

```
<?xml version="1.0" encoding="utf-8"?>
<!-- DRAFT TILE -->
<s:VGroup xmlns:fx="http://ns.adobe.com/mxml/2009"
          xmlns:s="library://ns.adobe.com/flex/spark"
          xmlns:component="com.futurescale.sa.view.component.*"
          height="100%" width="100%">

    <fx:Script>
        <![CDATA[
            import com.futurescale.sa.model.vo.DraftVO;
            import com.futurescale.sa.model.vo.SceneVO;
            import com.futurescale.sa.view.context.SelectionContext;
            import com.futurescale.sa.view.event.AppEvent;

            // Selection context
            [Bindable] public var context:SelectionContext;

            // The Draft
            [Bindable] public var draft:DraftVO;

            // Toggle the Draft selection
            public function selectDraft():void
            {
                context.scene.currentDraft = draft;
                var appEvent:AppEvent = new AppEvent( AppEvent.SELECT_DRAFT );
                appEvent.data = draft;
                appEvent.related = context.scene;
                dispatchEvent(appEvent);
            }

        ]]>
    </fx:Script>

    <!-- PADDING GROUP -->
    <s:HGroup width="100%"/>
```

```
                <!-- DRAFT BUTTON -->
                <s:ToggleButton id="draftButton" click="selectDraft()"
                                selected="{context.draft.uid == draft.uid}"
                                height="100%" width="100%" minWidth="75" minHeight="25"
                                label="{draft.name}"/>

        </s:VGroup>
```

The Selection Context

Class

SelectionContext.as

Responsibilities

- Expose public methods for selecting various `ValueObject` subclasses. These methods should ensure the deselection of related items or items below in the Story or Series hierarchy. For example, selecting a Part should clear the current Chapter, Scene, Draft, and Note selections, but not the Story, Season, or Series selections or the Cast and Milieu selections. Selecting a Story would also select its Cast and Milieu and clear the Part, Chapter, Scene, Draft, and Note selections.

- A bindable public `ValueObject` typed `selectedItem` property should always be set to the item being selected by a selection method. Thus, `select Story( story:StoryVO )` would not only set the `story` property to the inbound `StoryVO`, but also set the `selectedItem:ValueObject` property as well. The `selectedItem` property is used by the `ItemInfo` and `Notes` View Components, which work with any `ValueObject`.

- Expose bindable public properties for reading the currently selected `CastVO`, `ChapterVO`, `CharacterVO`, `DraftVO`, `CastVO`, `MilieuVO`, `NoteVO`, `PartVO`, `SceneVO`, `SeasonVO`, `SeriesVO`, `SettingVO`, `StoryVO`, and `ValueObject`.

Collaborations

The `SelectionContext` class knows `CastVO`, `ChapterVO`, `CharacterVO`, `DraftVO`, `CastVO`, `MilieuVO`, `NoteVO`, `PartVO`, `SceneVO`, `SeasonVO`, `SeriesVO`, `SettingVO`, `StoryVO`, and `ValueObject` classes, for which it maintains the entire system's notion of selected items for operations.

The `SelectionContext` class is known by most all View Components, which look to its properties to determine their selection-related behaviors. The `SelectionContext` class is also known by various `Commands`, including `AddItemCommand`, `DeleteItemCommand`, `Apply SelectionCommand`, `RemoveSelectionCommand`, `ApplyChangesCommand`, `DiscardChangesCommand`, `StartupCommand`, etc.

Code

```
package com.futurescale.sa.view.context
{
    import com.futurescale.sa.model.vo.CastVO;
    import com.futurescale.sa.model.vo.ChapterVO;
    import com.futurescale.sa.model.vo.CharacterVO;
    import com.futurescale.sa.model.vo.DraftVO;
    import com.futurescale.sa.model.vo.MilieuVO;
    import com.futurescale.sa.model.vo.NoteVO;
    import com.futurescale.sa.model.vo.PartVO;
    import com.futurescale.sa.model.vo.SceneVO;
    import com.futurescale.sa.model.vo.SeasonVO;
    import com.futurescale.sa.model.vo.SeriesVO;
    import com.futurescale.sa.model.vo.SettingVO;
    import com.futurescale.sa.model.vo.StoryVO;
    import com.futurescale.sa.model.vo.ValueObject;

    /**
     * The currently selected items in the UI.
     *
     * When calling the select methods, items
     * below the selection in the Series/Story
     * hierarchy as well as the selected Note,
     * Cast and Milieu are automatically nulled
     * as appropriate.
     */
    [Bindable] public class SelectionContext
    {
        public static const NAME:String = "SelectionContext";

        public function selectSeries( series:SeriesVO ):void
        {
            this.selectedItem = series;
            this.series  = series;
            this.season  = null;
            this.story   = null;
            this.part    = null;
            this.chapter = null;
            this.scene   = null;
            this.draft   = null;
            this.note    = null;
            if ( series ) {
                this.cast    = series.cast;
                this.milieu = series.milieu;
                this.setting   = null;
                this.character = null;
            }
        }

        public function selectSeason( season:SeasonVO ):void
        {
            this.selectedItem = season;
            this.season  = season;
            this.story   = null;
            this.part    = null;
```

```
        this.chapter = null;
        this.scene   = null;
        this.draft   = null;
        this.note    = null;
}

public function selectStory( story:StoryVO ):void
{
    this.selectedItem = story;
    this.story   = story;
    this.part    = null;
    this.chapter = null;
    this.scene   = null;
    this.draft   = null;
    this.note    = null;
    if ( story ) {
        this.cast    = story.cast;
        this.milieu = story.milieu;
        this.setting   = null;
        this.character = null;
    }
    selectedText = (story)? story.getText(true) : "";
}

public function selectPart( part:PartVO ):void
{
    this.selectedItem = part;
    this.part    = part;
    this.chapter = null;
    this.scene   = null;
    this.draft   = null;
    this.note    = null;
    selectedText = (part)? part.getText(true) : "";
}

public function selectChapter( chapter:ChapterVO ):void
{
    this.selectedItem = chapter;
    this.chapter = chapter;
    this.scene   = null;
    this.draft   = null;
    this.note    = null;
    selectedText = (chapter)? chapter.getText(true) : "";
}

public function selectScene( scene:SceneVO ):void
{
    this.selectedItem = scene;
    this.scene   = scene;
    this.draft   = null;
    this.note    = null;
    selectedText = (scene)? scene.getText(true) : "";
    if ( scene && scene.currentDraft ) selectDraft( scene.currentDraft );
}
```

```
public function selectDraft( draft:DraftVO ):void
{
    this.scene.currentDraft = draft;
    this.draft   = draft;
    this.note    = null;
    selectedText = (draft)? draft.text : "";
}

public function selectNote( note:NoteVO ):void
{
    this.note    = note;
}

public function selectCharacter( character:CharacterVO ):void
{
    this.selectedItem = character;
    this.character = character;
    this.note    = null;
}

public function selectSetting( setting:SettingVO ):void
{
    this.selectedItem = setting;
    this.setting = setting;
    this.note    = null;
}

public var selectedText:String;
public var selectedItem:ValueObject;

public var series:SeriesVO;
public var season:SeasonVO;
public var story:StoryVO;
public var part:PartVO;
public var chapter:ChapterVO;
public var scene:SceneVO;
public var draft:DraftVO;
public var note:NoteVO;
public var cast:CastVO;
public var milieu:MilieuVO;
public var character:CharacterVO;
public var setting:SettingVO;
}
```

The App Event

Class

AppEvent.as

Responsibilities

Some people like to build separate classes for every Event their system will use, and that is a perfectly valid approach. In this application, we will have one custom Event class with many possible types.

With the AppEvent, we are creating one part of a two-part protocol. The constants defined on the AppEvent class represent, in one place, all of the intentions that will arise from the user interface to be processed somewhere, either higher up in the display list, or deeper in the system by Mediators and Commands. The other part of that two-part protocol is the AppConstants file, where we will define, in a similar way, all of the notification names that will be shared by the View and Controller tiers. There will often be duplication between the two files, leading one to ponder whether they should be combined into a single file, and the answer is **no**. There will not always be a one-to-one relationship between event names and notification names, as you will shortly see. It is best to separate event and notification names and let the Mediators take care of translation. This two-part protocol approach is in keeping with the promise made earlier about being able to farm out the building of the entire UI to a developer or team that does not know anything about PureMVC. It lets the UI developer decide what events to dispatch and the PureMVC developers decide on how best to mediate those events.

Also notice we take the approach of defining verbs and nouns as private constants and then combine them in public constants that are used for AppEvent types. This is not necessary, but it can have a clarifying effect on your event naming.

- Extend the Flash Event class
- Define public static constants for valid AppEvent types
- Define public Object typed properties for data and related data
- Accept type, data, and related arguments on the constructor, setting them to the associated public properties
- Constructor should call superclass constructor with the passed in type, a true bubbling argument, and a true cancelable argument

Collaborations

The AppEvent class knows only the Flash Event class that it extends, and the ActionScript Object class that it has public properties for.

The AppEvent class is known by most all View Components, which dispatches events defined by its public, static type constants. The AppEvent class is also known by various Mediators, who listen to their View Components for them, and many Commands, including AddItemCommand, DeleteItemCommand, ApplySelectionCommand, RemoveSelectionCommand, ApplyChangesCommand, DiscardChangesCommand, which interpret the AppEvents relayed to them inside Notifications by Mediators in order to complete their business logic.

Code

```
package com.futurescale.sa.view.event
{
    import flash.events.Event;

    public class AppEvent extends Event
    {
        // Components of the AppEvent types
        private static const ADD:String            = "add";
        private static const DELETE:String         = "delete";
        private static const MANAGE:String         = "manage";
        private static const SELECT:String         = "delect";
        private static const DESELECT:String       = "deselect";
        private static const EXPORT:String         = "export";
        private static const OUTLINE:String        = "outline";
        private static const EDIT:String           = "edit";
        private static const DISCARD:String        = "discard";
        private static const SAVE:String           = "save";
        private static const REPORT:String         = "report";
        private static const MOVE:String           = "move";

        private static const SERIES:String         = "Series";
        private static const SEASON:String         = "Season";
        private static const EPISODE:String        = "Episode";
        private static const STORY:String          = "Story";
        private static const PART:String           = "Part";
        private static const CHAPTER:String        = "Chapter";
        private static const SCENE:String          = "Scene";
        private static const DRAFT:String          = "Draft";
        private static const CAST:String           = "Cast";
        private static const CHARACTER:String      = "Character";
        private static const MILIEU:String         = "Milieu";
        private static const SETTING:String        = "Setting";
        private static const NOTE:String           = "Note";
        private static const WORDCOUNT:String      = "WordCount";
        private static const AHEAD:String          = "Ahead";
        private static const BACK:String           = "Back";

        // AppEvent types
        public static const ADD_SERIES:String      = ADD+SERIES;
        public static const ADD_SEASON:String      = ADD+SEASON;
        public static const ADD_EPISODE:String     = ADD+EPISODE;
        public static const ADD_STORY:String       = ADD+STORY;
        public static const ADD_PART:String        = ADD+PART;
        public static const ADD_CHAPTER:String      = ADD+CHAPTER;
        public static const ADD_SCENE:String       = ADD+SCENE;
        public static const ADD_DRAFT:String        = ADD+DRAFT;
        public static const ADD_CHARACTER:String    = ADD+CHARACTER;
        public static const ADD_SETTING:String      = ADD+SETTING;
        public static const ADD_NOTE:String         = ADD+NOTE;

        public static const DELETE_SERIES:String    = DELETE+SERIES;
        public static const DELETE_SEASON:String     = DELETE+SEASON;
        public static const DELETE_EPISODE:String    = DELETE+EPISODE;
        public static const DELETE_STORY:String      = DELETE+STORY;
```

```
public static const DELETE_PART:String      = DELETE+PART;
public static const DELETE_CHAPTER:String    = DELETE+CHAPTER;
public static const DELETE_SCENE:String      = DELETE+SCENE;
public static const DELETE_DRAFT:String      = DELETE+DRAFT;
public static const DELETE_CHARACTER:String  = DELETE+CHARACTER;
public static const DELETE_SETTING:String    = DELETE+SETTING;
public static const DELETE_NOTE:String        = DELETE+NOTE;

public static const DISCARD_STORY:String     = DISCARD+STORY;
public static const DISCARD_SERIES:String    = DISCARD+SERIES;

public static const EXPORT_SERIES:String     = EXPORT+SERIES;
public static const EXPORT_STORY:String      = EXPORT+STORY;

public static const EDIT_SEREIES:String      = EDIT+SERIES;
public static const EDIT_STORY:String        = EDIT+STORY;

public static const SAVE_STORY:String        = SAVE+STORY;
public static const SAVE_SERIES:String       = SAVE+SERIES;

public static const MANAGE_SERIES:String     = MANAGE+SERIES;
public static const MANAGE_STORY:String      = MANAGE+STORY;
public static const MANAGE_CAST:String       = MANAGE+CAST;
public static const MANAGE_MILIEU:String     = MANAGE+MILIEU;

public static const MOVE_AHEAD:String        = MOVE+AHEAD;
public static const MOVE_BACK:String         = MOVE+BACK;

public static const OUTLINE_SERIES:String    = OUTLINE+SERIES;
public static const OUTLINE_STORY:String     = OUTLINE+STORY;

public static const REPORT_WORDCOUNT:String = REPORT+WORDCOUNT;

public static const SELECT_SERIES:String     = SELECT+SERIES;
public static const SELECT_SEASON:String     = SELECT+SEASON;
public static const SELECT_STORY:String      = SELECT+STORY;
public static const SELECT_PART:String       = SELECT+PART;
public static const SELECT_CHAPTER:String    = SELECT+CHAPTER;
public static const SELECT_SCENE:String      = SELECT+SCENE;
public static const SELECT_DRAFT:String      = SELECT+DRAFT;
public static const SELECT_CHARACTER:String  = SELECT+CHARACTER;
public static const SELECT_SETTING:String    = SELECT+SETTING;
public static const SELECT_NOTE:String        = SELECT+NOTE;

public static const DESELECT_PART:String     = DESELECT+PART;
public static const DESELECT_CHAPTER:String  = DESELECT+CHAPTER;
public static const DESELECT_SCENE:String    = DESELECT+SCENE;

public var data:Object;     // optional data object
public var related:Object;  // optional related data object

public function AppEvent( type:String, data:Object=null, related:Object=null )
{
    super(type, true, true);
    this.data = data;
```

```
            this.related = related;
        }
    }
}
```

CHAPTER 5

Proxying the Model

The PureMVC framework's `Proxy` class is a pretty simple affair. It has a few life cycle methods that are called when it is registered and removed; an `Object` typed data property with attendant `getData` and `setData` methods; and it can send notifications to communicate one-way with `Mediator`s or trigger execution of `Command`s.

It is so simple a class that it almost seems worthless, as a blank sheet of paper might once have appeared before receiving the first words of *Catcher in the Rye*. But because of this simplicity and the PureMVC `Model` that acts as a registry for `Proxy`s within the system, it turns out to be really useful. It does not impose much on you in the way of rules; as a best practice, it should not know any of the View or Controller tier classes, and that is really about it.

 Proxys are usually long-lived actors within your system, registered at startup and present throughout runtime. `Proxy` instances that may be created and removed dynamically are therefore referred to as *transient*.

You usually subclass the framework `Proxy` class, and then add your own functionality, but as you will see, our `Proxy` subclasses will also use transient `Proxy` instances to keep track of the individual VOs that we create or load into memory. This is the `Proxy` in its simplest form; a simple way of stashing an arbitrary piece of data so that we can retrieve it quickly by name later. We could as easily keep an `Array` of all `StoryVO`s as a property of the `StoryProxy`, for instance, but then when we wanted to find a specific one, we would have to iterate the `Array` until we found the right one, or treat the `Array` as a Java-style `Map` (i.e. a hash or associative array). But the PureMVC `Model` already does that for us, and it is unit-tested. The `Proxy` is a such a featherweight wrapper, it is the better answer in almost every case. Imagine the PureMVC `Model` as a bank vault and the transient `Proxy`s as safe deposit boxes within. Each simple box has a unique key and can contain anything you like.

The `Proxy` class has a `facade` property, a reference to your `Application Facade`. It can register, remove, and retrieve other `Proxys` or even `Mediators`. It has this property by virtue of being a `Notifier` subclass, where it also gets its `sendNotification()` convenience method. Use the Force for good and not evil; refrain from using the `Proxy`'s `facade` reference to do anything related to the View or Controller tiers.

Proxy Life Cycle

For the most part, the `Proxy` subclasses you write will add functionality to the basic framework `Proxy` to exchange data with remote services or filesystems, perform authentication, subscribe to RTMP (server-push) channels, perform socket communications, etc. To the rest of the system, `Proxys` are the keepers of the data and the gateway to the outside world. They are typically registered once in the "model preparation" phase of the startup process, which in its simplest form may just be the chunk of code before registering the `Mediators` in your `StartupCommand`.

Throughout runtime, `Commands` and `Mediators` will retrieve the `Proxys` they need to communicate with by name (usually a constant defined on the `Proxy` subclass itself), and call its methods or set and get the data it holds. `Proxys` cannot receive `Notifications`, however. This measure was taken to ensure that they would not find themselves referring to other classes in the system that might define the `Notification` names, and thus tie the `Proxy` subclass to its application, diminishing its reusability. It is also in keeping with the classic MVC diagram shown in Chapter 1; the Model tier is not a potential recipient of notification.

In the constructor of a `Proxy` subclass, we call the constructor of the superclass, passing it a unique name (which is used when the `Proxy` is registered with the `Model`), and a data object reference (possibly null, or often initialized to a collection type), which the superclass sets on the `data` property. Since `data` is type `Object`, we usually create a getter that casts `data` to its actual type and gives it a meaningful name like `cast` or `story`.

Sometimes, in order to preserve data integrity, `Proxys` need to communicate with each other as well. Once registered, they may, like any `Mediator` or `Command`, retrieve a `Proxy` and interact with it. However, that puts the onus on the `Controller` tier logic to register the `Proxys` in the right order, so the needed `Proxy` is sure to be there when requested. The dependency may not be obvious to a person editing the `StartupCommand` later. So, when one `Proxy` needs to talk to another, it is better to establish that relationship from the outset by requiring the dependent `Proxy` on the constructor, as this chapter will illustrate.

Finally, remember that the `Proxy` has `onRegister` and `onRemove` methods that are called by the framework at those junctures in the `Proxy`'s life cycle.

Things that you might normally put into the class constructor should really be deferred until `onRegister()` is called. Very few things are problematic, but getting the `Proxy` registered before doing anything else should be your plan of action; you will not save any CPU cycles by doing something in the constructor rather than onRegister(). Trying to get a service call out the door as quickly as possible is one of the things that in certain circumstances could get you into trouble. If the result of a service call will start a conversation with the rest of the app when the Proxy sends a notification saying that the data is ready, then starting the fetch before the Proxy is registered runs the risk that it will not be registered by the time the data gets back. In PureMVC MultiCore, you do not have access to the Facade until that time, so sending Notifications is not possible yet. Therefore if the call returns before the Proxy is registered, it cannot communicate with anyone about it anyway. By habitually using onRegister() rather than the constructor for everything, you will never have a problem or have to do things differently based on whether you are using the Standard or MultiCore version of PureMVC.

If you have created a service component like Flex's RemoteObject, you will have placed event listeners on it. If your Proxy subclass should have occasion to be removed before runtime is complete, onRemove() will be called by the framework. Unless you specified "weak references" in the event listeners you set in the onRegister() method, you should remove your listeners in onRemove(). If the life cycle of your Proxy is such that it may be removed before runtime is over, you may want to send out a final Notification from onRemove() so that Mediators that may be holding references to the Proxy can null them, ensuring that all references to the Proxy will be removed and the Proxy will be garbage collected.

Persistence Strategy Revisited

In our initial ruminations about persistence, we chose to write simple XML files to the filesystem as the persistence mechanism. But we also considered the possibility that at some point we would want to be able to store these files online somewhere, which sounds great, but presents an issue to be considered before we proceed. We do not want to put the cart before the horse and write a bunch of forward-looking code that may not turn out to be what is actually needed. But we also do not want to avoid painting ourselves into a corner by building a solution that precludes reaching a known future goal by not having at least thought out a strategy that we can iterate predictably.

At the heart of the issue is the difference between *synchronous* and *asynchronous* behavior.

When we communicate with remote services, we *always* do so asynchronously. Our client sends off a request to a server and the thread of execution continues about its business. Later, we will be interrupted with a response from the server. At that point, we will need to remember what we were doing when we made the call (using some variant of the Asynchronous Token pattern), so that we can figure out what to do with the response data from the server.

When we write to the filesystem using AIR, we have the option of doing so synchronously *or* asynchronously.

So at first blush, it would seem obvious to simply use AIR's async filesystem access methods and be done with it. Then, when we decide on an online service to use, we would either enhance the `Proxys` to be able to talk to the filesystem or the service. Or we could get really clever and augment the `Proxy` with the Delegate pattern, where the responsibility for the I/O is delegated to a class that can be swapped out interchangeably. The `Proxys` would use the appropriate Delegate class to talk to the filesystem or the service and would not be affected at all.

However, synchronous code is *much* easier to write and understand. A method can retrieve a file and immediately perform operations on it. Asynchronous code has to break such operations in two: operations up to retrieving the file, and operations after the file has come back to us. When you have to do that for every operation, it really has an impact on the size and complexity of the code, as well as its vulnerability to bugs. To implement async code at this stage would most definitely fall into the category of putting the cart before the horse. We would be writing more complicated code now, to serve a goal set in a future iteration. But when we get there, we do not want to find out that we have to completely rewrite all of our simple synchronous code to make it async. How can we write the simplest code now, but be assured it will still serve us when the more complicated requirements come?

Rather than assuming that the future system will only write to one location or the other, why not make it a two-stage process that writes synchronously to the local filesystem, and then subsequently mirrors to the online location asynchronously? This would give us a built-in offline mode of operation. We would need to build a syncing mechanism that checks the online service at startup if you are online, and pulls down any files that are newer than your local counterparts. So if you were collaborating with someone else, or were simply editing a Story on your desktop and then decided to retire to the veranda with a Mint Julep and an iPad to continue your work, you could do so seamlessly.

Therefore, we will write synchronously to the local filesystem, and reap the benefits of simpler code while being confident that we can easily add an online service later.

What Proxys Do We Need?

We know that our `Proxy`(s) must store XML on the local filesystem. Earlier, we defined `ValueObject` and quite a few subclasses, all of which wrap various bits of XML that are assembled into large hierarchies represented by the `StoryVO` and `SeriesVO`. So it seems pretty likely that we will want separate `Proxys` for managing persistence of `StoryVO` and `SeriesVO`. But we also have `CastVO` and `MilieuVO` to contend with. They are shared between a `SeriesVO` and all its `StoryVOs`. Even though we are not going to cover their use cases from the UI perspective in the book, managing their persistence presents an interesting problem, which we will address fully in this chapter. So we will also want `Proxys` for managing the `CastVOs` and `MilieuVOs`.

How will we store the data?

We have four `Proxy`s storing four different types of XML data, so we will logically store them in four different folders on the local filesystem: under AIR's *Application Storage Directory* for our application. And since we have made all the `ValueObjects` have their own unique IDs, we can just tack a *.xml* onto the end of the ID of the `StoryVO`, `SeriesVO`, `CastVO`, or `MilieuVO` and we have our filename.

So, is that it? Well, not quite...

Indexing

Look back at Figure 4-1 in Chapter 4. It shows the Chooser view of the application, where we see name-sorted lists of Stories and Series. How do you suppose we will get that list? Would we open every file in the Story and Series folders and read it just to get the names? What if we had a bunch of really large files in there? That would be the brute force approach. Surely we can improve on that. By deciding not to use SQLite, in favor of just writing XML files, we gave up the ability to get a list of items with just the fields we want using a quick query.

But remember that when we designed the VOs, we made an `isStub` property that tells us if a `ValueObject` subclass is a stub containing only the base class information, or if it is the full-blown object with all its data. This was done because we knew we would not want to store all the `StoryVO`s for a `SeriesVO` in the same file. Imagine if the text of all seven seasons of Lost—with about 26 episodes each—were stored in one file? It served our purpose of being able to store the `CastVO` and `MilieuVO` separately, while leaving stubs in the stored `StoryVO` and `SeriesVO` files. Well, it turns out that we can use those stubs as entries in an XML index file for each data type. When we save a new `StoryVO`, we can store the full XML in the data file, and add a stubbed representation to an index file that is a simple XMLList. See Figure 5-1 for a view of the Story files.

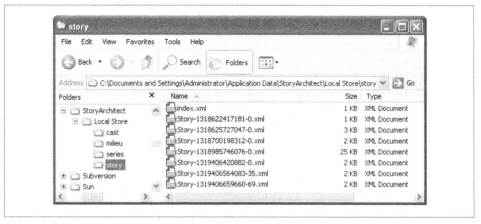

Figure 5-1. Story files in StoryArchitect's Application Storage Directory

A sample index.xml file

```xml
<?xml version="1.0" encoding="utf-8"?>
<index>
  <Story uid="Story-1319406659660-69" isStub="true">
    <name>Complex Story</name>
  </Story>
  <Story uid="Story-1318700198312-0" isStub="true">
    <name>Cthulu is Coming to Dinner</name>
    <description>arrrgh!</description>
  </Story>
  <Story uid="Story-1319406564083-35" isStub="true">
    <name>Normal Story</name>
  </Story>
  <Story uid="Story-1318985746076-0" isStub="true">
    <name>Once, Upon the Dark Matter Highway</name>
  </Story>
  <Story uid="Story-1319406420882-0" isStub="true">
    <name>Simple Story</name>
  </Story>
  <Story uid="Story-1318625727047-0" isStub="true">
    <name>Something Good, Something Bad</name>
    <description>That's life.</description>
  </Story>
  <Story uid="Story-1318622417181-0" isStub="true">
    <name>Zombie Apocalypse</name>
    <description>Braaaains!</description>
  </Story>
</index>
```

Building the Proxys

So far, we are sure that we need these four Proxy subclasses:

- CastProxy
- MilieuProxy
- SeriesProxy
- StoryProxy

We know there are dependencies between the structures that they store and that we will manage these dependencies by allowing the Proxys to collaborate with each other. And we know that these Proxys will all be doing a lot of the same things with regard to filesystem I/O and indexing.

This is a classic OOP decision point: do we add that similar functionality by inheritance or composition? Some say you should always favor one over the other, but you really need to make those decisions when you come to them based on the pressures at hand.

The Delegate pattern that was described in passing earlier would be an example of the composition approach. If you want to vary this common functionality, then composition is a good choice. If the object that adds this functionality to your class implements an interface, you can swap it out easily with a different implementer of the interface.

But in this case (filesystem and indexing), we are not really interested in swapping out the functionality. We will always be using AIR to synchronously interact with the filesystem first, even later when we add asynchronous mirroring to the cloud. So in our case, inheritance is the most logical approach.

We will create an `AbstractProxy` class that extends `Proxy` and adds all this common functionality. Our `Proxy`s listed above will extend the `AbstractProxy` and add the functions that the application will need in order to persist the VOs and have the dependencies between them taken care of automatically. In the design of this `Abstract Proxy`, we have the opportunity to hide the messy details of the actual filesystem interaction and indexing, allowing our subclasses to deal strictly with `ValueObjects`.

Note that the composition approach will be represented here as well. When we give the `SeriesProxy` and `StoryProxy` references to the `CastProxy` and `MilieuProxy` and allow the former set to delegate some of their responsibilities to the latter, it is an example of composition.

 As previously discussed, if you want to unit-test your `Proxy` classes, you should use PureMVC MultiCore where you can have a fresh PureMVC core for each test. But if you use the Delegate pattern to create a nonframework class that handles I/O, and use composition to give the `Proxy` a reference to this nonframework Delegate, you can easily unittest the delegate functions without involving the framework at all.

The Abstract Proxy

Class

AbstractProxy.as

Responsibilities

The `AbstractProxy` will never be instantiated, but always subclassed. It will provide those subclasses with everything needed to persist and retrieve VOs while hiding the filesystem access in private methods, so that the only methods and properties the subclasses know about work with VOs. It will automatically produce a sorted index in memory and on disk of the VO type its subclass is in charge of managing.

- Provide a function for connecting to the folder name specified by the subclass, creating it if it does not exist, and ensuring that it always contains an index file even if there are no items in the folder
- Provide functions for adding, saving, and deleting `ValueObjects`, automatically updating the index on the filesystem and in memory

- Provide a function that returns an ArrayCollection of the `ValueObject` stubs in the connected folder's index
- Make sure the index is sorted by the name field of the `ValueObject`

Collaborations

The `AbstractProxy` class knows the Flash `File`, `FileMode`, and `FileStream` classes for performing filesystem I/O. It knows the Flex `ArrayCollection`, `Sort`, and `SortField` classes for creating a name-sorted index. And of course, it knows the PureMVC `Proxy` class, which it extends, and our custom `ValueObject` class, which it persists.

The `AbstractProxy` class is known only by its subclasses: the `SeriesProxy`, `StoryProxy`, `CastProxy`, and `MilieuProxy`.

Code

```
package com.futurescale.sa.model.proxy
{
    import com.futurescale.sa.model.vo.ValueObject;

    import flash.filesystem.File;
    import flash.filesystem.FileMode;
    import flash.filesystem.FileStream;

    import mx.collections.ArrayCollection;

    import org.puremvc.as3.patterns.proxy.Proxy;

    import spark.collections.Sort;
    import spark.collections.SortField;

    /**
     * Provides subclasses with a simple VO-to-disk
     * API with automatic name-sorted indexing.
     */
    public class AbstractProxy extends Proxy
    {

        // Extension for files
        private const FILE_EXT:String = ".xml";

        // Index filename
        private const INDEX:String    = "index"+FILE_EXT;

        // The folder to access. Set by connectToFolder()
        private var folder:File;

        /**
         * Constructor.
         *
         * Name provided by subclass, data property
         * (used for the index of stubbed VOs) is
         * initialized to ArrayCollection.
```

```
 */
public function AbstractProxy( name:String )
{
    super( name, new ArrayCollection() );
}

/**
 * The name-sorted index of stubbed VOs.
 */
public function get index():ArrayCollection
{
    return data as ArrayCollection;
}

/**
 * Abstract factory method to create stubbed VOs
 * for the index. Must be overridden in subclass
 * and return a stubbed VO of the appropriate type
 * for inclusion in the index.
 */
protected function getVoInstance( xml:XML ):ValueObject
{
    return null;
}

/**
 * Sets the protected folder property.
 *
 * Also, if the folder does not exist, it is
 * created and an empty index written. Otherwise,
 * the index is read from the existing folder.
 */
protected function connectToFolder( name:String ):void
{
    folder = File.applicationStorageDirectory.resolvePath( name );
    if ( !folder.exists ) {
        folder.createDirectory();
        writeIndex();
    } else {
        readIndex();
    }
}

/**
 * Write the Value Object's XML property to a file
 * and update the index on disk and in memory.
 */
protected function writeVO( vo:ValueObject ):void
{
    var file:File = getFile( vo );
    writeFile( file, vo.xml );
    updateIndex( vo );
}

/**
```

```
 * From the stub passed in, read the corresponding VO
 * from the disk and return the XML.
 */
protected function readVO( voStub:ValueObject ):XML
{
    var file:File = getFile( voStub );
    return XML ( readFile( file ) );
}

/**
 * From the VO passed in, delete the corresponding VO
 * from the disk and update the index.
 */
protected function deleteVO( vo:ValueObject ):void
{
    var file:File = getFile( vo );
    if ( file.exists ) file.deleteFile();
    updateIndex( vo, true );
}

/**
 * Read the index XML from disk and create the
 * in memory index of stubbed VOs.
 */
private function readIndex():void
{
    // read in the index XML
    var file:File = folder.resolvePath( INDEX );
    var xml:XML = readFile( file );

    // build the index from the XML
    var ac:ArrayCollection =  new ArrayCollection();
    for each ( var ix:XML in xml.children() )
    {
        var vo:ValueObject = getVoInstance( ix );
        ac.addItem( vo );
    }

    // Sort the index by name
    var sort:Sort = new Sort();
    var field:SortField = new SortField( "name" );
    sort.fields = [ field ];
    ac.sort = sort;
    ac.refresh();

    // set the index as the proxy data
    setData( ac );
}

/**
 * Read the in memory index of stubbed VOs to
 * the index XML file on disk.
 */
private function writeIndex():void
{
```

```
        var file:File = folder.resolvePath( INDEX );
        var xml:XML = <index></index>;
        var ivo:ValueObject;
        for ( var i:int=0; i < index.length; i++ ){
            ivo = ValueObject( index.getItemAt(i) );
            xml.appendChild( ivo.getStub() );
        }
        writeFile( file, xml );
}

/**
 * Update the in memory index of stubbed VOs, replacing or
 * removing the stubbed VO passed in, sort the index, and
 * write the index XML file on disk.
 */
private function updateIndex( vo:ValueObject, removing:Boolean=false ):void
{
    // Find and remove existing item if present
    for ( var i:int=0; i < index.length; i++ ){
        var ivo:ValueObject = ValueObject( index.getItemAt(i) );
        if ( ivo.uid == vo.uid ) {
            index.removeItemAt( i );
            break;
        }
    }

    // add the new or updated item to index if not removing
    if ( ! removing ) index.addItem( getVoInstance( vo.getStub() ) );

    // re-sort the index
    index.refresh();

    // persist the index
    writeIndex();
}

/**
 * Write xml to a file.
 */
private function writeFile( file:File, xml:XML ):void
{
    var stream:FileStream = new FileStream()
    stream.open( file, FileMode.WRITE );
    stream.writeUTFBytes( xml );
    stream.close();
}

/**
 * Read XML from a file and return it.
 */
private function readFile( file:File ):XML
{
    var stream:FileStream = new FileStream()
    stream.open( file, FileMode.READ );
    var xml:XML = XML( stream.readUTFBytes( stream.bytesAvailable ) );
```

```
            stream.close();
            return xml;
        }

        /**
         * Get the corresponding File object for a given VO.
         */
        private function getFile( vo:ValueObject ):File
        {
            var filename:String = vo.uid + FILE_EXT;
            return folder.resolvePath( filename );
        }
    }
}
```

The Cast Proxy

Class

CastProxy.as

Responsibilities

The CastProxy only needs to worry about creating, saving, and deleting CastVOs, and making sure that loaded VOs are cached in memory and removed when deleted. In a future iteration, where editing of the Cast is enabled, the CastProxy will also handle loading of the CastVO.

- Extend AbstractProxy to inherit persistence and indexing functionality
- When the CastProxy is registered (*not* in the constructor), connect to the cast folder
- Override the superclass getVoInstance method, returning a CastVO instance created with the XML passed into the method (necessary because the superclass only knows ValueObject, so when the XML is read by superclass, this method provides the facility for creating the right ValueObject subclass)
- Provide a function that creates a new CastVO, caches it in a transient Proxy instance by its ID, and writes it to the filesystem, returning a stubbed CastVO
- Provide a function for saving a CastVO
- Provide a function for deleting a CastVO, ensuring that its associated transient Proxy is removed from memory

Collaborations

The CastProxy class knows the CastVO, ValueObject, AbstractProxy, and Proxy classes.

The CastProxy is known by the StoryProxy, SeriesProxy, and, in the next iteration, by Commands used for editing the Cast of a Story or Series.

Code

```
package com.futurescale.sa.model.proxy
{
    import com.futurescale.sa.model.vo.CastVO;
    import com.futurescale.sa.model.vo.ValueObject;

    import org.puremvc.as3.patterns.proxy.Proxy;

    /**
     * The CastProxy provides persistence,
     * indexing, and caching of CastVOs
     */
    public class CastProxy extends AbstractProxy
    {
        // Registered name
        public  static const NAME:String        = "CastProxy";

        // Filesystem folder name for storage
        private static const FOLDER:String       = "cast";

        // Notes sent from this Proxy
        public static const CAST_CREATED:String = NAME+"/"+FOLDER+"/created";
        public static const CAST_SAVED:String   = NAME+"/"+FOLDER+"/saved";
        public static const CAST_DELETED:String = NAME+"/"+FOLDER+"/deleted";

        /**
         * Constructor.
         */
        public function CastProxy( )
        {
            super( NAME );
        }

        /**
         * Called by the framework when the Proxy is registered.
         */
        override public function onRegister():void
        {
            connectToFolder( FOLDER );
        }

        /**
         * Create, save, cache, and return a new CastVO.
         *
         * A new CastVO is only created when a new StoryVO or SeriesVO
         * is saved. It is created, saved, and cached with a
         * transient Proxy instance, so that it does not have
         * to be loaded again later to be used. The stub is
         * returned because it will only be used in a StoryVO
         * or SeriesVO that is saved.
         */
        public function createCast( name:String ):CastVO
        {
            // Create and name the Cast
            var cast:CastVO = new CastVO();
```

```
        cast.name = name;

        // Cache the Cast
        facade.registerProxy( new Proxy( cast.uid, cast ) );

        // Save the Cast and update index
        writeVO( cast );

        // Notify any observers
        sendNotification( CAST_CREATED, cast );

        // Return the stub to caller
        return new CastVO( cast.getStub() );
    }

    /**
     * Save a CastVO.
     */
    public function saveCast( cast:CastVO ):void
    {
        // Save the Cast and update index
        writeVO( cast );

        // Notify any observers
        sendNotification( CAST_SAVED, cast );
    }

    /**
     * Delete a Cast.
     *
     * Removes the transient Proxy holding the cached
     * CastVO if present, then removes the CastVO from
     * filesystem. Index will be automatically updated.
     */
    public function deleteCast( cast:CastVO ):void
    {
        // Remove cached Cast
        if ( facade.hasProxy( cast.uid ) ) {
            facade.removeProxy( cast.uid );
        }
        // Delete Cast from filesystem and update index
        deleteVO( cast );

        // Notify any observers with stub so CastVO is GC'd
        sendNotification( CAST_DELETED, new CastVO( cast.getStub() ) );
    }

    /**
     * VO Factory Method. Required for indexing in superclass.
     */
    override protected function getVoInstance( xml:XML ):ValueObject
    {
        return new CastVO( xml );
    }
```

```
        }
    }
```

The Milieu Proxy

Class

```
MilieuProxy.as
```

Responsibilities

The MilieuProxy is equally simple, and only has to create, save, and delete MilieuVOs, making sure that loaded VOs are cached in memory and removed when deleted. In a future iteration where editing of the Milieu is enabled, the MilieuProxy will also handle loading the MilieuVO.

- Extend AbstractProxy to inherit persistence and indexing functionality
- When the MilieuProxy is registered (*not* in the constructor), connect to the milieu folder
- Override the superclass getVoInstance method, returning a MilieuVO instance created with the XML passed into the method
- Provide a function that creates a new MilieuVO, caches it in a transient Proxy instance by its ID, and writes it to the filesystem, returning a stubbed MilieuVO
- Provide a function for saving a MilieuVO
- Provide a function for deleting a MilieuVO, ensuring that its associated transient Proxy is removed from memory

Collaborations

The MilieuProxy class knows the CastVO, ValueObject, AbstractProxy, and Proxy classes.

The MilieuProxy is known by the StoryProxy, SeriesProxy, and, in the next iteration, by Commands used for editing the Cast of a Story or Series.

Code

```
package com.futurescale.sa.model.proxy
{
    import com.futurescale.sa.model.vo.MilieuVO;
    import com.futurescale.sa.model.vo.ValueObject;

    import org.puremvc.as3.patterns.proxy.Proxy;

    /**
     * The MilieuProxy provides persistence,
     * indexing, and caching of MilieuVOs
     */
    public class MilieuProxy extends AbstractProxy
```

```
{
    // Registered name
    public  static const NAME:String          = "MilieuProxy";

    // Filesystem folder name for storage
    private static const FOLDER:String         = "milieu";

    // Notes sent from this Proxy
    public static const MILIEU_CREATED:String = NAME+"/"+FOLDER+"/created";
    public static const MILIEU_SAVED:String   = NAME+"/"+FOLDER+"/saved";
    public static const MILIEU_DELETED:String = NAME+"/"+FOLDER+"/deleted";

    /**
     * Constructor.
     */
    public function MilieuProxy( )
    {
        super( NAME );
    }

    /**
     * Called by the framework when the Proxy is registered.
     */
    override public function onRegister():void
    {
        connectToFolder( FOLDER );
    }

    /**
     * Create, save, cache, and return a new MilieuVO.
     *
     * A new MilieuVO is only created when a new StoryVO or SeriesVO
     * is saved. It is created, saved, and cached with a transient
     * Proxy instance, so that it does not have to be loaded again
     * later to be used. The stub is returned because it will only
     * be used in a StoryVO or SeriesVO that is saved.
     */
    public function createMilieu( name:String ):MilieuVO
    {
        // Create and name the Milieu
        var milieu:MilieuVO = new MilieuVO();
        milieu.name = name;

        // Cache the Milieu
        facade.registerProxy( new Proxy( milieu.uid, milieu ) );

        // Save the Milieu and update index
        writeVO( milieu );

        // Notify any observers
        sendNotification( MILIEU_CREATED, milieu );

        // Return the stub to caller
        return new MilieuVO( milieu.getStub() );
    }
```

```
/**
 * Save a MilieuVO.
 */
public function saveMilieu( milieu:MilieuVO ):void
{
    // Save the Milieu and update index
    writeVO( milieu );

    // Notify any observers
    sendNotification( MILIEU_SAVED, milieu );
}

/**
 * Delete a MilieuVO.
 *
 * Removes the transient Proxy holding the cached
 * Milieu if present, then removes the Milieu from
 * filesystem. Index will be automatically updated.
 */
public function deleteMilieu( milieu:MilieuVO ):void
{
    // Remove cached Milieu
    if ( facade.hasProxy( milieu.uid ) ) {
        facade.removeProxy( milieu.uid );
    }

    // Delete Milieu from filesystem and update index
    deleteVO( milieu );

    // Notify any observers with stub so Milieu is GC'd
    sendNotification( MILIEU_DELETED, new MilieuVO( milieu.getStub() ) );
}

/**
 * VO Factory Method. Required for indexing in superclass.
 */
override protected function getVoInstance( xml:XML ):ValueObject
{
    return new MilieuVO( xml );
}
    }
}
```

The Story Proxy

Class

StoryProxy.as

Responsibilities

The StoryProxy is concerned with creating, loading, saving, and deleting StoryVOs, and making sure that loaded VOs are cached in memory and removed when deleted. It has some responsibility that involves the CastProxy and MilieuProxy. When adding a Story, if it is not part of a Series, a new Cast and Milieu must be created and persisted. Upon deletion of a Story that is not part of a Series, the Cast and Milieu must be removed from memory and disk. Also, when adding a Story, the StoryProxy must, based on the Story type, create a new Chapter, Part, or Scene, so that the Story is ready for editing and the user does not have to add it manually. Due to the logic in the VO, this will cause all the sections below to be created as well. For instance, before being saved, a complex Story will have a Part created, which will automatically include a Chapter with one Scene with one Draft.

- Extend AbstractProxy to inherit persistence and indexing functionality
- Require references to the CastProxy and MilieuProxy as constructor arguments and save them in private properties
- When the StoryProxy is registered (*not* in the constructor), connect to the story folder
- Override the superclass getVoInstance method, returning a StoryVO instance created with the XML passed into the method
- Provide a function for adding a new StoryVO, caching it in a transient Proxy instance by ID
- When adding the StoryVO, if the cast and milieu properties are null, have the CastProxy and MilieuProxy create a new CastVO and MilieuVO, and save the stubs with the StoryVO (they would be null if the Story is not part of a Series)
- When adding the StoryVO, make sure it has a default Scene, Chapter, or Part depending upon the Story type before saving it
- Provide a function for loading a StoryVO, using the cached version if present, and caching it if loading was necessary and allowing for explicit recaching (in the case of discarding changes)
- Provide a function for saving a StoryVO
- Provide a function for deleting a StoryVO, ensuring that its associated transient Proxy is removed from memory, and remove the CastVO and MilieuVO if not part of a Series

Collaborations

The StoryProxy class knows the StoryTypeEnum, StoryVO, ValueObject, AbstractProxy, and Proxy classes.

The StoryProxy is known by the SeriesProxy, and by various Commands including StartupCommand, ManageStoryCommand, EditStoryCommand, ApplyChangesCommand, and DiscardChangesCommand.

Code

```
package com.futurescale.sa.model.proxy
{
    import com.futurescale.sa.model.enum.StoryTypeEnum;
    import com.futurescale.sa.model.vo.StoryVO;
    import com.futurescale.sa.model.vo.ValueObject;

    import org.puremvc.as3.interfaces.IProxy;
    import org.puremvc.as3.patterns.proxy.Proxy;

    /**
     * The StoryProxy provides persistence,
     * indexing, and caching of StoryVOs
     */
    public class StoryProxy extends AbstractProxy
    {
        // Registered name
        public static  const NAME:String        = "StoryProxy";

        // Filesystem folder name for storage
        private static const FOLDER:String       = "story";

        // Notes sent from this Proxy
        public static const STORY_ADDED:String   = NAME+"/"+FOLDER+"/added";
        public static const STORY_SAVED:String   = NAME+"/"+FOLDER+"/saved";
        public static const STORY_DELETED:String = NAME+"/"+FOLDER+"/deleted";

        // Known Collaborators
        private var milieuProxy:MilieuProxy;
        private var castProxy:CastProxy;

        /**
         * Constructor.
         *
         * The StoryProxy collaborates with the
         * MilieuProxy and CastProxy to ensure
         * consistency of the domain data. Requiring
         * them on the constructor both ensures they
         * will be present and encapsulates their
         * relationship.
         */
        public function StoryProxy( milieuProxy:MilieuProxy,
                                    castProxy:CastProxy )
        {
            super( NAME );

            this.milieuProxy = milieuProxy;
            this.castProxy   = castProxy;
        }
```

```
/**
 * Called by the framework when the Proxy is registered.
 */
override public function onRegister():void
{
    connectToFolder( FOLDER );
}

/**
 * Load a Story.
 *
 * If Story is already cached from having been
 * previously loaded or added, the cached VO will be
 * returned, otherwise it will be loaded and cached first.
 *
 * Optionally allows forced re-caching from disc
 * (as when user changes are discarded).
 */
public function loadStory( storyStub:StoryVO,
                           recache:Boolean = false ):StoryVO
{
    // Optionally force loading from disc and recaching
    if ( recache ) facade.removeProxy( storyStub.uid );

    var cacheProxy:IProxy;
    if ( facade.hasProxy( storyStub.uid ) ) {
        cacheProxy = facade.retrieveProxy( storyStub.uid );
    } else {
        var story:StoryVO = new StoryVO( readVO( storyStub ) );
        cacheProxy = new Proxy( story.uid, story );
        facade.registerProxy( cacheProxy );
    }
    return cacheProxy.getData() as StoryVO;
}

/**
 * Add a Story.
 *
 * Story is written to the filesystem and cached in memory
 * with a transient Proxy instance, so that it does not have
 * to be loaded again later to be used. Also this method
 * populates the Story down to the first draft.
 */
public function addStory( story:StoryVO ):void
{
    // Cache Story
    facade.registerProxy( new Proxy( story.uid, story ) );

    // If this story is part of a series, it will already
    // have a cast and milieu, otherwise create them.
    if ( story.cast == null ) {
        story.cast = castProxy.createCast( story.name );
    }
    if ( story.milieu == null ) {
```

```
                story.milieu = milieuProxy.createMilieu( story.name );
        }
        // Populate story
        switch ( story.type )
        {
            case StoryTypeEnum.SIMPLE:
                story.getNewScene();
                break;

            case StoryTypeEnum.NORMAL:
                story.getNewChapter();
                break;

            case StoryTypeEnum.COMPLEX:
                 story.getNewPart();
                break;
        }

        // Save to the filesystem, updating the index
        writeVO( story );

        // Notify any observers
        sendNotification( STORY_ADDED, story );
}

/**
 * Save a Story.
 */
public function saveStory( story:StoryVO ):void
{
    // save to the filesystem, updating the index
    writeVO( story );

    // Notify any observers
    sendNotification( STORY_SAVED, story );
}

/**
 * Delete a Story.
 *
 * Removes the transient Proxy holding the cached
 * Story if present, then removes the Story from
 * filesystem. Index will be automatically updated.
 */
public function deleteStory( story:StoryVO ):void
{
    // Remove the cached story
    if ( facade.hasProxy( story.uid ) ) {
        facade.removeProxy( story.uid );
    }

    // remove cast and milieu if not part of a series
    if ( ! story.isEpisode ) {
        castProxy.deleteCast( story.cast );
        milieuProxy.deleteMilieu( story.milieu );
```

```
        }

        // remove from filesystem and update index
        deleteVO( story );

        // Notify any observers with stub so that story is GC'd
        sendNotification( STORY_DELETED, new StoryVO( story.getStub() ) );
    }

    /**
     * VO Factory Method. Required for indexing in superclass.
     */
    override protected function getVoInstance( xml:XML ):ValueObject
    {
        return new StoryVO( xml );
    }
}
}
```

The Series Proxy

Class

SeriesProxy.as

Responsibilities

The SeriesProxy is concerned with creating, loading, saving, and deleting SeriesVOs, and making sure that loaded VOs are cached in memory and removed when deleted. When adding a Series, a new Cast and Milieu must be created and persisted. Also, when adding a Series, if it uses Seasons, then it is populated with a single new Season. When deleting a Series, the Cast, Milieu, and all Stories must also be deleted.

- Extend AbstractProxy to inherit persistence and indexing functionality
- Require references to StoryProxy, CastProxy, and MilieuProxy as constructor arguments and save them in private properties
- When the SeriesProxy is registered (*not* in the constructor), connect to the series folder
- Override the superclass getVoInstance method, returning a SeriesVO instance created with the XML passed into the method
- Provide a function for adding a new SeriesVO, caching it in a transient Proxy instance by ID
- When adding the SeriesVO, if the cast and milieu properties are null, have the CastProxy and MilieuProxy create a new CastVO and MilieuVO and save the stubs with the SeriesVO

- Provide a function for loading a SeriesVO, using the cached version if present, caching it if loading was necessary, and allowing for explicit re-caching (in the case of discarding changes)

- Provide a function for saving a SeriesVO

- Provide a function for deleting a SeriesVO, ensuring that its associated transient Proxy is removed from memory

- When deleting the SeriesVO, remove each of its StoryVOs as well as the CastVO and MilieuVO from the filesystem and memory

Collaborations

The SeriesProxy class knows the SeriesVO, StoryVO, ValueObject, AbstractProxy, and Proxy classes.

The SeriesProxy is known by various Commands including StartupCommand, Manage SeriesCommand, EditStoryCommand, ApplyChangesCommand, and DiscardChangesCommand.

Code

```
package com.futurescale.sa.model.proxy
{
    import com.futurescale.sa.model.vo.SeriesVO;
    import com.futurescale.sa.model.vo.StoryVO;
    import com.futurescale.sa.model.vo.ValueObject;

    import org.puremvc.as3.interfaces.IProxy;
    import org.puremvc.as3.patterns.proxy.Proxy;

    /**
     * The SeriesProxy provides persistence,
     * indexing, and caching of SeriesVOs
     */
    public class SeriesProxy extends AbstractProxy
    {
        // Registered name
        public  static const NAME:String        = "SeriesProxy";

        // Filesystem folder name for storage
        private static const FOLDER:String       = "series";

        // Notes sent from this Proxy
        public static const SERIES_ADDED:String   = NAME+"/"+FOLDER+"/added";
        public static const SERIES_SAVED:String   = NAME+"/"+FOLDER+"/saved";
        public static const SERIES_DELETED:String = NAME+"/"+FOLDER+"/deleted";

        // Known Collaborators
        private var storyProxy:StoryProxy;
        private var milieuProxy:MilieuProxy;
        private var castProxy:CastProxy;

        /**
```

```
 * Constructor.
 *
 * The SeriesProxy collaborates with the StoryProxy,
 * MilieuProxy and CastProxy to ensure
 * consistency of the domain data. Requiring
 * them on the constructor both ensures they
 * will be present and encapsulates their
 * relationship.
 */
public function SeriesProxy( storyProxy:StoryProxy,
                             milieuProxy:MilieuProxy,
                             castProxy:CastProxy )
{
    super( NAME );

    this.storyProxy  = storyProxy;
    this.milieuProxy = milieuProxy;
    this.castProxy   = castProxy;
}

/**
 * Called by the framework when the Proxy is registered.
 */
override public function onRegister():void
{
    connectToFolder( FOLDER );
}

/**
 * Load a Series.
 *
 * If Series is already cached from having been
 * previously loaded or added, the cached VO will be
 * returned, otherwise it will be loaded and cached first.
 * The index will be automatically updated.
 *
 * Optionally allows forced re-caching from disc
 * (as when user changes are discarded).
 */
public function loadSeries( seriesStub:SeriesVO,
                            recache:Boolean = false ):SeriesVO
{
    if ( recache ) facade.removeProxy( seriesStub.uid );

    var cacheProxy:IProxy;
    if ( facade.hasProxy( seriesStub.uid ) ) {
        cacheProxy = facade.retrieveProxy( seriesStub.uid );
    } else {
        var series:SeriesVO = new SeriesVO( readVO( seriesStub ) );
        cacheProxy = new Proxy( series.uid, series );
        facade.registerProxy( cacheProxy );
    }
    return cacheProxy.getData() as SeriesVO;
}
```

```
/**
 * Add a Series.
 *
 * Series is written to the filesystem and cached in memory
 * with a transient Proxy instance, so that it does not have
 * to be loaded again later to be used.
 *
 * Cast and Milieu will be created, cached, saved and stubs
 * added to the
 */
public function addSeries( series:SeriesVO ):void
{
    // Cache the Series
    facade.registerProxy( new Proxy( series.uid, series ) );

    // Create the Cast and Milieu
    series.cast   = castProxy.createCast( series.name );
    series.milieu = milieuProxy.createMilieu( series.name );

    // Populate series
    if (series.useSeasons) series.getNewSeason();

    // Save the Series and update index
     writeVO( series );

     // Notify any observers
     sendNotification( SERIES_ADDED, series );
}

/**
 * Save a Series.
 */
public function saveSeries( series:SeriesVO ):void
{
    // Save the Series and update index
    writeVO( series );

    // Notify any observers
    sendNotification( SERIES_SAVED, series );
}

/**
 * Delete a Series.
 *
 * Removes the transient Proxy holding the cached
 * Series if present, then removes the Series from
 * filesystem. Index will be automatically updated.
 *
 * Also removes Cast, Milieu, and all Episodes.
 */
public function deleteSeries( series:SeriesVO ):void
{
    // Remove the cached Series
    if ( facade.hasProxy( series.uid ) ) {
        facade.removeProxy( series.uid );
```

```
        }

        // Delete Cast and Milieu
        castProxy.deleteCast( series.cast );
        milieuProxy.deleteMilieu( series.milieu );

        // Delete Episodes
        var episode:StoryVO;
        for each ( episode in series.stories ) {
            storyProxy.deleteStory( episode );
        }

        // Delete Series from filesystem and update index
        deleteVO( series );

        // Notify any observers with stub so Series is GC'd
        sendNotification( SERIES_DELETED, new SeriesVO( series.getStub() ) );
    }

    /**
     * VO Factory Method. Required for indexing in superclass.
     */
    override protected function getVoInstance( xml:XML ):ValueObject
    {
        return new SeriesVO( xml );
    }
  }
}
```

CHAPTER 6

Mediating the View

As the old saying goes, communication is a two-way street. That is the central truism of the `Mediator`'s existence.

The `Mediator` exists to facilitate two-way communication between a View Component and the rest of the application. Therefore, the bulk of the `Mediator`'s responsibilities will be handling `Events` from the View Component and `Notifications` from the rest of the application. This decouples the other actors in the application from the component and vice versa.

If a `Mediator` is the only class in the application that actually knows a View Component, and the implementation of the component has to change, the impact to the rest of the system will be minimized. And if the View Component has been properly encapsulated, changes to the internal implementation (such as changing a `List` to a `ComboBox`) will not change its collaboration patterns or have any impact at all on the `Mediator`.

The `Mediator` class has a `facade` property: a reference to your `ApplicationFacade`. It can register, remove, and possibly retrieve other `Mediators`, `Proxys`, and `Commands`. It has this property by virtue of being a `Notifier` subclass, where it also gets its `sendNotification()` convenience method. Of all these things, only retrieving other `Mediators` is considered a bad practice. We will discuss that below.

Mediator Life Cycle

Generally, you will pass a View Component into a `Mediator` subclass constructor, most often in the "view preparation" phase of your `StartupCommand`. When the main application is created, it will pass a reference to itself into a `startup()` method of the `ApplicationFacade`, triggering the `StartupCommand`, where it will usually be mediated, along with some of its top-level subcomponents.

There are other ways a `Mediator` might come by its View Component, including creating one itself or receiving one in a `Notification` sometime after registration. We will consider some of those cases in the Advanced View Topics chapter, but for the most part, the scenario just described is the most common.

Our `Mediator` subclass constructor usually accepts a strongly typed View Component as a sole argument. For instance, the `ChooserMediator` will only expect a `Chooser` component. Inside the constructor, we call the superclass constructor, passing it a unique name (usually defined in the `Mediator` subclass in a `NAME` constant), and the View Component reference (which the superclass sets on the `viewComponent` property). Since `viewComponent` is type `Object` we usually create a `private` or `protected` getter that casts `viewComponent` to its actual type and gives it a meaningful name like `app` or `chooser` that the rest of the methods in the class will refer to when handling the View Component.

Usually a `Mediator` is long-lived, remaining registered throughout runtime, though this may not always be the case. For instance, in Flex Mobile projects that use a `ViewNavigator` as the main application, the life cycle of the View Components (called `Views`) are radically different. The `ViewNavigator` acts as a stack that you push and pop `Views` onto. Mediation is a moving target in that environment because the `ViewNavigator` destroys the component when you move away from it. You can listen for added `Events` coming from the application and have a `Command` to remove the old `Mediator` and add a new one with the new `View`. For an example of mediation in a Flex Mobile application, see Chapter 9.

Regardless of how long a Mediator will live or when it is created, if there are `Events` that the View Component will dispatch that the `Mediator` needs to hear, we set listeners for them in the `onRegister()` method of the `Mediator` subclass. You will also use this method to retrieve any `Proxys` the `Mediator` will collaborate with. And unless you specified "weak references" in the listeners you set in the `onRegister()` method, be sure to remove them in the `onRemove()` method. This ensures all references to the `Mediator` that exist are gone when it is removed from the PureMVC `View`, and thus, it can be garbage-collected.

Communicating with the Component

When writing a View Component, we do not have it reach into the application and retrieve a `Proxy` in order to get its data. Instead we expose properties and methods whereby that data can be passed into the component. Likewise, we will not retrieve the component from other places in the system and act upon it, but instead send `Notifications` to its `Mediator`, who will take care of informing the component.

Let the View Component act like an overpaid CEO that sits around his office and has everything brought to him. He does not go to the kitchen and get his own coffee, it is brought to him as a matter of course by his secretary. If he needs some important signed document to be rushed by courier to another company, he simply calls his secretary and she fetches it from his desk and arranges the courier pickup.

An inbound courier with an important dispatch intended for our CEO would not just barge into his office, but would instead direct the parcel to his secretary who would notify him the way he prefers.

The Mediator plays the role of the secretary in this scenario. It is a simple but universal pattern in business, and it works perfectly for ensuring the View Component is well tended by one class who understands its needs implicitly.

In our Mediators, event handlers for the listeners we set on the View Component, we usually end up translating the Event to a Notification, which we then send off to be heard by other Mediators or a Command.

We might simply send Notification X when we get Event Y. We might also include the Event itself (or a property from it) in the body of the Notification, or we might pluck some data from the View Component and send that in body property of the Notification.

 One thing we do not want to do is use the Mediator to maintain state, do a lot of calculations, or other data manipulation. A Mediator should *mediate*, not *cogitate*; leave the thinking to the Commands, they are just a Notification away.

Dependency Injection

There has been a lot of talk in the Flex community over the last few years about the power of "dependency injection" or "DI." Some alternative framework devotees have touted DI as some mystical new feature that PureMVC lacks. However, this is precisely what the Mediator does when it passes a VO into a View Component, whether through calling a method or setting a property. The View Component is *dependent* upon the Value Object to do its work. The Mediator *injects* that VO into the View Component.

What PureMVC does lack is DI with *Compiler Dependency*. For instance, Flex Data Binding is DI via compiler directives. Each time you add a [Bindable] tag to a property in a View Component, you are telling the Flex compiler that you would like the dependent components that reference that property in a binding expression to have the data re-injected into them whenever it changes. This forms a dependency on the Flex compiler and framework to interpret and fulfill, limiting the portability of the application.

Our View Components would not be directly portable anyway; we would have to rewrite them completely in, say, Python. In lieu of a direct equivalent of data binding, we would add a little more intelligence to the View Component to encapsulate the binding behaviors. However, if PureMVC *itself* required custom compiler directives in order to work, it (and your app's architecture) would not be so easily portable to other languages.

Communicating with the Application

Notification Interests

When a `Mediator` handles an `Event` from a View Component, the most common response is to send off a corresponding `Notification` using the `sendNotification()` method. This could trigger a single `Command` or notify any number of interested `Mediators` (including the `Mediator` sending the `Notification`). What does it mean to be an *interested* `Mediator`?

The PureMVC `Notification` system is a publish/subscribe approach that complements the Flash `Event` system rather than seeking to replace it. A `Mediator` expresses its interest in `Notifications` that it would like to receive by listing their names in an `Array` returned from the `listNotificationInterests()` method, which is called by the framework when the `Mediator` is registered. This means that the `Mediator` does not need to have a reference to the actor it wishes to receive the `Notification` from; it could come from anywhere. The framework has registered the `Mediator` as an `Observer` to this `Notification`, so whenever another actor sends that note, the interested `Mediators` will be notified by having their `handleNotification()` method called.

Handling Notifications

Inside the `handleNotification()` method, just as in the `Event` handlers, we will generally perform a simple operation, such as setting a property or making a method call on the View Component with some data from the `Notification` body. Since we aim to avoid performing logic and data manipulation in response to `Notifications`, the best practice is to use a simple `switch` statement with a `case` for each `Notification` name the `Mediator` is interested in. The simplicity of this approach is a virtue. The `Mediator` does not have to implement or provide references to handler methods for each `Notification` it is interested in. The `switch` approach to `Notification` handling exerts a gentle pressure to keep the response simple (e.g. setting a View Component property, calling a method, or perhaps sending out another `Notification`).

Collaboration with Proxys

Something else we might do in response to a `Notification` (or in `Event` handlers) is communicate directly with a `Proxy`. As you may remember, a `Proxy` cannot listen for `Notifications`, instead it is manipulated by `Commands`, `Mediators`, or other `Proxys`. Recall the classic MVC diagram from Chapter 1. The View tier is allowed to update the Model tier directly, as is the Controller tier. So, when do you send off a Notification to be handled by a Command as opposed to communicating with Proxys directly? If you are going to take only a single piece of data from the View Component and route it to a Proxy method, then take the shortest path and just call the Proxy directly. If you are going to be performing logic, transforming or validating the data, and/or talking to several Proxys, then it is best to do all that in a Command triggered by a simple Notification from the Mediator. Another good reason to send a Notification to be handled by a Command is the case where you need to trigger the same functionality from several places in the user interface such as a button, a keyboard shortcut, and an options menu; all being listened to by different Mediators. If the Mediators all send the same Notification name, they can trigger the same Command. Alternatively, the same Command can be registered to be triggered by several different Notification names.

 If a Mediator needs to collaborate with a Proxy, it should retrieve a reference to the Proxy in the onRegister() method. This is the main reason we prepare the Model before the View during the startup process, so that the Proxy will already be registered by the time the Mediator is registered and looking to form a collaboration.

Avoid Retrieving Other Mediators

One thing we should refrain from in a Mediator is retrieving another Mediator to call methods or set and get its properties. While the Proxys may freely collaborate via direct references to each other in order to maintain the integrity of the data model, we have no reason to resort to such tight coupling with Mediators. Our Mediators can send and receive Notifications, and that allows us to more loosely couple them.

With regard to loose coupling in the View tier, consider the possibility of a Story Viewer Flex application that lets readers view your Story (from the XML file created by StoryArchitect) in a web browser. It would be navigable with the Timeline View Component, but without the trappings of the Editor. We might create a Viewer component that reuses just the Timeline and a TextArea. That would mean we would register a ViewerMediator instead of an EditorMediator. Assume the Chooser has a new mode where it never shows the editing buttons, just dispatches a selection Event. Now if the ChooserMediator normally responded to a selection by retrieving the EditorMediator and giving it the selected StoryVO, we would have an undesired tight coupling to the EditorMediator. Instead, the ChooserMediator should send a Notification that the EditorMediator is interested in, even if it is a request that the EditorMediator send some piece of information back in a response Notification. That way, the ChooserMediator has dispatched its responsibility without accepting a dependency on another actor. That the ViewerMediator can just as easily be interested in that selection note is the beauty of publish/subscribe.

Mediator Multiplicity

Usually, you have a single instance of a given `Mediator` subclass registered for the life of the View Component it tends, often for the duration of runtime. But what if you need more than one mediated instance of a View Component in your app? A `Notification` also has a `type` property. This can be used to pass extra information about the `Notification` (in `String` form), to be interpreted as needed by the `Mediator`. This can allow us to have multiple instances of a `Mediator` registered.

Imagine we decided in a future iteration of `StoryArchitect` that we want to open multiple Stories at once, inside a tabbed container with a separate `Editor` component instance on each tab. In that case we would need to register the `EditorMediator` multiple times, one to tend each `Editor`. We could do that by supplying the unique `uid` property of the associated `StoryVO` to the `Mediator` super constructor for a name. But when handling `Notifications`, how would any given `EditorMediator` instance know if the note were directed to it and therefore respond? The type property of the `Notification` can help. To direct a `Notification` to the `Mediator` handling the `Editor` for StoryVO *Story-123456789-0*, you would simply provide that Story `uid` as the `type` argument to the `sendNotification()` method. Then, in the `EditorMediator`'s `handleNotification()` method, you would only take action if the `Notification`'s type was equal to the `Mediator` name (retrieved with the `getMediatorName()`method).

Determining Granularity of Mediation

We have a fairly deep hierarchy of View Components in places. Inside the `Timeline` component alone, we can have a hierarchy of `StoryTile`, `PartTile`, `ChapterTile`, `SceneTile`, and `DraftTile`. Do we need a `Mediator` for each of these components? Do we need a `Mediator` for the `Timeline` instead? Or is it even necessary to have a `Mediator` for the `Timeline`, which itself is only a child of the `Controls` component, which is a child of the `Editor`? Confusing, right? How much mediation is too much? Does every button need a `Mediator`? Well, that depends on how our view hierarchy is built and how much custom tending each component really needs. The best approach is to consider your needs from the top down, not from the bottom up.

We usually assume that the App itself will require a `Mediator`. In our case, `StoryArchitect` has simple needs. It must have `SelectionContext` injected, and we will want to be able tell the `ApplicationMediator` to toggle `StoryArchitect`'s display mode. For example, returning you to `Chooser` after discarding or saving changes in the `Editor`.

The `Chooser` and the `Editor` are the two main views in our UI, and they are different enough in their needs to make separate mediation a better choice than lumping it all into a single huge `ApplicationMediator`. The information that the child components need can be supplied by their parents via binding or composition. For instance, the `SelectionContext` is bound down all the way from the `StoryArchitect` through the `Editor` to the `Controls` to the `Timeline`. From there, the tile components construct their own children, passing down the SelectionContext like a family heirloom through the generations. The AppEvents generated by those tiles when the user clicks on the buttons all bubble back up through the display list where they can be listened for by the EditorMediator and will be sent off in Notifications to be processed by Commands.

Building the Mediators

In StoryArchitect, we make use of the view hierarchy itself to pass down a shared SelectionContext and to bubble events up from the deepest subcomponents. Thus we do not really need much mediation. We are going to use some pop ups to get things done as well, but we will talk about how we handle them in Chapter 9.

So far, we are sure that we need these three Mediator subclasses:

- ApplicationMediator
- ChooserMediator
- EditorMediator

In our case, there is no common functionality we need to share between these Mediator subclasses, so there is no need to create an AbstractMediator as we did with AbstractProxy. All these classes will extend Mediator and override or add the methods necessary to communicate with their View Components and the rest of the system. In the following implementations, note how every View Component does not necessarily dispatch (or bubble through) events that the Mediator needs to handle. Similarly, some Mediators have no Notification interests. The balance of Event and Notification handling responsibilities is different for every Mediator/View Component pair, but usually includes some of both. It just so happens that these particular Mediators ended up doing one or the other.

The Application Mediator

Class

ApplicationMediator.as

Responsibilities

The ApplicationMediator does not need to listen for any Events from the app. It needs to tell StoryArchitect to display the Chooser at registration time. Thereafter it merely needs to respond to Notifications to display the Editor (e.g. when you have chosen a Story in the Chooser and clicked the "Write" button) or the Chooser (e.g. when you have saved or discarded your changes in the Editor).

- At registration time, retrieve the transient Proxy holding the SelectionContext and set the SelectionContext on StoryArchitect's context property

- Also set the application to `StoryArchitect.MODE_CHOOSER` at registration time
- Note that the `StoryArchitect` does not currently dispatch (or bubble through) any Events we need to handle
- Declare interest in the `AppConstants.SHOW_EDITOR` and `AppConstants.SHOW_CHOOSER` `Notifications`
- Handle those `Notifications` by setting the application to the appropriate display mode
- Define a `private` getter called `app` casting the `viewComponent` property to type `Story Architect`

Collaborations

The `ApplicationMediator` class knows the `StoryArchitect`, `AppConstants`, `SelectionCon text`, `Proxy`, and `Mediator` classes.

The `ApplicationMediator` component is known only by the `StartupCommand` that registers it.

Code

```
package com.futurescale.sa.view.mediator
{
    import com.futurescale.sa.controller.constant.AppConstants;
    import com.futurescale.sa.view.context.SelectionContext;

    import org.puremvc.as3.interfaces.INotification;
    import org.puremvc.as3.interfaces.IProxy;
    import org.puremvc.as3.patterns.mediator.Mediator;

    /**
     * Mediate communications with the Application component.
     */
    public class ApplicationMediator extends Mediator
    {
        /**
         * Mediator registration name.
         */
        public static const NAME:String = "ApplicationMediator";

        /**
         * Construct with an instance of the application.
         */
        public function ApplicationMediator( app:StoryArchitect )
        {
            super( NAME, app );
        }

        /**
         * Called when Mediator is registered.
         */
        override public function onRegister():void
```

```
{
    // Set the SelectionContext
    var scProxy:IProxy = facade.retrieveProxy( SelectionContext.NAME );
    app.context = SelectionContext( scProxy.getData() );

    // Set the initial display mode
    app.setMode( StoryArchitect.MODE_CHOOSER );
}

/**
 * Notifications this Mediator is interested in.
 */
override public function listNotificationInterests():Array
{
    return [ AppConstants.SHOW_EDITOR,
             AppConstants.SHOW_CHOOSER,
           ];
}

/**
 * Handle the notifications this Mediator is interested in.
 */
override public function handleNotification( note:INotification ):void
{
    switch ( note.getName() )
    {
        case AppConstants.SHOW_EDITOR:
            app.setMode( StoryArchitect.MODE_EDITOR );
            break;

        case AppConstants.SHOW_CHOOSER:
            app.setMode( StoryArchitect.MODE_CHOOSER );
            break;
    }
}

/**
 * Cast the View Component to the correct type
 */
private function get app():StoryArchitect
{
    return viewComponent as StoryArchitect;
}
    }
}
```

The Chooser Mediator

Class

ChooserMediator.as

Responsibilities

The ChooserMediator is not interested in any Notifications, but it does listen to the Chooser for a number of AppEvents, (e.g. AppEvent.EDIT_STORY when you choose a Story from the list and click the "Write" button). It handles all these events in a single method, using a switch statement to send the corresponding Notifications rather than having separate handler methods. Since Mediators should rarely do more than this with an Event, using a single method with a switch statement is an efficient and readable way to handle Events. It also mirrors the handling of Notifications and keeps Mediator classes short.

- At registration time, retrieve the StoryProxy and SeriesProxy and populate the Chooser's storyList and seriesList
- Set listeners on the View Component for the important AppEvents dispatched from the Chooser
- Handle the AppEvents by dispatching appropriate Notifications (note that these particular AppEvents are translated one-to-one with some corresponding Notification and so can be handled with a single method containing a switch statement, in the same way handleNotification() is usually implemented)
- Define a private getter called chooser, casting the viewComponent property to type Chooser

Collaborations

The ChooserMediator class knows the Chooser, AppConstants, AppEvent, and Mediator classes. It also collaborates with the StoryProxy and SeriesProxy to retrieve the Story and Series lists needed by the Chooser.

The ChooserMediator component is known only by the StartupCommand that registers it.

Code

```
package com.futurescale.sa.view.mediator
{
    import com.futurescale.sa.controller.constant.AppConstants;
    import com.futurescale.sa.model.proxy.SeriesProxy;
    import com.futurescale.sa.model.proxy.StoryProxy;
    import com.futurescale.sa.view.component.chooser.Chooser;
    import com.futurescale.sa.view.event.AppEvent;

    import org.puremvc.as3.patterns.mediator.Mediator;

    public class ChooserMediator extends Mediator
    {
        /**
         * Mediator registration name.
         */
        public static const NAME:String = "ChooserMediator";
```

```
/**
 * Construct with an instance of the StoryChooser component.
 */
public function ChooserMediator( chooser:Chooser )
{
    super( NAME, chooser );
}

/**
 * Called when mediator is registered.
 */
override public function onRegister():void
{
    // Form collaborations with required proxies
    storyProxy = StoryProxy( facade.retrieveProxy( StoryProxy.NAME ) );
    seriesProxy = SeriesProxy( facade.retrieveProxy( SeriesProxy.NAME ) );

    // Set required data
    chooser.storyList  = storyProxy.index;
    chooser.seriesList = seriesProxy.index;

    // Set component event listeners
    chooser.addEventListener( AppEvent.ADD_EPISODE,   handleAppEvent );
    chooser.addEventListener( AppEvent.ADD_STORY,     handleAppEvent );
    chooser.addEventListener( AppEvent.ADD_SERIES,    handleAppEvent );
    chooser.addEventListener( AppEvent.EDIT_STORY,    handleAppEvent );
    chooser.addEventListener( AppEvent.MANAGE_STORY,  handleAppEvent );
    chooser.addEventListener( AppEvent.MANAGE_SERIES, handleAppEvent );
}

/**
 * Handle AppEvents from the View Component.
 */
private function handleAppEvent( event:AppEvent ):void
{
    switch ( event.type )
    {
        case AppEvent.ADD_EPISODE:
            sendNotification( AppConstants.ADD_EPISODE );
            break;

        case AppEvent.ADD_STORY:
            sendNotification( AppConstants.MANAGE_STORY );
            break;

        case AppEvent.ADD_SERIES:
            sendNotification( AppConstants.MANAGE_SERIES );
            break;

        case AppEvent.EDIT_STORY:
            sendNotification( AppConstants.EDIT_STORY, event.data );
            break;

        case AppEvent.MANAGE_STORY:
            sendNotification( AppConstants.MANAGE_STORY, event.data );
```

```
                    break;

                case AppEvent.MANAGE_SERIES:
                    sendNotification( AppConstants.MANAGE_SERIES, event.data );
                    break;
            }
        }

        /**
         * Cast the View Component to the correct type
         */
        private function get chooser():Chooser
        {
            return viewComponent as Chooser;
        }

        private var storyProxy:StoryProxy;
        private var seriesProxy:SeriesProxy;
    }
}
```

The Editor Mediator

Class

EditorMediator.as

Responsibilities

Like the ChooserMediator, the EditorMediator is not interested in any Notifications. However, it does listen to the Editor for a number of AppEvents, for which it sends corresponding Notifications. The major difference is that each of the Notifications that the EditorMediator sends is triggered by two or more different AppEvent types, so it sends the AppEvent along in the body of the note to be processed by the recipient. As you read on to Chapter 7, you will see that the Commands triggered by these notes all examine the AppEvent and take a similar but specific action for each AppEvent type. For instance, the ApplySelectionCommand (triggered by the AppConstants.APPLY_SELECTION) will call the appropriate method on the SelectionContext for whatever item is being selected, such as a Story or Scene. This approach is much more economical than having different Commands for every item that can be selected (such as a SelectStoryCommand, SelectPartCommand, etc., which all do essentially the same thing).

- At registration time, set listeners on the View Component for the important AppE vents dispatched from (and bubbled up through) the Editor
- Handle the AppEvents by dispatching appropriate Notifications (note how this Mediator is translating a large number of specific AppEvents into a smaller number of Notifications by functional category; the Commands triggered by these notes will inspect the AppEvent to determine the correct action to take)

- Define a `private` getter called `editor` casting the `viewComponent` property to type `Editor`

Collaborations

The `EditorMediator` class knows the `Editor`, `AppConstants`, `AppEvent`, and `Mediator` classes.

The `EditorMediator` component is known only by the `StartupCommand` that registers it.

Code

```
package com.futurescale.sa.view.mediator
{
    import com.futurescale.sa.controller.constant.AppConstants;
    import com.futurescale.sa.view.component.editor.Editor;
    import com.futurescale.sa.view.event.AppEvent;

    import org.puremvc.as3.patterns.mediator.Mediator;

    /**
     * Mediate communications with the Editor component.
     */
    public class EditorMediator extends Mediator
    {
        /**
         * Mediator registration name.
         */
        public static const NAME:String = "EditorMediator";

        /**
         * Construct with an instance of the Editor component.
         */
        public function EditorMediator( editor:Editor )
        {
            super( NAME, editor );
        }

        /**
         * Called when mediator is registered.
         */
        override public function onRegister():void
        {
            // Set component event listeners
            editor.addEventListener( AppEvent.ADD_STORY,      handleAppEvent );
            editor.addEventListener( AppEvent.ADD_PART,       handleAppEvent );
            editor.addEventListener( AppEvent.ADD_CHAPTER,    handleAppEvent );
            editor.addEventListener( AppEvent.ADD_SCENE,      handleAppEvent );
            editor.addEventListener( AppEvent.ADD_DRAFT,      handleAppEvent );
            editor.addEventListener( AppEvent.ADD_NOTE,       handleAppEvent );
            editor.addEventListener( AppEvent.DELETE_STORY,   handleAppEvent );
            editor.addEventListener( AppEvent.DELETE_PART,    handleAppEvent );
            editor.addEventListener( AppEvent.DELETE_CHAPTER, handleAppEvent );
            editor.addEventListener( AppEvent.DELETE_SCENE,   handleAppEvent );
```

```
        editor.addEventListener( AppEvent.DELETE_DRAFT,      handleAppEvent );
        editor.addEventListener( AppEvent.DELETE_NOTE,       handleAppEvent );
        editor.addEventListener( AppEvent.SELECT_STORY,      handleAppEvent );
        editor.addEventListener( AppEvent.SELECT_PART,       handleAppEvent );
        editor.addEventListener( AppEvent.SELECT_CHAPTER,    handleAppEvent );
        editor.addEventListener( AppEvent.SELECT_SCENE,      handleAppEvent );
        editor.addEventListener( AppEvent.SELECT_DRAFT,      handleAppEvent );
        editor.addEventListener( AppEvent.SELECT_NOTE,       handleAppEvent );
        editor.addEventListener( AppEvent.DESELECT_PART,     handleAppEvent );
        editor.addEventListener( AppEvent.DESELECT_CHAPTER,  handleAppEvent );
        editor.addEventListener( AppEvent.DESELECT_SCENE,    handleAppEvent );
        editor.addEventListener( AppEvent.DISCARD_STORY,     handleAppEvent );
        editor.addEventListener( AppEvent.DISCARD_SERIES,    handleAppEvent );
        editor.addEventListener( AppEvent.SAVE_STORY,        handleAppEvent );
        editor.addEventListener( AppEvent.SAVE_SERIES,       handleAppEvent );
    }

    /**
     * Handle AppEvents from the view component.
     */
    private function handleAppEvent( event:AppEvent ):void
    {
        switch ( event.type )
        {
            // AppEvents for adding items.
            case AppEvent.ADD_STORY:
            case AppEvent.ADD_PART:
            case AppEvent.ADD_CHAPTER:
            case AppEvent.ADD_SCENE:
            case AppEvent.ADD_DRAFT:
            case AppEvent.ADD_NOTE:
                sendNotification(  AppConstants.ADD_ITEM, event );
                break;

            // AppEvents for deleting items.
            case AppEvent.DELETE_STORY:
            case AppEvent.DELETE_PART:
            case AppEvent.DELETE_CHAPTER:
            case AppEvent.DELETE_SCENE:
            case AppEvent.DELETE_DRAFT:
            case AppEvent.DELETE_NOTE:
                sendNotification( AppConstants.DELETE_ITEM, event );
                break;

            // AppEvents for selecting items.
            case AppEvent.SELECT_STORY:
            case AppEvent.SELECT_PART:
            case AppEvent.SELECT_CHAPTER:
            case AppEvent.SELECT_SCENE:
            case AppEvent.SELECT_DRAFT:
            case AppEvent.SELECT_NOTE:
                sendNotification( AppConstants.APPLY_SELECTION, event );
                break;

            // AppEvents for deselecting items.
```

```
            case AppEvent.DESELECT_PART:
            case AppEvent.DESELECT_CHAPTER:
            case AppEvent.DESELECT_SCENE:
                sendNotification( AppConstants.REMOVE_SELECTION, event );
                break;

            // AppEvents for discarding changes.
            case AppEvent.DISCARD_STORY:
            case AppEvent.DISCARD_SERIES:
                sendNotification( AppConstants.DISCARD_CHANGES, event );
                break;

            // AppEvents for saving changes.
            case AppEvent.SAVE_STORY:
            case AppEvent.SAVE_SERIES:
                sendNotification( AppConstants.APPLY_CHANGES, event );
                break;
        }
    }

    /**
     * Cast the view component to the correct type;
     */
    private function get editor():Editor
    {
        return viewComponent as Editor;
    }
  }
}
```

CHAPTER 7

Applying Business Logic

With the actors of our Model and View tiers now defined, we are ready to stitch them together and get things done. That is certainly the speciality of the Controller tier. But what *kind* of things do we want to do here?

Two Shades of Logic

Domain Logic

All of that code in `ValueObject`, `AbstractProxy`, and their subclasses is *Domain Logic*. It deals strictly with representing and persisting the data structures of our domain model.

The VOs encapsulate any logic necessary to represent data as typed objects and properties for manipulation by the rest of the program (in this case, marshaling data into and out of an XML structure). Often there is no logic, only properties on the VOs, or XML parsing logic might end up in your `Proxys`, if it is relatively simple, or in some form of delegate or helper used by the `Proxys` if there is a lot of it.

The `Proxys` and VOs take care of persisting and retrieving the data in a reliable way. We do not want to rely on `Commands` in the application to ensure the integrity of our data or be directly responsible for its persistence.

Business Logic

By contrast, *Business Logic* has to do with the aims, or business, of the application itself, fulfilling its use cases. For example, opening a Story for editing by taking the `StoryVO` and making the appropriate calls on the `SelectionContext` to select the current Draft of the very last Scene in the Story, however its Scenes are grouped. This code works with the domain model data, but for the purpose of preparing the View tier to present it. That functionality is specific to a use case for the application saying that when the Editor opens, we should be sitting at the end of the Story, ready to add more suspense and action. It has nothing whatsoever to do with the data representation or its persistence. If we decided to do a Viewer application that did not do any editing, we would not have this particular use case, so it should be clear that it does not belong in the Model tier, which should remain independent of the whims of application use cases.

Why the Distinction?

Always consider the possibility that you would want to repackage the Model tier for reuse in another application, such as a Viewer version of StoryArchitect. We would like pretty much everything needed to represent and persist the domain model to live in our model package, where it is easily moved into a library (see Chapter 8). So if we had our domain logic mixed in with our business logic in Commands, then repackaging the Model tier for reuse in another application would not be as clean cut an operation as it should be. We would have to remember which specific Commands need to be brought over to the library and registered in both applications. And of course, if we are not making the distinction between domain and business logic at all, they might well be muddled inside a single Command. Moving such a fuzzily defined Command over to a library to share its domain logic might not be so easy if it also performs business logic that is only relevant in the app it was written for.

Command Life Cycle

Commands are typically registered in your ApplicationFacade's initializeController() method, where you register one or more Notification names to a given Command class.

Unlike the Proxy and Mediator, there are no onRegister() and onRemove() methods for a Command; it is a short-lived actor. A Command is instantiated when any of the Notifications it was registered to are sent by any other actor. Once the Command has done its work, the framework does not keep any reference to it, so it should be garbage-collected as long as no other actor has a reference. Thus, you should avoid setting listeners on anything in a Command. In addition, Commands should be stateless, but if you need to track, for instance, how many times a Command has run, you might hold that in a class variable rather than an instance variable.

There are two flavors of Command: SimpleCommand and MacroCommand.

In a SimpleCommand, you will simply override the execute() method and place your logic inside. It will be executed immediately after construction, and the Notification that triggered it will be passed in.

In a MacroCommand, you will override the initializeMacroCommand() method, and call addSubCommand() one or more times, passing in Command class names. When a MacroCommand's execute() method is called, it will simply execute one "subcommand" after the other in FIFO order. Those subcommands can be a mixture of MacroCommands and SimpleCommands. Each subcommand will receive the original Notification, which can be modified along the way. Also, note that unless you want to run them separately as well, the subcommands are only registered with the `MacroCommand`, not with the `Controller` (via your `ApplicationFacade`'s `initializeController()` method).

The `Commands` we will see in this chapter are all `SimpleCommands`; we are going to focus on some of the business logic in our app. Later, in Chapter 8, we will see a good example of a `MacroCommand` when we break the `StartupCommand` into two `SimpleCommands` triggered by a `MacroCommand` in our repackaging of our domain model into a separate library.

The `SimpleCommand` class has a `facade` property: a reference to your `ApplicationFacade`. This means it can register, remove, and retrieve `Mediators`, `Proxys`, and it can register and remove `Commands`. It has this `facade` property by virtue of being a `Notifier` subclass, where it also gets its `sendNotification()` convenience method.

Building the Commands

We will begin our tour of the application's business logic with a look at the `StartupCommand` where we will prepare the Model and View tiers for use. Then, we will have a look at some of the `Commands` that are triggered by the `Chooser` and the `Editor`. In this chapter, we will focus on the `Commands` associated with editing a Story, applying and removing selection, applying and discarding changes to the Story, and adding items to a Story (Parts, Chapters, Scenes, Drafts, and Notes).

We will defer discussion of the `Commands` for creating, deleting, or changing the name of a Story or Series until Chapter 9 since they use a special pop up management subsystem created for this app (but easily reusable).

The Startup Command

Class

`StartupCommand.as`

Responsibilities

The `StartupCommand` has somewhat unique responsibilities. At the time it is run, none of the `Proxys` or `Mediators` have yet been registered, so we will register them, preparing the `Model` with its `Proxys` before preparing the `View` with its `Mediators`. The order is important because `Mediators` that form relationships with `Proxys` often do so by retrieving them in `onRegister()`, thus the `Proxys` should already be available at that time.

- Extend `SimpleCommand`
- Implement the common phases of the startup process
- Register all our `AbstractProxy` subclasses, in the proper order so that their constructor-enforced interdependencies can be served

- Create the instance of SelectionContext that is shared with many View Components and Commands, caching it in a transient Proxy using SelectionContext.NAME as the Proxy name
- Retrieve the reference to the StoryArchitect app from the Notification body
- Mediate the StoryArchitect application and its two top-level components chooser and editor
- Register mediators for pop ups (covered in Chapter 9)

Collaborations

The StartupCommand class knows all the Proxy and Mediator subclasses. It is a pretty unique actor in terms of number of known collaborators. In Chapter 8, we will split the Model and View preparation phases into two different Commands, which makes this somewhat saner.

The StartupCommand component is known only by the ApplicationFacade, which registers it in its initializeController() method.

Code

```
package com.futurescale.sa.controller.command.startup
{
    import com.futurescale.sa.model.proxy.CastProxy;
    import com.futurescale.sa.model.proxy.MilieuProxy;
    import com.futurescale.sa.model.proxy.SeriesProxy;
    import com.futurescale.sa.model.proxy.StoryProxy;
    import com.futurescale.sa.view.context.SelectionContext;
    import com.futurescale.sa.view.mediator.ApplicationMediator;
    import com.futurescale.sa.view.mediator.ChooserMediator;
    import com.futurescale.sa.view.mediator.EditorMediator;
    import com.futurescale.sa.view.popup.mediator.AlertPopupMediator;
    import com.futurescale.sa.view.popup.mediator.ConfirmationPopupMediator;
    import com.futurescale.sa.view.popup.mediator.SeriesPopupMediator;
    import com.futurescale.sa.view.popup.mediator.StoryPopupMediator;

    import org.puremvc.as3.interfaces.INotification;
    import org.puremvc.as3.patterns.command.SimpleCommand;
    import org.puremvc.as3.patterns.proxy.Proxy;

    public class StartupCommand extends SimpleCommand
    {
        override public function execute( note:INotification ):void
        {
            // MODEL PREPARATION PHASE
            //
            // Create and register the Proxys for the domain model.
            var castProxy:CastProxy     = new CastProxy();
            var milieuProxy:MilieuProxy = new MilieuProxy();
            var storyProxy:StoryProxy   = new StoryProxy( milieuProxy, castProxy );
            var seriesProxy:SeriesProxy = new SeriesProxy( storyProxy, milieuProxy,
                                                           castProxy);
```

```
facade.registerProxy( castProxy );
facade.registerProxy( milieuProxy );
facade.registerProxy( storyProxy );
facade.registerProxy( seriesProxy );

// VIEW PREPARATION PHASE
//
// Get the application from the note body
var app:StoryArchitect = StoryArchitect( note.getBody() );

// Register a convenience Proxy to hold the SelectionContext.
//
// The SelectionContext tracks the selected items in the View
// and is not part of the domain model, but we can utilize
// the framework Proxy class as a quick way to cache this data
// entity used solely by the View and Controller tiers.
var selectionContext:SelectionContext = new SelectionContext();
var scProxy:Proxy = new Proxy( SelectionContext.NAME, selectionContext );
facade.registerProxy( scProxy );

// Mediate the initial View Components
facade.registerMediator( new ApplicationMediator( app ) );
facade.registerMediator( new EditorMediator( app.editor ) );
facade.registerMediator( new ChooserMediator( app.chooser ) );

// Register the popup mediators
facade.registerMediator( new AlertPopupMediator() );
facade.registerMediator( new ConfirmationPopupMediator() );
facade.registerMediator( new StoryPopupMediator() );
facade.registerMediator( new SeriesPopupMediator() );
        }
    }
}
```

The Edit Story Command

Class

EditStoryCommand.as

Responsibilities

When the user has chosen a story in the Chooser and clicks the big "Write" button, the EditStoryCommand retrieves the full StoryVO and SelectionContext. It finds and selects the last Scene of the Story, regardless of type, and selects all the proper things in the SelectionContext (e.g. the very last Chapter, Part, Scene, and Draft in a complex Story). Then, it triggers display of the Editor, which will open up to the selected location since it has a reference to the SelectionContext.

- Extend SimpleCommand

- Get the `StoryVO` from the `Notification` body
- Retrieve the `SelectionContext` from its transient `Proxy`
- If the `StoryVO` is a stub, load the full `StoryVO` from disk
- Select the farthest point in the Story for editing by finding the current Draft of the last scene (however Scenes happen to be grouped in this Story)
- When selecting the Draft, we must also select all elements of the Story structure above it on the `SelectionContext`
- Send the `AppConstants.SHOW_EDITOR` Notification (it is not necessary to pass the `StoryVO` in the note body, the `Editor` will act on the selected Story in the `Selection Context`)

Collaborations

The `EditStoryCommand` class knows the `StoryVO`, `PartVO`, `ChapterVO`, `SceneVO`, the `Selec tionContext`, and `AppConstants`. It is triggered when a user selects a Story in the `Chooser` and clicks the "Write" button. Our goal here is to set the `SelectionContext` to the current Draft of the very last scene of the Story and place the user in the `Editor` at that point, ready to add more text.

The `EditStoryCommand` component is known only by the `ApplicationFacade`, which registers it in its `initializeController()` method.

Code

```
package com.futurescale.sa.controller.command.story
{
    import com.futurescale.sa.controller.constant.AppConstants;
    import com.futurescale.sa.model.proxy.StoryProxy;
    import com.futurescale.sa.model.vo.ChapterVO;
    import com.futurescale.sa.model.vo.PartVO;
    import com.futurescale.sa.model.vo.SceneVO;
    import com.futurescale.sa.model.vo.StoryVO;
    import com.futurescale.sa.view.context.SelectionContext;

    import org.puremvc.as3.interfaces.INotification;
    import org.puremvc.as3.interfaces.IProxy;
    import org.puremvc.as3.patterns.command.SimpleCommand;

    /**
     * Prepare a story for editing.
     */
    public class EditStoryCommand extends SimpleCommand
    {
        override public function execute( note:INotification ):void
        {
            // Get the story from the note body.
            var story:StoryVO = StoryVO( note.getBody() );

            // Get the SelectionContext
```

```
var scProxy:IProxy = facade.retrieveProxy( SelectionContext.NAME );
var context:SelectionContext = SelectionContext( scProxy.getData() );

// Get the StoryProxy
var storyProxy:StoryProxy =
                StoryProxy( facade.retrieveProxy( StoryProxy.NAME ) );

// Be sure we have the full Story
if ( story.isStub ) {
    story = storyProxy.loadStory( story );
}

// Select the farthest point in the story for editing
context.selectStory( story );
var part:PartVO;
var chapter:ChapterVO;
var scene:SceneVO;
if ( story.useScenes )
{
    scene = story.scenes[ story.scenes.length-1 ];
    context.selectScene( scene );
    context.selectDraft( scene.currentDraft );
}
else if ( story.useChapters )
{
    chapter = story.chapters[ story.chapters.length-1 ];
    scene   = chapter.scenes[ chapter.scenes.length-1 ];
    context.selectChapter( chapter );
    context.selectScene( scene );
    context.selectDraft( scene.currentDraft );
}
else if ( story.useParts )
{
    part    = story.parts[ story.parts.length-1 ];
    chapter = part.chapters[ part.chapters.length-1 ];
    scene   = chapter.scenes[ chapter.scenes.length-1 ];
    context.selectPart( part );
    context.selectChapter( chapter );
    context.selectScene( scene );
    context.selectDraft( scene.currentDraft );
}

// Tell the View to edit the story.
sendNotification( AppConstants.SHOW_EDITOR );
            }
        }
    }
```

The Apply Selection Command

Class

ApplySelectionCommand.as

Responsibilities

When the user opens a section of a Story in the Timeline (or a Note in the Details component), the ApplySelectionCommand is executed and passed an AppEvent. The ApplySelectionCommand evaluates the AppEvent to figure out what to select on the SelectionContext, which is shared with the View Components who use it to determine what to display.

- Extend SimpleCommand
- Get the AppEvent from the Notification body
- Retrieve the SelectionContext from its transient Proxy
- Based on the type of the AppEvent call the appropriate selection method on the SelectionContext
- When calling the selection method on the SelectionContext, call it first with null, then with the data property of the AppEvent (this is necessary to force the bindings in the view hierarchy to be re-evaluated if the selection is the same object that is already selected so that the view will redraw itself)
- Additionally, when selecting a Story, replace the StoryVO in the AppEvent.data property (which could be a stub) with a fully populated StoryVO by calling the StoryProxy's loadStory() method (if the StoryVO is already loaded, it will be returned from its transient Proxy cache, otherwise it will be loaded, cached, and returned)

Collaborations

The ApplySelectionCommand class knows AppEvent, most of the ValueObject subclasses, SelectionContext, and Proxy. In future iterations, we will add selection of SeasonVO, CharacterVO, and SettingVO.

The ApplySelectionCommand component is known only by the ApplicationFacade, which registers it in its initializeController() method.

Code

```
package com.futurescale.sa.controller.command.edit
{
    import com.futurescale.sa.model.proxy.StoryProxy;
    import com.futurescale.sa.model.vo.ChapterVO;
    import com.futurescale.sa.model.vo.DraftVO;
    import com.futurescale.sa.model.vo.NoteVO;
    import com.futurescale.sa.model.vo.PartVO;
    import com.futurescale.sa.model.vo.SceneVO;
    import com.futurescale.sa.model.vo.StoryVO;
    import com.futurescale.sa.view.context.SelectionContext;
    import com.futurescale.sa.view.event.AppEvent;

    import org.puremvc.as3.interfaces.INotification;
    import org.puremvc.as3.interfaces.IProxy;
```

```
import org.puremvc.as3.patterns.command.SimpleCommand;

/**
 * Handle a request to select some new item, which
 * comes in the form of an AppEvent. Here, we will
 * interpret the event, selecting the item in the
 * SelectionContext shared by the View Components.
 */
public class ApplySelectionCommand extends SimpleCommand
{
    override public function execute( note:INotification ):void
    {
        // Get the event from the note body
        var event:AppEvent = AppEvent( note.getBody() );

        // Get the SelectionContext
        var scProxy:IProxy = facade.retrieveProxy( SelectionContext.NAME );
        var context:SelectionContext = SelectionContext( scProxy.getData() );

        switch ( event.type )
        {
            case AppEvent.SELECT_STORY:
                context.selectStory( null );
                context.selectStory( getStory( StoryVO( event.data ) ) );
                break;

            case AppEvent.SELECT_PART:
                context.selectPart( null );
                context.selectPart( PartVO( event.data ) );
                break;

            case AppEvent.SELECT_CHAPTER:
                context.selectChapter( null );
                context.selectChapter( ChapterVO( event.data ) );
                break;

            case AppEvent.SELECT_SCENE:
                context.selectScene( null );
                context.selectScene( SceneVO( event.data ) );
                break;

            case AppEvent.SELECT_DRAFT:
                context.selectDraft( null );
                context.selectDraft( DraftVO( event.data ) );
                break;

            case AppEvent.SELECT_NOTE:
                context.selectNote( null );
                context.selectNote( NoteVO( event.data ) );
                break;
        }
    }

    /**
      * Get the full StoryVO from a stub.
```

```
        */
        private function getStory( stub:StoryVO ):StoryVO
        {
          var proxy:StoryProxy = StoryProxy( facade.retrieveProxy( StoryProxy.NAME ) );
            return proxy.loadStory( stub );
        }
      }
    }
```

The Remove Selection Command

Class

RemoveSelectionCommand.as

Responsibilities

When the user closes a section of the Timeline (such as clicking a "Chapter" button when the Timeline is already displaying its Scenes), then it and the sections below it in the hierarchy must be removed from the SelectionContext. For instance, when a selected Chapter is clicked to deselect it, the Story or Part containing it should be selected, causing the Chapter and its Scenes to be deselected by the logic inside the corresponding selection method on the SelectionContext.

- Extend SimpleCommand
- Get the AppEvent from the Notification body
- Retrieve the SelectionContext from its transient Proxy
- Based on the type of the AppEvent, call the appropriate selection method on the SelectionContext (we will be selecting the *parent* of the item in the data property of the AppEvent, which clears the selection of anything below it in the Story hierarchy)
- When deselecting a PartVO, we will call the SelectionContext's selectStory() method and the StoryVO will be in the related property of the AppEvent
- When deselecting a ChapterVO, the related property of the AppEvent may contain a StoryVO or a PartVO; select the appropriate one
- When deselecting a SceneVO, the related property of the AppEvent may contain a StoryVO or a ChapterVO; select the appropriate one
- When calling a selection method, call it with null first, causing the view hierarchy bindings to be re-evaluated if the object is the same as the currently selected one for its type (forcing the view to redraw)

Collaborations

The RemoveSelectionCommand class knows AppEvent, several of the ValueObject subclasses, SelectionContext, and Proxy.

The RemoveSelectionCommand component is known only by the ApplicationFacade, which registers it in its initializeController() method.

Code

```
package com.futurescale.sa.controller.command.edit
{
    import com.futurescale.sa.model.proxy.StoryProxy;
    import com.futurescale.sa.model.vo.ChapterVO;
    import com.futurescale.sa.model.vo.PartVO;
    import com.futurescale.sa.model.vo.StoryVO;
    import com.futurescale.sa.view.context.SelectionContext;
    import com.futurescale.sa.view.event.AppEvent;

    import org.puremvc.as3.interfaces.INotification;
    import org.puremvc.as3.interfaces.IProxy;
    import org.puremvc.as3.patterns.command.SimpleCommand;

    /**
     * Handle a request to deselect some item, which
     * comes in the form of an AppEvent. Here, we will
     * interpret the event, selecting the item in the
     * SelectionContext shared by the View Components.
     */
    public class RemoveSelectionCommand extends SimpleCommand
    {
        override public function execute( note:INotification ):void
        {
            // Get the event from
            var event:AppEvent = AppEvent( note.getBody() );

            // Get the SelectionContext
            var scProxy:IProxy = facade.retrieveProxy( SelectionContext.NAME );
            var context:SelectionContext = SelectionContext( scProxy.getData() );

            switch ( event.type )
            {
                case AppEvent.DESELECT_PART:
                    context.selectStory(null);
                    context.selectStory( StoryVO( event.related ) );
                    break;

                case AppEvent.DESELECT_CHAPTER:
                    if ( event.related is PartVO ) {
                        context.selectPart(null);
                        context.selectPart( PartVO( event.related ) );
                    } else {
                        context.selectStory(null);
                        context.selectStory( StoryVO( event.related ) );
                    }
                    break;

                case AppEvent.DESELECT_SCENE:
                    if ( event.related is ChapterVO ) {
                        context.selectChapter(null);
```

```
                context.selectChapter( ChapterVO( event.related ) );
            } else {
                context.selectStory(null);
                context.selectStory( StoryVO( event.related ) );
            }
            break;
        }
      }
    }
}
```

The Apply Changes Command

Class

ApplyChangesCommand.as

Responsibilities

When the user is in the Editor and clicks the "Save" button, the ApplyChangesCommand is executed. It simply saves the Story or Series that was being edited and returns the user to the Chooser.

- Extend SimpleCommand
- Get the AppEvent from the Notification body
- If the type of the AppEvent is SAVE_STORY, retrieve the StoryProxy and call its saveStory() method with the StoryVO from the data property of the AppEvent
- If the type of the AppEvent is SAVE_SERIES, retrieve the SeriesProxy and call its saveSeries() method with the SeriesVO from the data property of the AppEvent

Collaborations

The ApplyChangesCommand class knows AppConstants, AppEvent, StoryProxy, SeriesProxy, StoryVO, and SeriesVO. The AppEvent is sent when you are in the Editor editing a Story (or in future iterations, a Series) and you click the "Save" button.

The ApplyChangesCommand component is known only by the ApplicationFacade, which registers it in its initializeController() method.

Code

```
package com.futurescale.sa.controller.command.edit
{
    import com.futurescale.sa.controller.constant.AppConstants;
    import com.futurescale.sa.model.proxy.SeriesProxy;
    import com.futurescale.sa.model.proxy.StoryProxy;
    import com.futurescale.sa.model.vo.SeriesVO;
    import com.futurescale.sa.model.vo.StoryVO;
    import com.futurescale.sa.view.event.AppEvent;
```

```
import org.puremvc.as3.interfaces.INotification;
import org.puremvc.as3.patterns.command.SimpleCommand;

public class ApplyChangesCommand extends SimpleCommand
{
    override public function execute( note:INotification ):void
    {
        // Get the event from
        var event:AppEvent = AppEvent( note.getBody() );

        // Proxys we may need
        var storyProxy:StoryProxy;
        var seriesProxy:SeriesProxy;

        // Save entity to disk
        switch ( event.type )
        {
            case AppEvent.SAVE_STORY:
               storyProxy = StoryProxy( facade.retrieveProxy( StoryProxy.NAME ) );
                var story:StoryVO = StoryVO( event.data );
                storyProxy.saveStory( story );
                break;

            case AppEvent.SAVE_SERIES:
              seriesProxy = SeriesProxy( facade.retrieveProxy( StoryProxy.NAME ) );
                var series:SeriesVO = SeriesVO( event.data );
                seriesProxy.saveSeries( series );
                break;

        }

        // Send the user back to the chooser
        sendNotification( AppConstants.SHOW_CHOOSER );
    }
  }
}
```

The Discard Changes Command

Class

DiscardChangesCommand.as

Responsibilities

When the user is in the Editor and clicks the "Discard" button, the DiscardChangesCom mand is executed. It clears the reference to the modified Story or Series in the Selection Context, then reloads the Story or Series, overwriting the cached version we were editing. Then it returns the user to the Chooser.

- Extend SimpleCommand

- Get the AppEvent from the Notification body
- If the type of the AppEvent is DISCARD_STORY, call the SelectionContext's selectStory() method with null, retrieve the StoryProxy and call its loadStory() method with the StoryVO from the data property of the AppEvent, and a true recache argument, ensuring the cached StoryVO will be removed and replaced with one loaded from disk
- If the type of the AppEvent is DISCARD_SERIES, call the SelectionContext's selectSeries() method with null, retrieve the SeriesProxy and call its loadSeries() method with the SeriesVO from the data property of the AppEvent, and a true recache argument, ensuring the cached SeriesVO will be removed and replaced with one loaded from disk
- Send an AppConstants.SHOW_CHOOSER Notification to return the user to the Chooser

Collaborations

The DiscardChangesCommand class knows AppConstants, AppEvent, StoryProxy, SeriesProxy, StoryVO, SeriesVO, and SelectionContext. The AppEvent is sent when you are in the Editor editing a Story (or in future iterations, a Series) and you click the "Discard" button.

The DiscardChangesCommand component is known only by the ApplicationFacade, which registers it in its initializeController() method.

Code

```
package com.futurescale.sa.controller.command.edit
{
    import com.futurescale.sa.controller.constant.AppConstants;
    import com.futurescale.sa.model.proxy.SeriesProxy;
    import com.futurescale.sa.model.proxy.StoryProxy;
    import com.futurescale.sa.model.vo.SeriesVO;
    import com.futurescale.sa.model.vo.StoryVO;
    import com.futurescale.sa.view.context.SelectionContext;
    import com.futurescale.sa.view.event.AppEvent;

    import org.puremvc.as3.interfaces.INotification;
    import org.puremvc.as3.interfaces.IProxy;
    import org.puremvc.as3.patterns.command.SimpleCommand;

    public class DiscardChangesCommand extends SimpleCommand
    {
        override public function execute( note:INotification ):void
        {
            // Get the event from
            var event:AppEvent = AppEvent( note.getBody() );

            // Get the SelectionContext
            var scProxy:IProxy = facade.retrieveProxy( SelectionContext.NAME );
            var context:SelectionContext = SelectionContext( scProxy.getData() );
```

```
        // Proxys we may need
        var storyProxy:StoryProxy;
        var seriesProxy:SeriesProxy;

        // Remove entity from selection context and re-cache from disk
        switch ( event.type )
        {
            case AppEvent.DISCARD_STORY:
              storyProxy = StoryProxy( facade.retrieveProxy( StoryProxy.NAME ) );
                var story:StoryVO = context.story;
                context.selectStory( null );
                storyProxy.loadStory( story, true );
                break;

            case AppEvent.DISCARD_SERIES:
              seriesProxy = SeriesProxy( facade.retrieveProxy( StoryProxy.NAME ) );
                var series:SeriesVO = context.series;
                context.selectSeries( null );
                seriesProxy.loadSeries( series, true );
                break;
        }

        // Send the user back to the chooser
        sendNotification( AppConstants.SHOW_CHOOSER );
      }
    }
  }
```

The Add Item Command

Class

AddItemCommand.as

Responsibilities

When the user adds an item in the Timeline or Details components (such as adding a Chapter to a Part, or a Note to a Scene), the AddItemCommand is executed. Based on the type of AppEvent (e.g. AppEvent.ADD_CHAPTER or AppEvent.ADD_NOTE), it will add the appropriate item and select it in the SelectionContext.

- Extend SimpleCommand
- Get the AppEvent from the Notification body
- Retrieve the SelectionContext from its transient Proxy
- If the type of the AppEvent is ADD_PART, get the selected Story, call its getNewPart() method, then call the SelectionContext's selectStory() method with null followed by the selected Story, causing the view hierarchy to redraw with the new Part shown

- If the type of the AppEvent is ADD_CHAPTER, get the selected Part if it exists, or the Story otherwise, call its getChapter() method, then call the SelectionContext's appropriate selection method with null followed by the selected Part or Story, causing the view hierarchy to redraw with the new Chapter shown

- If the type of the AppEvent is ADD_SCENE, get the selected Chapter if it exists, or the Story otherwise, call its getScene() method, then call the SelectionContext's appropriate selection method with null followed by the selected Chapter or Story, causing the view hierarchy to redraw with the new Scene shown

- If the type of the AppEvent is ADD_DRAFT, get the selected Scene, call its getNew Draft() method, then call the SelectionContext's selectScene() method with null followed by the selected Scene, causing the view hierarchy to redraw with the new Draft shown

- If the type of the AppEvent is ADD_NOTE, get the selected item (a ValueObject typed reference to whatever the actual selection is), call its addNote() method, then set the SelectionContext's selectedItem property with null followed by the selected item, causing the view hierarchy to redraw with the new Note shown

Collaborations

The AddItemCommand class knows ValueObject and most of its subclasses, AppEvent, SeriesVO, and SelectionContext. The AppEvent is sent when you are in the Editor editing a Story (or in future iterations, a Series) and you click the one of the "Add" (+) buttons to add a Note, Draft, Scene, Chapter, or Part. In future iterations, this Command will also add Episodes and Seasons to a Series.

The AddItemCommand component is known only by the ApplicationFacade, which registers it in its initializeController() method.

Code

```
package com.futurescale.sa.controller.command.edit
{
    import com.futurescale.sa.model.vo.ChapterVO;
    import com.futurescale.sa.model.vo.DraftVO;
    import com.futurescale.sa.model.vo.NoteVO;
    import com.futurescale.sa.model.vo.PartVO;
    import com.futurescale.sa.model.vo.SceneVO;
    import com.futurescale.sa.model.vo.SeasonVO;
    import com.futurescale.sa.model.vo.StoryVO;
    import com.futurescale.sa.model.vo.ValueObject;
    import com.futurescale.sa.view.context.SelectionContext;
    import com.futurescale.sa.view.event.AppEvent;

    import org.puremvc.as3.interfaces.INotification;
    import org.puremvc.as3.interfaces.IProxy;
    import org.puremvc.as3.patterns.command.SimpleCommand;

    /**
```

```
 * A request to add some new item has arisen from the
 * View in the form of an AppEvent. Here, we will
 * interpret the event, add the item, then trigger
 * selection of that item.
 */
public class AddItemCommand extends SimpleCommand
{
    override public function execute( notification:INotification ):void
    {
        var event:AppEvent = AppEvent( notification.getBody() );

        // Get the SelectionContext
        var scProxy:IProxy = facade.retrieveProxy( SelectionContext.NAME );
        var context:SelectionContext = SelectionContext( scProxy.getData() );

        var season:SeasonVO;
        var story:StoryVO;
        var part:PartVO;
        var chapter:ChapterVO;
        var scene:SceneVO;
        var draft:DraftVO;
        var vo:ValueObject;

        switch ( event.type )
        {
            case AppEvent.ADD_PART:
                // add part to selected story
                story = context.story;
                part = story.getNewPart();
                context.selectStory( null );
                context.selectStory( story );
                break;

            case AppEvent.ADD_CHAPTER:
                if ( context.part )
                {
                    // add chapter to selected part
                    part = context.part;
                    chapter =  part.getNewChapter( );
                    context.selectPart( null );
                    context.selectPart( part );
                } else {
                    // add chapter to selected story
                    story = context.story;
                    chapter =  story.getNewChapter( );
                    context.selectStory( null );
                    context.selectStory( story );
                }
                break;

            case AppEvent.ADD_SCENE:
                if ( context.chapter )
                {
                    // add scene to selected chapter
                    chapter = context.chapter;
```

```
            scene =  chapter.getNewScene( );
            context.selectChapter( null );
            context.selectChapter( chapter );
        } else {
            // add scene to selected story
            story = context.story;
            scene =  story.getNewScene( );
            context.selectStory( null );
            context.selectStory( story );
        }
        break;

    case AppEvent.ADD_DRAFT:
        // add draft to selected scene
        scene = context.scene;
        draft = scene.getNewDraft();
        context.selectScene( null );
        context.selectScene( scene );
        break;

    case AppEvent.ADD_NOTE:
        // add note to selected item
        context.note = new NoteVO();
        vo = context.selectedItem;
        vo.addNote( context.note );
        context.selectedItem = null
        context.selectedItem = vo;
        break;
        }
    }
  }
}
```

Registering the Commands

The reason we do not also register Commands in the StartupCommand is that we usually override intializeController() in the ApplicationFacade to bootstrap the app with a minimum of a STARTUP Notification, so it makes sense to just do all the Command registrations in one place. However, that is also a lot of classes for a long-lived actor like the ApplicationFacade to know if it only registers them once.

You may move the rest of the Command registrations (other than STARTUP, of course) to the StartupCommand if you would like. If you decide to do so, you might consider putting them in their own SimpleCommand executed as a subcommand of a StartupCommand that is a MacroCommand. It would call its addSubCommand() method with PrepareController Command, PrepareModelCommand, and PrepareViewCommand, in that order (so that Com mands can respond to notifications arising from both Proxy and Mediator onRegister() methods).

Regardless of where you choose to do your Command registrations, remember that Commands will not be executed if you forget to register them!

After building the View Components and their Mediators in previous chapters, you saw how the AppEvents dispatched from the user interface will be translated into various Notifications that will trigger Commands. Let's revisit the ApplicationFacade's intiali zeController() with the first iteration's Command registrations in place.

Application Facade / initializeController()

Class
ApplicationFacade.as

Method
initializeController()

Responsibilities
We generally register all of the Commands in an overridden ApplicationFacade.initiali zeController() method since, at a minimum, the StartupCommand must be registered by the ApplicationFacade. However, see Chapter 8 for an example and discussion of why and how you would want to refactor this to a Command.

- Must call super.initializeController()
- Call registerCommand() for each Notification / Command pair
- Only one Command can be registered to a given Notification name, but the same Command can be registered to more than one Notification name

Code

```
/**
 * Register the Commands.
 */
override protected function initializeController():void
{
    super.initializeController();

    // Initiated by the App
    registerCommand( AppConstants.STARTUP,          StartupCommand );

    // Initiated by the Chooser
    registerCommand( AppConstants.MANAGE_STORY,     ManageStoryCommand );
    registerCommand( AppConstants.MANAGE_SERIES,    ManageSeriesCommand );
    registerCommand( AppConstants.EDIT_STORY,       EditStoryCommand );
```

```
        registerCommand( StoryProxy.STORY_ADDED,      EditStoryCommand );

        // Initiated by the Editor
        registerCommand( AppConstants.ADD_ITEM,          AddItemCommand );
        registerCommand( AppConstants.DELETE_ITEM,       DeleteItemCommand );
        registerCommand( AppConstants.APPLY_SELECTION,   ApplySelectionCommand );
        registerCommand( AppConstants.REMOVE_SELECTION,  RemoveSelectionCommand);
        registerCommand( AppConstants.DISCARD_CHANGES,   DiscardChangesCommand );
        registerCommand( AppConstants.APPLY_CHANGES,     ApplyChangesCommand);
    }
```

CHAPTER 8

Advanced Model Topics

In this chapter, we will have a look at a couple of common Model related issues: Synchronous versus Asynchronous behavior, and reuse of the Model tier.

Handling Synchronous Behavior

In the StoryArchitect application, our Proxy subclasses interacted with the filesystem in a *synchronous* fashion. That is to say, the result of reading a file is available to the next line of code, and you may begin working with the retrieved data immediately. This is nice because the calling code is usually in the middle of doing something when it makes the call and would probably like to get on with it.

Here is an example from StoryArchitect of a Proxy method and the calling Command using the fetched data immediately as it carries out a use case. The ApplySelectionCommand has to select a Story (a view-related endeavor), but needs to be sure that if the Story is a stub (as it would be from a list), it is fully loaded when placed on the SelectionContext. Notice the ease with which the result is consumed in the Command.

The Story Proxy

Class

StoryProxy.as

Method

loadStory()

Code

```
/**
 * Load a Story.
 *
 * If Story is already cached from having been
```

```
 * previously loaded or added, the cached VO will be
 * returned, otherwise it will be loaded and cached first.
 *
 * Optionally allows forced re-caching from disc
 * (as when user changes are discarded).
 */
public function loadStory( storyStub:StoryVO, recache:Boolean = false ):StoryVO
{
    // Optionally force loading from disk and recaching
    if ( recache ) facade.removeProxy( storyStub.uid );

    var cacheProxy:IProxy;
    if ( facade.hasProxy( storyStub.uid ) ) {
        cacheProxy = facade.retrieveProxy( storyStub.uid );
    } else {
        var story:StoryVO = new StoryVO( readVO( storyStub ) );
        cacheProxy = new Proxy( story.uid, story );
        facade.registerProxy( cacheProxy );
    }
    return cacheProxy.getData() as StoryVO;
}
```

The Apply Selection Command

Class

ApplySelectionCommand.as

Methods

execute(), getStory()

Code

```
override public function execute( note:INotification ):void
{
    // Get the event from
    var event:AppEvent = AppEvent( note.getBody() );

    // Get the SelectionContext
    var scProxy:IProxy = facade.retrieveProxy( SelectionContext.NAME );
    var context:SelectionContext = SelectionContext( scProxy.getData() );

    switch ( event.type )
    {
            ...

        case AppEvent.SELECT_STORY:
            context.selectStory( null );
            context.selectStory( getStory( StoryVO( event.data ) ) );
            break;

            ...
```

```
        }
    }

    /**
     * Get the full StoryVO from a stub.
     */
    private function getStory( stub:StoryVO ):StoryVO
    {
      var proxy:StoryProxy = StoryProxy( facade.retrieveProxy( StoryProxy.NAME ) );
        return proxy.loadStory( stub );
    }
```

Handling Asynchronous Behavior

As discussed previously in the book, a future version of the StoryArchitect application may mirror its data to a server, so that you can do your work on multiple devices. That will require remote server communication.

When we communicate with remote servers, we always do so *asynchronously*. We send off a request, and some time later we are interrupted by an incoming response from the server. If you are retrieving an object, you cannot work with it immediately after making the call; you must instead wait for the result. Moreover, you must remember what you were doing when you sent the request, as that may have a bearing on what you do with the result.

Inside the Proxy, that just means you split the calling code and the subsequent result handling code into at least two methods: one for invoking the call, one for handling the result, and perhaps another for handling a fault response.

As the synchronous example above shows, often persistence or retrieval operations are invoked on a Proxy while the middle of a larger block of code in a Command that is carrying out a use case for the application. That means that the way we build our App (Media tors and Commands) is somewhat dependent on whether our Proxys exhibit synchronous or asynchronous behavior, or a mixture of both. This is one of the reasons we built the Proxys before we built the Mediators and Commands. In StoryArchitect, we knew we were going to be communicating synchronously, so that worked out fine. But let's consider a situation where we are using an async service, which is a far more common situation.

Imagine a Command that simply invokes an async method on a Proxy. Later a response comes back, and is sent out in a Notification from the Proxy.

What happens then?

- Can another Command be executed and/or some number of Mediators notified?
- Can the calling Command get the result somehow and carry on with it?

Yes and yes.

These are a couple of ways to go about handling the async break in the use case and we will discuss them here. In either case, there will have to be a more complex response handling mechanism due to the nature of async communications. Just remember, the goal is not finding the shortest possible path to the data but to completely hide the nature of the remote communication from the Commands that are executing business logic. Encapsulate the retrieval in the Proxy so that if you later have to change the nature of that server communication (say, from reading and parsing XML from flat files to talking to a WebORB server and getting back fully formed ActionScript objects), your business logic will remain unaffected. The View and Controller tiers request and receive typed objects, regardless of how they look coming in from the service.

Separate Invoker and Responder(s)

This is by far the most common approach. One actor invokes the request on the Proxy, while one or more other actors (Mediators and/or a Command) handle the result.

We have talked previously about a hypothetical Viewer application that will probably utilize some cloud service API, but for now let's imagine we created our own WebORB, BlazeDS, or LCDS backend and we have a remote Java service that we publish access to our StoryVOs from. And we have a Viewer application that is a Flex app in a web browser (and possibly desktop and mobile versions) that basically just lets the user browse a list of Stories and open one to read.

Let's discuss a use case where the user has chosen a Story from the list, and we have triggered a LoadStoryCommand. Since we do not have a big need for the selection of parts of a Story in the Viewer, we have not even registered a SelectionContext, so the Mediator has sent the selected StoryVO stub in the Notification body for the Command to work with. LoadStoryCommand is going to talk with a special StoryReadingProxy that communicates with the remote reading service and fetches the full StoryVO.

- LoadStoryCommand makes a call on StoryReadingProxy, passing it the StoryVO stub to load, sends an AppConstants.READ_STORY note, and exits
- ViewerAppMediator is interested in AppConstants.READ_STORY and responds by telling its View Component, the ViewerApp, to change from the Chooser to the Reader
- Later, the response comes back from the server, the StoryReadingProxy sends a StoryReadingProxy.STORY_RETRIEVED note with the StoryVO in the body
- ReaderMediator is interested in StoryReadingProxy.STORY_RETRIEVED and responds by taking the StoryVO from the note and setting it on its View Component Reader
- The View Component Reader immediately displays the StoryVO for reading

This does not really require an illustration code here. If you recall, back in Chapter 1, we showed a very similar example where the PerformEmailTestCommand invoked the EmailProxy's testConfiguration() method, the async result of which was later sent out in a EmailProxy.TEST_RESULT note, handled by the EmailConfigMediator.

Single Invoker/Responder

Occasionally, we would like to have the same `SimpleCommand` instance that invokes a remote retrieval method on a `Proxy` receive an async response so that it can carry on its business logic with the retrieved information.

The biggest problem with this approach is decoupling the `Command` from the domain logic.

It is a common practice in Flex development to have a `Command`-like class implement the Flex `IResponder` interface and either make the call itself or have the `Proxy` make the call, setting the `Command` as the responder. Then the result comes back directly to the `result` or `fault` methods of the `Command`. The problem with this is that we muddle the responsibilities of the `Command`, making it implicitly involved in the persistence mechanism by implementing `IResponder` and handling `ResultEvents` and `FaultEvents`.

As was discussed in Chapter 7, we really want the persistence mechanism to be encapsulated by the Model tier, and for the `Command` to focus on business logic. It just needs a piece of data, it does not need to know that it came from a service, or to parse `ResultEvents` and `FaultEvents`. If it does, and you change the persistence mechanism later, your business logic will be impacted as well as your domain logic, because this `Command` will have to be refactored.

In this example, let's imagine that we have selected a Story in the `Chooser` and we want to perform a text search on it, but we have to load the full Story first. We will load the Story with the `SearchStoryCommand`, which will subsequently be notified when the Story is loaded, so that it can then perform the search operation.

We will formalize the request and encapsulate the callback mechanism in a single class called `ServiceRequest`. It makes use of the little-known PureMVC `Observer` class, which is used by the framework to notify interested `Mediators` and trigger `Commands` (hint: the `Controller` is the interested `Observer` for all `Notifications` in `Command` registrations). `ServiceRequest` will extend `Observer` (allowing the caller to identify itself) and expose properties for the request data and response data. The `StoryReadingProxy` will take a `ServiceRequest` instead of the `StoryVO`. It will hold onto the `ServiceRequest` until the result comes back and then call its `notifyObserver()` method to send a `Notification` back to the calling `Command`. The reason the `Command` still exists, and is not garbage-collected after its `execute()` method finishes, is that the `ServiceRequest` still has a reference to it. As long as the `Proxy` keeps the `ServiceRequest` around, the `Command` is still able to be responded to.

- `SearchStoryCommand`, in its `execute()` method:
  — Extracts the `StoryVO` stub and the search term from the `Notification` body and type, respectively
  — Creates a `ServiceRequest` with the `StoryVO` stub as the `requestData`, its own `searchStory()` method as the `callback`, and itself as the `caller`

- — Makes a call on `StoryReadingProxy.loadStory()`, passing in the `ServiceRequest`
- `StoryReadingProxy`, in its `loadStory()` method:
  - — Calls a method on a Flex `RemoteObject` instance, and receives a Flex `AsyncToken` as the immediate return value (the token will remain in memory and be returned along with the response from the service)
  - — Stores the `ServiceRequest` on the `AsyncToken` object, which accepts dynamic properties
  - — Calls the `AsyncToken`'s `addResponder()` method, setting itself as a responder for the call (since `StoryReadingProxy` implements the Flex `IResponder` interface, its `result()` and `fault()` methods will now be called)
- Later, the response comes back from the server and the `StoryReadingProxy`'s `result()` method is called and does the following:
  - — Takes the `StoryVO` from the `ResultEvent`'s result property
  - — Takes the `AsyncToken` from the `ResultEvent`'s token property
  - — Takes the `ServiceRequest` from the `AsyncToken`'s dynamically set `request` property
  - — Sets the loaded `StoryVO` on the `ServiceRequest` `resultData` property
  - — Creates a `Notification` with the `ServiceRequest` in the body
  - — Notifies the `Observer` (`SearchStoryCommand`) by calling `notifyObserver()` on the `ServiceRequest`
- `SearchStoryCommand` is notified on its callback method `searchStory()` where it evaluates the note name and takes one of two actions:
  - — For `ServiceRequest.RESULT_OK`, it searches the full text of the Story for the search term and sends off the location of the first occurrence in an `AppConstants.SEARCH_RESULT` note
  - — For `ServiceRequest.RESULT_FAIL`, it sends off the failure message in an `AppConstants.REPORT_FAILURE` note, to be handled by a standard error reporting mechanism in the View tier

The Service Request

Class

`ServiceRequest.as`

Code

```
package com.futurescale.sa.model.request
{
    import org.puremvc.as3.patterns.observer.Observer;

    public class ServiceRequest extends Observer
```

```
{
    public static const RESULT_OK:String = "result/ok";
    public static const RESULT_FAIL:String = "result/fail";

    public var hasCallback:Boolean = false;
    public var requestData:Object;
    public var resultData:Object;

    public function ServiceRequest( requestData:Object = null,
                                    callback:Function = null,
                                    caller:Object      = null ) {
        // Store the Observer info
        super( callback, caller );

        // Store the request data
        this.requestData = requestData;

        // Remember whether complete Observer info was specified
        hasCallback = ( callback != null && caller != null );
    }
}
}
```

The Search Story Command

Class

SearchStoryCommand.as

Code

```
package com.futurescale.sa.controller.command.story
{
    import com.futurescale.sa.controller.constant.AppConstants;
    import com.futurescale.sa.model.proxy.StoryReadingProxy;
    import com.futurescale.sa.model.request.ServiceRequest;
    import com.futurescale.sa.model.vo.StoryVO;

    import org.puremvc.as3.interfaces.INotification;
    import org.puremvc.as3.interfaces.IProxy;
    import org.puremvc.as3.patterns.command.SimpleCommand;

    public class SearchStoryCommand extends SimpleCommand
    {
        private var term:String; // the search term

        override public function execute( note:INotification ):void
        {
            // Get the search term from the note type
            term = note.getType();

            // Get the story stub from the note body
            var storyVO:StoryVO = StoryVO( note.getBody );
```

```
            // Get the StoryReadingProxy
            var proxy:IProxy = facade.retrieveProxy( StoryReadingProxy.NAME );
            var readerProxy:StoryReadingProxy = StoryReadingProxy( proxy );

            // Create the ServiceRequest
            var request:ServiceRequest =
                new ServiceRequest( storyVO, searchStory, this );

            // Load the story
            readerProxy.loadStory( request );
        }

        private function searchStory( note:INotification ):void
        {
            // Get the completed request from the note body
            var request:ServiceRequest = ServiceRequest( note.getBody() );

            // Handle the result
            switch ( note.getName() ) {

                // RESULT_OK: Search for first occurance, send note with result
                case ServiceRequest.RESULT_OK:
                    var story:StoryVO = StoryVO( request.resultData );
                    var firstOccurance:int = story.getText().indexOf( term );
                    sendNotification( AppConstants.SEARCH_RESULT, firstOccurance );
                    break;

                // RESULT_FAIL: Send failure message in a note to be displayed
                case ServiceRequest.RESULT_FAIL:
                    var message:String = String( request.resultData );
                    sendNotification( AppConstants.REPORT_FAILURE, message );
                    break;
            }
        }
    }
}
```

The Story Reading Proxy

Class

StoryReadingProxy.as

Code

```
package com.futurescale.sa.model.proxy
{
    import com.futurescale.sa.model.request.ServiceRequest;
    import com.futurescale.sa.model.vo.StoryVO;

    import mx.rpc.AsyncToken;
    import mx.rpc.IResponder;
    import mx.rpc.events.FaultEvent;
    import mx.rpc.events.ResultEvent;
```

```
import mx.rpc.remoting.RemoteObject;

import org.puremvc.as3.patterns.observer.Notification;
import org.puremvc.as3.patterns.proxy.Proxy;

public class StoryReadingProxy extends Proxy implements IResponder
{
    public static const NAME:String = "StoryReadingProxy";
    private var service:RemoteObject;

    public function StoryReadingProxy()
    {
        super( NAME );
    }

    // Create the service at registration time
    override public function onRegister():void
    {
        service = new RemoteObject("StoryReadingService");
    }

    // Load Story from remote service
    public function loadStory( request:ServiceRequest ):void
    {
        var story:StoryVO = request.requestData as StoryVO;
        var token:AsyncToken =  service.loadStory( story );
        token.request = request;    // hang onto the request
        token.addResponder( this ); // this proxy will respond
    }

    // Handle loaded story
    public function result( data:Object ):void
    {
        var event:ResultEvent      = ResultEvent(data);
        var token:AsyncToken       = event.token;
        var request:ServiceRequest = token.request;
        request.resultData         = event.result; // the loaded story
        if ( request.hasCallback ) {
            var note:Notification;
            note = new Notification( ServiceRequest.RESULT_OK, request );
            request.notifyObserver( note );
        }
    }

    // Handle a failed story load
    public function fault( info:Object ):void
    {
        var event:FaultEvent       = FaultEvent(data);
        var token:AsyncToken       = event.token;
        var request:ServiceRequest = token.request;
        request.resultData         = event.message.toString();
        if ( request.hasCallback ) {
            var note:Notification;
            note = new Notification( ServiceRequest.RESULT_FAIL, request );
            request.notifyObserver( note );
```

```
                    }
                }
            }
        }
    }
```

Reusing the Model Tier

It has been stressed often throughout this book that the Model tier should remain unaware of the rest of the application. This means Proxys should never know (i.e. import) View Components, Mediators, or Commands. This also extends to not sending Notifications defined on the ApplicationFacade, AppConstants, or any other application-specific location.

When you are developing a small application, like StoryArchitect, you may suspect that eventually you will want companion applications, say for tablet and mobile. Those potential apps may have their own View Components, use cases, and business logic. You will be well served if you keep your Model reusable, but you do not have to move it to a separate project if you are sure you are taking the proper precautions. You could wait until you start work on your first companion app and at that time, move the Model tier code to its own library project. If you are positive the other apps will be built (perhaps they are being built in parallel), you may want to start out with the model package in a library project.

Another good reason to package the Model tier in a separate library is so that you can build unit tests against its classes. We all know that the realities of software development do not always give us time for unit tests, and that developers do not all have the discipline, experience, or inclination to write them. Regardless of your time for, and attitude toward, unit testing, the most important coverage to try for is the Model tier. In my experience, user interface behavior and business logic are better tested by competent and incentivized QA individuals. But the representation and persistence of your data is quite tractable to unit testing, and since the application's behavior and appearance depend on the reliability of the Model tier, it makes sense to spend at least a little time testing it. In Adobe FlashBuilder, you can create a new unit test for a class quickly and it automatically creates a testing application right there alongside your main application in the project. But crowding your unit tests and your application in the same project can lead to tedious time spent waiting for tests to compile each time you make a change in your application. It can really be a drag on productivity. During the creation of the unit tests for StoryArchitect, it became unbearable and forced the separation, but once the App, Model, and Tests were all in separate projects, sanity and productivity were fully restored.

So whether you are sharing your Model tier with two applications, want to test it in a separate project, or just want the peace of mind to know that your Model tier is fully decoupled from your app in anticipation of reuse, the simple exercise of moving your Model tier to a new library project is worthwhile. It should not take more than 10 minutes, and you will be better off for it. The steps you will take depend on your IDE and your code repository if you are using one.

Step 1: Create a New Flex Library Project

This is intended to be an IDE-agnostic book. Dialogs change as new project options appear, and the Flex and AIR products are still evolving rapidly. But the basic steps that have been valid for years with Flex and its libraries are the same. Since I know what they are, I will mention the FlashBuilder menu shortcuts here. I believe most of these menu paths are valid to most other Eclipse-based Flex IDEs, but your mileage may vary. At any rate, screenshots of the dialogs would be out of date quickly (and useless to other IDE users), so we will skip them.

1. Create a new Flex Library Project.

    In FlashBuilder: File➡New➡Flex Library Project➡StoryArchitectModel

2. Add a `libs` folder to the project and place in it a copy of `PureMVC_AS3_2_0_4.swc`, which can be found in the downloadable archive for the PureMVC AS3 Standard Version (*http://trac.puremvc.org/PureMVC_AS3/wiki/Downloads*).

    In FlashBuilder: New➡Folder➡`libs`

3. Add the `libs` folder to the Build Path for the library project.

    In FlashBuilder: Project➡Properties➡Flex Library Build Path➡Add SWC Folder➡`libs`

4. Create the basic package structure, (e.g. `com.futurescale.sa`), in the `src` folder of the library project and then copy over the `model` package from your app.

    If you are using a repository like SVN and you are moving classes out of a project, do not copy from the one project tree and paste into another because the repository information for the source project will be carried over and confuse your IDE when you try to check in the new project. Instead, right click on the project's `src` folder and choose Team➡Export and write the folder structure to your desktop. Then copy the folders and classes in from there.

5. Compile the library and see that it builds a `StoryArchitectModel.swc` file in the `bin` folder.

    In FlashBuilder: Project➡Clean...➡StoryArchitectModel

6. Add the project to your code repository following your ordinary procedures for sharing a project.

Step 2: Add Library Project to Flex Build Path in App Projects

Now that you have created a separate project with a copy of your Model tier and it is successfully building a SWC file, you are ready to use that library in your applications (main app, unit test app, mobile version, etc).

1. Remove the `model` package from your application; you are going to reference the library project now.

2. Add the library project to the application project Build Path.

   In FlashBuilder: Project→Properties→Flex Build Path→Add Project→StoryArchitect

3. Compile the application and see that it builds a `StoryArchitectModel.swf` file in the `bin-debug` folder.

   In FlashBuilder: Project→Clean...→StoryArchitect

4. Launch and interactively test the application.

5. Commit the project to your code repository following your ordinary procedures.

Extra Credit: Refactor the Startup Process

Your Model tier is now a standalone, reusable library. Your App and Test projects reference it but it does not reference them, ensuring that the most important separation of concerns in your app is enforced. There is one more thing you might want to do at this point, particularly if you are planning (or are already building) another app, which will use this Model tier—reuse the "model preparation" phase of the `StartupCommand`.

- In the library project:

  1. Create a new `controller` package, sibling to `model` (e.g. `com.futures cale.sa.controller`).

  2. Copy the `StartupCommand` over from the App project into the controller package, renaming it `PrepareModelCommand`.

  3. Inside `PrepareModelCommand`, make sure the class name is correct, remove all the "view preparation" code and the associated `import` statements.

  4. Compile the library and see that it builds a `StoryArchitectModel.swc` file in the `bin` folder.

     In FlashBuilder: Project→Clean...→StoryArchitectModel

- In the main application project:

  1. Rename `StartupCommand` to `PrepareViewCommand` (make sure to deselect the option to update references!).

  2. Inside the `PrepareViewCommand`, make sure the class name is correct, remove all the "model preparation" code and the associated `import` statements.

  3. Create a new `StartupCommand` class based on `MacroCommand`.

  4. In an overridden `initializeMacroCommand()` method, add the `PrepareModelCommand` and `PrepareViewCommand` as subcommands (in that order).

  5. Compile the application and see that it builds a `StoryArchitect.swf` file in the `bin-debug` folder.

In FlashBuilder: Project➞Clean...➞StoryArchitect

6. Launch and interactively test the application.

- Now that you have a `MacroCommand` that executes separate `SimpleCommands` to handle the "view preparation" and "model preparation" phases, you might as well take advantage of the situation by also moving the `Command` registrations out of your `ApplicationFacade` and into a `SimpleCommand`.

In your App project:

1. Make a copy of `PrepareViewCommand` called `PrepareControllerCommand`.

2. Inside the `PrepareControllerCommand`, make sure the class name is correct, remove all the code within the `execute()` method and the associated `import` statements.

3. Inside the `StartupCommand`'s overridden `initializeMacroCommand()` method, add the `PrepareControllerCommand` a subcommand prior to the other subcommands.

4. Inside the `ApplicationFacade`, copy all the block of `Command` registrations and paste them into the `PrepareControllerCommand`'s `execute()` method. In the `Command` you will need to prepend `facade.` to each of the `registerCommand()` calls, e.g. `facade.registerCommand` (AppConstants.MY_NOTE, MyCommand).

5. Move the `StartupCommand` registration into the `startup()` method before sending the `STARTUP` note.

6. Remove the `ApplicationFacade`'s `initializeController()` method and all associated imports.

7. Marvel at how tiny the `ApplicationFacade` is now.

8. Compile the application and see that it builds a `StoryArchitectModel.swf` file in the `bin-debug` folder.

In FlashBuilder: Project➞Clean...➞StoryArchitect

9. Launch and interactively test the application.

10. Commit the project to your code repository following your ordinary procedures.

The Application Facade

Class

`ApplicationFacade.as`

Code

```
package com.futurescale.sa
{
```

```
import com.futurescale.sa.controller.command.startup.StartupCommand;
import com.futurescale.sa.controller.constant.AppConstants;

import org.puremvc.as3.patterns.facade.Facade;

public class ApplicationFacade extends Facade
{
    /**
     * The Singleton instance factory method.
     */
    public static function getInstance( ) : ApplicationFacade
    {
        if ( instance == null ) instance = new ApplicationFacade( );
        return instance as ApplicationFacade;
    }

    /**
     * A convenience method for starting up the PureMVC
     * apparatus from the application.
     */
    public function startup( app:StoryArchitect ):void
    {
        registerCommand( AppConstants.STARTUP, StartupCommand );
        sendNotification( AppConstants.STARTUP, app );
    }
}
}
```

The Startup Command

Class

StartupCommand.as

Code

```
package com.futurescale.sa.controller.command.startup
{
    import org.puremvc.as3.patterns.command.MacroCommand;

    /**
     * Execute separate commands for each phase of startup
     */
    public class StartupCommand extends MacroCommand
    {
        override protected function initializeMacroCommand():void
        {
            addSubCommand( PrepareControllerCommand );
            addSubCommand( PrepareModelCommand );
            addSubCommand( PrepareViewCommand );
        }
    }
}
```

The Prepare Controller Command

Class

PrepareControllerCommand.as

Code

```
package com.futurescale.sa.controller.command.startup
{
    import com.futurescale.sa.controller.command.edit.AddItemCommand;
    import com.futurescale.sa.controller.command.edit.ApplyChangesCommand;
    import com.futurescale.sa.controller.command.edit.ApplySelectionCommand;
    import com.futurescale.sa.controller.command.edit.DeleteItemCommand;
    import com.futurescale.sa.controller.command.edit.DiscardChangesCommand;
    import com.futurescale.sa.controller.command.edit.RemoveSelectionCommand;
    import com.futurescale.sa.controller.command.series.ManageSeriesCommand;
    import com.futurescale.sa.controller.command.story.EditStoryCommand;
    import com.futurescale.sa.controller.command.story.ManageStoryCommand;
    import com.futurescale.sa.controller.constant.AppConstants;
    import com.futurescale.sa.model.proxy.StoryProxy;

    import org.puremvc.as3.interfaces.INotification;
    import org.puremvc.as3.patterns.command.SimpleCommand;

    /**
     * Prepare the Controller.
     *
     * Register all Commands other than StartupCommand
     */
    public class PrepareControllerCommand extends SimpleCommand
    {
        override public function execute( note:INotification ):void
        {
            // Initiated by the Chooser
            facade.registerCommand( AppConstants.MANAGE_STORY,
                                    ManageStoryCommand );
            facade.registerCommand( AppConstants.MANAGE_SERIES,
                                    ManageSeriesCommand );
            facade.registerCommand( AppConstants.EDIT_STORY,
                                    EditStoryCommand );
            facade.registerCommand( StoryProxy.STORY_ADDED,
                                    EditStoryCommand );

            // Initiated by the Editor
            facade.registerCommand( AppConstants.ADD_ITEM,
                                    AddItemCommand );
            facade.registerCommand( AppConstants.DELETE_ITEM,
                                    DeleteItemCommand );
            facade.registerCommand( AppConstants.APPLY_SELECTION,
                                    ApplySelectionCommand );
            facade.registerCommand( AppConstants.REMOVE_SELECTION,
                                    RemoveSelectionCommand );
            facade.registerCommand( AppConstants.DISCARD_CHANGES,
```

```
                                        DiscardChangesCommand );
            facade.registerCommand( AppConstants.APPLY_CHANGES,
                                     ApplyChangesCommand );
        }
    }
}
```

The Prepare Model Command

Class

PrepareModelCommand.as

Code

```
package com.futurescale.sa.controller.command.startup
{
    import com.futurescale.sa.model.proxy.CastProxy;
    import com.futurescale.sa.model.proxy.MilieuProxy;
    import com.futurescale.sa.model.proxy.SeriesProxy;
    import com.futurescale.sa.model.proxy.StoryProxy;

    import org.puremvc.as3.interfaces.INotification;
    import org.puremvc.as3.patterns.command.SimpleCommand;

    /**
     * Prepare the Model.
     */
    public class PrepareModelCommand extends SimpleCommand
    {
        override public function execute( note:INotification ):void
        {
            // Create the Proxys
            var castProxy:CastProxy     = new CastProxy();
            var milieuProxy:MilieuProxy = new MilieuProxy();
            var storyProxy:StoryProxy   =
                new StoryProxy( milieuProxy, castProxy );
            var seriesProxy:SeriesProxy =
                new SeriesProxy( storyProxy, milieuProxy, castProxy);

            // Register the Proxys
            facade.registerProxy( castProxy );
            facade.registerProxy( milieuProxy );
            facade.registerProxy( storyProxy );
            facade.registerProxy( seriesProxy );
        }
    }
}
```

The Prepare View Command

Class

PrepareViewCommand.as

Code

```
package com.futurescale.sa.controller.command.startup
{
    import com.futurescale.sa.view.context.SelectionContext;
    import com.futurescale.sa.view.mediator.ApplicationMediator;
    import com.futurescale.sa.view.mediator.ChooserMediator;
    import com.futurescale.sa.view.mediator.EditorMediator;
    import com.futurescale.sa.view.popup.mediator.AlertPopupMediator;
    import com.futurescale.sa.view.popup.mediator.ConfirmationPopupMediator;
    import com.futurescale.sa.view.popup.mediator.SeriesPopupMediator;
    import com.futurescale.sa.view.popup.mediator.StoryPopupMediator;

    import org.puremvc.as3.interfaces.INotification;
    import org.puremvc.as3.patterns.command.SimpleCommand;
    import org.puremvc.as3.patterns.proxy.Proxy;

    /**
     * Prepare the View.
     *
     * Create a SelectionContext, cache it for access from Commands,
     * and inject it into the app for sharing with the display list.
     * Also, mediate the initial View Components and register popup
     * mediators.
     */
    public class PrepareViewCommand extends SimpleCommand
    {
        override public function execute( note:INotification ):void
        {
            // Get the application from the note body
            var app:StoryArchitect = StoryArchitect( note.getBody() );

            // Register a convenience Proxy to hold the SelectionContext.
            //
            // The SelectionContext tracks the selected items in the View
            // and is not part of the domain model, but we can utilize
            // the framework Proxy class as a quick way to cache this data
            // entity used solely by the View and Controller tiers.
            var selectionContext:SelectionContext = new SelectionContext();
            var scProxy:Proxy = new Proxy( SelectionContext.NAME,
                                           selectionContext );
            facade.registerProxy( scProxy );

            // Mediate the initial View Components
            facade.registerMediator( new ApplicationMediator( app ) );
            facade.registerMediator( new EditorMediator( app.editor ) );
            facade.registerMediator( new ChooserMediator( app.chooser ) );
```

```
        // Register the popup mediators (See Chapter 9)
        facade.registerMediator( new AlertPopupMediator() );
        facade.registerMediator( new ConfirmationPopupMediator() );
        facade.registerMediator( new StoryPopupMediator() );
        facade.registerMediator( new SeriesPopupMediator() );
    }
  }
}
```

The Refactored Projects

Here is a look at the source code structure of the Story Architect Model (Figure 8-1),
App (Figure 8-2), and Test (Figure 8-3) projects at the end of the first iteration of development.

Figure 8-1. The StoryArchitect Model

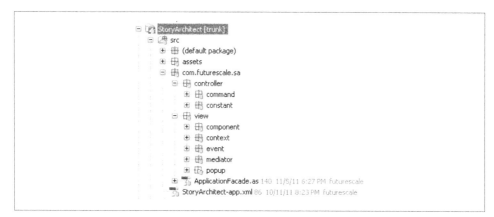

Figure 8-2. The StoryArchitect Application

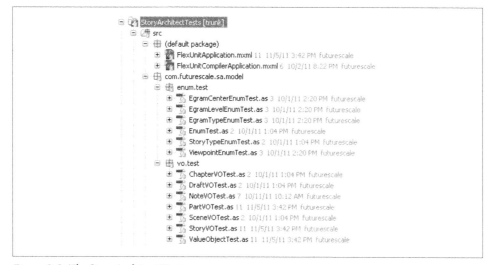

Figure 8-3. The StoryArchitect Tests

CHAPTER 9

Advanced View Topics

Much of your application's user interface may already be created by the time the PureMVC apparatus is initialized, and is therefore ready for mediation at startup. But there many situations that do not fit this easy approach. We will look at the major categories of problematic View Component life cycles in this chapter.

Managing Pop Ups

So far in the book, we have only covered mediation and interaction with View Components that are in the display list by way of the main application declaring a few top-level components, which in turn declare other components, and so forth. In the case of `StoryArchitect`, the application and its two top-level components are mediated easily in the `PrepareViewCommand` and receive `Event`s from all the subcomponents within.

However, the application also makes use of some pop ups, which require an inherently different mediation strategy. They are transient objects that are displayed and removed randomly throughout runtime. In Flex, the `PopUpManager` Singleton is used to manage the display, centering, and removal of pop ups. If you want to center the pop up over the application, you have to pass in a reference to the application itself, which traditionally was accessed from another Flex Singleton, `Application.application`. However that has been deprecated in favor of `FlexGlobals.topLevelApplication`. So if you have been working on a really large application where pop ups are created frequently throughout, you may see lots of warnings in your IDE's Problems View telling you about this deprecation, burying other (possibly more important) warnings until you become blind to them all, and gently reminding you that Flex is a moving target. In one client's application, I saw upward of 100 such warnings. That means laborious revisiting of all that code over a deprecated framework method.

Past Approaches

The PureMVC community has wrestled with the best way to manage pop ups for quite sometime. The basic approaches have been:

- *In any* Command *that needs one, create a pop up, set* Event *listeners on it, open and center it with the* PopUpManager, *and close it from inside the pop up or* Event *handler in the* Command.

  Singletons do have a reputation for being evil, and as the flood of warnings about deprecation I mentioned before illustrate, they can be pretty bad. Since we can reach them from anywhere, we do, and our code ends up littered with unreasonable dependencies, not to mention a lot of duplicated code for interacting with Pop-UpManager, since the five or six lines of code you use is almost always the same, regardless of the pop up.

- *Have a* PopupMediator *that handles all pop ups, creating the pop ups for you in response to a note. Results go out from the* PopupMediator *in a note that triggers another* Command *or* Mediator.

  This gets all the PopUpManager interaction into a single actor, which is nice, but it also puts us back to the "separate invoker and responder" paradigm we saw with asynchronous Proxy interaction in Chapter 8. We have to break up our use case into multiple steps to cope with the async break of displaying the pop up and waiting for the user to submit some data.

- *Have a* PopupMediator *that handles the* PopUpManager *interaction, but the* Command *creates the pop up, sets listeners for the* Events *the pop up dispatches, and sends your component to the* PopupMediator *in a note.*

  This preserves our ability to put all or most of the logic of a use case in a single Command, but it also couples the Command to the View Component. Now, in the Classic MVC diagram back in Chapter 1, you will notice it does say the Controller tier can update the View tier directly. It would not seem unreasonable to create or manipulate a View Component inside a Command. While the job of the Mediator is to be the single point of contact for any View Component in the application, in this case it seems like a good idea to do the creation and listening in the Command, otherwise the temptation to put a bunch of business logic in the Mediator will win out, which is to be avoided.

  As it turns out, it really *is not* such a good idea to tie your Commands to your concrete View Components, even for seemingly difficult scenarios like handling pop ups. I was recently working on a large project, with a lot of business logic that uses Halo (Flex 3) components for pop ups. Halo Alert.show() is also used quite a bit. All this code is shared between a Flex web app, an AIR desktop app, and now a Flex mobile app. But a Flex mobile project can only use Spark (Flex 4) components. Halo is out of the question. We knew our main UI was going to be totally different, but figured the pop ups and alerts would work. Not the case. So now our shared business logic all has to be refactored to remove dependencies on View Components. This was a good reminder of the importance of insulating the business logic from boundary objects.

A Different Approach

All of the above solutions have worked in the past, but are clearly lacking in one way or another. We need a different approach that is widely recommendable as a best practice.

Remember back to Chapter 8 and the way we allowed a Command to send a formal request to a Proxy for an asynchronous operation and later be notified with the results? If you think about it, that is the exact same problem we have with pop ups. In both cases, the Command is doing some business logic and at some point needs a piece of data that has to be retrieved asynchronously. We want the Command to be notified with the result, so we do not want to have to break our business logic into multiple steps because of the async break.

A Proxy retrieves the data from a service and a pop up retrieves it from the user; that is the only difference. They are examples of *Asynchronous Boundary Interaction*. We can reapply the same pattern we used in Chapter 8 and achieve decoupled interaction with pop ups via a formal request mechanism that encapsulates the request data and ability to notify the caller by basing the request on the PureMVC Observer class.

The Add, Change, and Delete Story Use Cases

StoryArchitect has several pop ups for creating, modifying, or deleting StoryVOs and SeriesVOs, displaying alerts, or requesting confirmation before a destructive activity.

Take, for example, creating a new Story. In that use case you click on the "Add Story" (+) button, as shown in Figure 9-1, on the Chooser component, and the StoryPopup (see Figure 9-2) is displayed to collect the basic information to create a new StoryVO. Unless you cancel or close the dialog, when you submit your information the pop up is closed, the new Story is created, stored on disk, and the index is updated with the new Story. You are then taken to the Editor, where you may immediately begin writing.

Figure 9-1. The Add Story Button

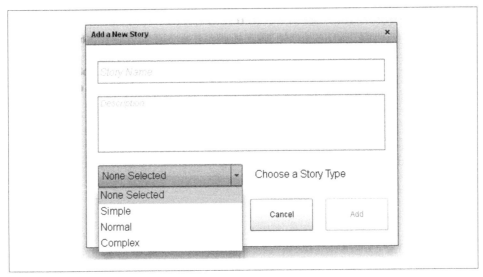

Figure 9-2. The Add Story Pop Up

You can examine the code earlier in the book for the `Chooser` and the `ChooserMedia tor` to see how the `ManageStoryCommand` ends up being executed when you click the "Add Story" (+) button. We will go through how the pop up itself is managed momentarily, but before we start looking at the code, let's consider a couple of other associated use cases that get served by the `ManageStoryCommand` and the same pop up class.

We also need to be able to change the name and description of a Story that exists (but not its Story Type), or delete it. And when we choose to delete a Story, we want to ask for confirmation first, using a reusable confirmation pop up.

When we select a Story in the `Chooser` and click the "Manage" button, shown in Figure 9-3, we trigger this same pop up (see Figure 9-4), but Story type is not editable. Instead we see a description of the Story type that was selected when the Story was created. The window title is different, and there is a "Delete" button that was not visible in the Add Story use case.

The Delete Story confirmation, shown in Figure 9-5, represents yet another async break in the same use case that could otherwise leave you with yet another `Command` if you are breaking things up into a series of `Commands` and `Notifications`. But with this new approach, we are able to handle Add, Change, and Delete/Confirm use cases all with a single command that is not coupled of any of the individual pop ups itself.

Figure 9-3. The Manage Story Button

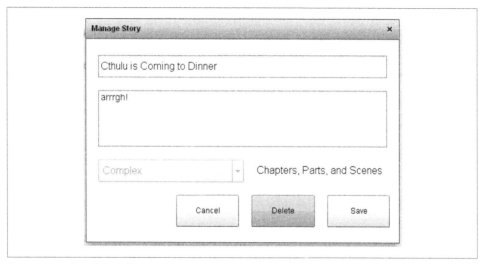

Figure 9-4. The Manage Story Pop Up

Figure 9-5. The Delete Story Confirmation Pop Up

Since communication with pop ups can be more complex than the binary Result/Fault paradigm when communicating this way with the Model tier, a slightly different implementation was built for pop ups. In addition to the formal request class, we will also have a custom `PopupActionEvent` class that comes back to the caller in the async `Notification` rather than the original request carrying the result. This allows a pop up to dispatch a number of different `PopupActionEvent` types and to flag whether the pop up should be closed.

All the messy pop up handling will be placed in an `AbstractPopupMediator`, where the pop up will be interrogated when it is created and asked for a list of `PopupActionEvent` types it might dispatch. This allows the `AbstractPopupMediator` to know what event listeners to set, so that it does not have to be done by its subclasses or the calling `Command`.

Each pop up will have an associated `AbstractPopupMediator` subclass, and all it will need to do is be interested in a single `Notification` for invoking its pop up and override a factory method returning a new instance of its pop up. This allows us, if need be, to register a different version of the `Mediator` for a pop up if, say, we have a Halo version for our desktop and web apps, but a Spark version for our mobile app.

We will now review the code class by class, but first a brief overview of the moving parts:

The Pop Up Request
 Based on `Observer`, combines the ability to request and customize a pop up with asynchronous notification when the pop up dispatches `PopupActionEvent`s

The Pop Up Action Event
 A special event for pop ups to communicate back to their callers

The Pop Up Interface
 Interface for pop ups, requires methods `setData()` and `getEvents()`

The Confirmation Pop Up
 Implements `IPopup`; has adjustable size, prompt, title; sends `PopupActionEvent.OK` and `CANCEL`

The Story Pop Up
 Implements `IPopup`; has adjustable title; sends `PopupActionEvent.ADD`, `SAVE`, `DELETE`, and `CANCEL`

The Abstract Pop Up Mediator
 Base class that encapsulates all direct pop up handling including interrogating the pop up for its `PopupActionEvent`s, listening for them, opening, closing, centering, and notifying the requester

The Story Pop Up Mediator
 Subclass of `AbstractPopupMediator`, creates `StoryPopup`

The Confirmation Pop Up Mediator
 Subclass of `AbstractPopupMediator`, creates `ConfirmationPopup`

A SimpleCommand that manages Add, Change, and Delete logic and Proxy interaction for StoryVOs, including invoking and consuming PopupActionEvents from the Story Popup and ConfirmationPopup

The Pop Up Request

Class

PopupRequest.as

Code

```
package com.futurescale.sa.view.popup.request
{
    import flash.display.DisplayObject;

    import mx.core.FlexGlobals;
    import mx.managers.PopUpManagerChildList;

    import org.puremvc.as3.patterns.observer.Observer;

    /**
     * PopupRequest carries all the information necessary
     * to request a popup be created by its mediator.
     */
    public class PopupRequest extends Observer
    {
        // Prefix for all request notification names
        private static const NAME:String = "PopupRequest/";

        // Add new request notification names here...
        public static const ALERT_POPUP:String        = NAME + "AlertPopup";
        public static const CONFIRMATION_POPUP:String = NAME + "ConfirmationPopup";
        public static const SERIES_POPUP:String       = NAME + "SeriesPopup";
        public static const STORY_POPUP:String        = NAME + "StoryPopup";
        public static const CHARACTER_POPUP:String    = NAME + "CharacterPopup";
        public static const SETTING_POPUP:String      = NAME + "SettingPopup";

        /**
         * Constructor.
         * Example: new PopupRequest( handlePopupNotification, this );
         */
        public function PopupRequest( callback:Function=null,
                                      caller:Object=null )
        {
            super( callback, caller );
            hasCallback = ( callback != null && caller != null );
        }

        // Request has a callback. (Set by constructor)
        public var hasCallback:Boolean = false;
```

```
                // Parent in the display list to open the popup over.
                public var parent:DisplayObject =
                    FlexGlobals.topLevelApplication as DisplayObject;

                // Child list to place the popup in
                public var childList:String = PopUpManagerChildList.PARENT;

                // Should the popup be centered?
                public var center:Boolean = true;

                // Should the popup be modal?
                public var modal:Boolean = true;

                // Optional data for the popup to use,
                //such as a title or width and height
                public var data:Object = {};

                // Convenience method for creating a new Alert Request
                public static function getAlertRequest( message:String,
                                                        windowTitle:String="Alert",
                                                        callback:Function=null,
                                                        caller:Object = null):PopupRequest {
                    var request:PopupRequest = new PopupRequest( callback, caller );
                    request.childList = PopUpManagerChildList.POPUP;
                    request.data.windowTitle = windowTitle;
                    request.data.message = message;
                    return request;
                }
            }
        }
```

The Pop Up Action Event

Class

PopupActionEvent.as

Code

```
    package com.futurescale.sa.view.popup.event
    {
        import flash.events.Event;

        public class PopupActionEvent extends Event
        {
            // Prefix for all popup action event types
            private static const NAME:String = "PopupEvent/";

            // Add new event names here...
            public static const CANCEL:String  = NAME + "cancel";
            public static const OK:String       = NAME + "ok";
            public static const ADD:String      = NAME + "add";
            public static const SAVE:String     = NAME + "save";
```

```
            public static const DELETE:String  = NAME + "delete";

            /**
             * Constructor.
             *
             * Dispatched from a popup, captured by PopupMediatorBase and sent
             * back to the original caller for interpretation.
             */
            public function PopupActionEvent( type:String,
                                              data:Object = null,
                                              closePopup:Boolean=true ) {
                super( type );
                this.data       = data;
                this.closePopup = closePopup;
            }

            public var data:Object;          // optional data
            public var closePopup:Boolean;    // close the popup?

        }
    }
```

The Pop Up Interface

Class

IPopup.as

Code

```
    package com.futurescale.sa.view.popup.component
    {
        import mx.core.IFlexDisplayObject;

        /**
         * Interface for popups
         */
        public interface IPopup extends IFlexDisplayObject
        {
            function setData( data:Object ):void;
            function getEvents():Array;
        }
    }
```

The Confirmation Pop Up

Class

ConfirmationPopup.mxml

Code

```xml
<?xml version="1.0" encoding="utf-8"?>
<!-- CONFIRMATION POPUP -->
<s:TitleWindow xmlns:fx="http://ns.adobe.com/mxml/2009"
               xmlns:s="library://ns.adobe.com/flex/spark"
               title="{windowTitle}" width="200" height="150" close="onCancel()"
               implements="com.futurescale.sa.view.popup.component.IPopup">

    <fx:Script>
        <![CDATA[
            import com.futurescale.sa.view.popup.event.PopupActionEvent;

            // Required by IPopup interface
            public function setData( data:Object ):void
            {
                if ( data.windowTitle ) windowTitle = data.windowTitle;
                if ( data.promptText )  promptText  = data.promptText;
                if ( data.width )       width       = data.width;
                if ( data.height )      height      = data.height;
            }

            // Required by IPopup interface
            public function getEvents( ):Array
            {
                return [ PopupActionEvent.OK, PopupActionEvent.CANCEL ]
            }

            private function onOk():void
            {
                dispatchEvent( new PopupActionEvent( PopupActionEvent.OK ) )
            }

            private function onCancel():void
            {
                dispatchEvent( new PopupActionEvent( PopupActionEvent.CANCEL ) )
            }

            [Bindable] private var windowTitle:String = "Confirmation";
            [Bindable] private var promptText:String  = "Are you sure?";

        ]]>
    </fx:Script>

    <!-- LAYOUT -->
    <s:VGroup width="100%" height="100%" gap="20"
              horizontalAlign="center" verticalAlign="middle">

        <!-- MESSAGE -->
        <s:Label text="{promptText}"/>

        <!-- BUTTONS -->
        <s:HGroup gap="20">
            <s:Button label="Cancel" click="onCancel()"/>
            <s:Button label="OK"     click="onOk()"/>
        </s:HGroup>
```

```
            </s:VGroup>

    </s:TitleWindow>
```

The Story Pop Up

Class

StoryPopup.mxml

Code

```
<?xml version="1.0" encoding="utf-8"?>
<!-- STORY POPUP -->
<s:TitleWindow implements="com.futurescale.sa.view.popup.component.IPopup"
               xmlns:fx="http://ns.adobe.com/mxml/2009"
               xmlns:s="library://ns.adobe.com/flex/spark"
               xmlns:mx="library://ns.adobe.com/flex/mx"
               close="onCancel()" title="{windowTitle}"
               width="500" height="350">

    <fx:Script>
        <![CDATA[
            import com.futurescale.sa.model.enum.StoryTypeEnum;
            import com.futurescale.sa.model.vo.StoryVO;
            import com.futurescale.sa.view.popup.event.PopupActionEvent;

            import mx.controls.Text;

            // Required by IPopup interface
            public function setData( data:Object ):void
            {
                if ( data.story ) {
                    editing = true;
                    windowTitle = "Manage Story";
                    story = data.story as StoryVO;
                }
            }

            // Required by IPopup interface
            public function getEvents( ):Array
            {
                return [ PopupActionEvent.ADD,
                         PopupActionEvent.SAVE,
                         PopupActionEvent.DELETE,
                         PopupActionEvent.CANCEL ]
            }

            private function reapFields( vo:StoryVO ):void
            {
                vo.name = txtStoryName.text;
                vo.description = txtStoryDesc.text;
                vo.type = cmbStoryType.selectedItem;
```

```
        }

        private function onAdd():void
        {
            var newStory:StoryVO = new StoryVO();
            reapFields( newStory );
            dispatchEvent(
              new PopupActionEvent( PopupActionEvent.ADD, newStory ) );
        }

        private function onSave():void
        {
            reapFields( story );
            dispatchEvent(
              new PopupActionEvent( PopupActionEvent.SAVE, story ) );
        }

        private function onDelete():void
        {
            dispatchEvent(
              new PopupActionEvent( PopupActionEvent.DELETE, story ) );
        }

        private function onCancel():void
        {
            dispatchEvent(
              new PopupActionEvent( PopupActionEvent.CANCEL ) );
        }

        [Bindable] private var windowTitle:String = "Add a New Story";
        [Bindable] private var editing:Boolean=false;
        [Bindable] private var story:StoryVO;


</fx:Script>

<!-- LAYOUT -->
<s:layout>
    <s:VerticalLayout gap="20" horizontalAlign="center" verticalAlign="middle"/>
</s:layout>

<!-- STORY NAME -->
<s:TextInput id="txtStoryName" width="460" height="35" fontSize="16"
             prompt="Story Name" text="{story.name}"/>

<!-- STORY DESCRIPTION -->
<s:TextArea id="txtStoryDesc" width="460" height="88" fontSize="14"
            prompt="Description" text="{story.description}"/>

<!-- STORY TYPE-->
<s:HGroup gap="20" horizontalAlign="center"
          verticalAlign="middle">

    <!-- COMBO -->
    <s:DropDownList id="cmbStoryType" width="232" height="35"
```

```
                        selectedItem="{(editing)?story.type:StoryTypeEnum.NONE}"
                        dataProvider="{StoryTypeEnum.comboList}" fontSize="16"
                        labelField="name" enabled="{!(editing)}"/>

        <!-- LABEL -->
        <s:Label id="lblStoryType" width="208" height="35" fontSize="16"
                text="{StoryTypeEnum(cmbStoryType.selectedItem).description}"
                verticalAlign="middle"/>
    </s:HGroup>

    <!-- BUTTONS -->
    <s:HGroup gap="20" width="100%" horizontalAlign="right" paddingRight="15">

        <!-- CANCEL -->
        <s:Button width="100" height="50" label="Cancel" click="onCancel()"/>

        <!-- ADD -->
        <s:Button width="100" height="50" label="Add" click="onAdd()"
                visible="{!(editing)}" includeInLayout="{!(editing)}"
                enabled="{cmbStoryType.selectedItem != StoryTypeEnum.NONE
                &amp;&amp; txtStoryName.text != ''}"/>

        <!-- DELETE -->
        <s:Button width="100" height="50" label="Delete" click="onDelete()"
                visible="{editing &amp;&amp; !story.isEpisode}"
                includeInLayout="{editing}"/>

        <!-- SAVE -->
        <s:Button width="100" height="50" label="Save" click="onSave()"
                visible="{editing}" includeInLayout="{editing}"
                enabled="{cmbStoryType.selectedItem != StoryTypeEnum.NONE
                        &amp;&amp; txtStoryName.text != ''}"/>
    </s:HGroup>

</s:TitleWindow>
```

The Abstract Pop Up Mediator

Class

AbstractPopupMediator.as

Code

```
package com.futurescale.sa.view.popup.mediator
{
    import com.futurescale.sa.view.popup.component.IPopup;
    import com.futurescale.sa.view.popup.event.PopupActionEvent;
    import com.futurescale.sa.view.popup.request.PopupRequest;

    import mx.managers.PopUpManager;

    import org.puremvc.as3.interfaces.INotification;
    import org.puremvc.as3.patterns.mediator.Mediator;
```

```
import org.puremvc.as3.patterns.observer.Notification;

public class AbstractPopupMediator extends Mediator
{
    public function AbstractPopupMediator( name:String )
    {
        super( name );
    }

    /**
     * Override in subclass.
     * Just create and the concrete popup.
     */
    protected function popupFactory():IPopup
    {
        return null;
    }

    /**
     * Called from the handleNotification method when a request notification
     * is received. Creates the popup with popupFactory(), gives it the data
     * from the request, calls setEventInterests to add the listeners, then
     * pops up the popup and optionally centers it.
     */
    protected function openPopup( ) : void
    {
        var popup:IPopup = popupFactory();
        if (popup) {
            popup.setData( request.data );
            setEventInterests( popup );
            PopUpManager.addPopUp( popup,
                                   request.parent,
                                   request.modal,
                                   request.childList );
            if ( request.center ) PopUpManager.centerPopUp( popup );
        }
    }

    /**
     * Called from openPopup when the request is set, before
     * popping up the popup. Interrogates the popup for the
     * events it will dispatch and sets listeners for each.
     */
    protected function setEventInterests( popup:IPopup ):void
    {
        for each ( var interest:String in popup.getEvents() )
        {
            popup.addEventListener( interest,
                                    handlePopupAction,
                                    false, 0, true );
        }
    }

    /**
     * Subclasses will register a single notification interest,
```

```
 * which will be handled here in the same way for all subclasses.
 */
override public function handleNotification( note:INotification ):void
{
    request = note.getBody() as PopupRequest;
    openPopup( );
}

/**
 * Subclasses will set a single notification interest,
 * which will be handled here in the same way for all subclasses.
 * The popup will be closed if specified by the event, and then the
 * caller will be notified with the PopupEvent and the
 */
protected function handlePopupAction( event:PopupActionEvent ):void
{
    var popup:IPopup = event.target as IPopup;
    if ( event.closePopup ) removePopup( popup );
    var note:Notification = new Notification( event.type, event );
    if (request.hasCallback) request.notifyObserver( note );
    request = null;
}

/**
 * Called if the PopupActionEvent's closePopup property is true
 */
protected function removePopup( popup:IPopup ):void
{
    PopUpManager.removePopUp( popup );
}

// The request is stored temporarily while the popup is alive
// so that the mediator can notify the caller.
protected var request:PopupRequest;

    }
}
```

Story Pop Up Mediator

Class

StoryPopupMediator.as

Code

```
package com.futurescale.sa.view.popup.mediator
{
    import com.futurescale.sa.view.popup.component.IPopup;
    import com.futurescale.sa.view.popup.component.StoryPopup;
    import com.futurescale.sa.view.popup.request.PopupRequest;

    public class StoryPopupMediator extends AbstractPopupMediator
    {
```

```
        public static const NAME:String = "StoryPopupMediator";

        public function StoryPopupMediator()
        {
            super( NAME );
        }

        override public function listNotificationInterests():Array
        {
            return [ PopupRequest.STORY_POPUP ];
        }

        override protected function popupFactory():IPopup
        {
            return new StoryPopup();
        }
    }
}
```

The Confirmation Pop Up Mediator

Class

ConfirmationPopupMediator.as

Code

```
package com.futurescale.sa.view.popup.mediator
{
    import com.futurescale.sa.view.popup.component.ConfirmationPopup;
    import com.futurescale.sa.view.popup.component.IPopup;
    import com.futurescale.sa.view.popup.request.PopupRequest;

    public class ConfirmationPopupMediator extends AbstractPopupMediator
    {
        public static const NAME:String = "ConfirmationPopupMediator";

        public function ConfirmationPopupMediator()
        {
            super( NAME );
        }

        override public function listNotificationInterests():Array
        {
            return [ PopupRequest.CONFIRMATION_POPUP ];
        }

        override protected function popupFactory():IPopup
        {
            return new ConfirmationPopup();
        }

    }
}
```

The Manage Story Command

Class

ManageStoryCommand.as

Code

```
package com.futurescale.sa.controller.command.story
{
    import com.futurescale.sa.model.proxy.StoryProxy;
    import com.futurescale.sa.model.vo.StoryVO;
    import com.futurescale.sa.view.popup.event.PopupActionEvent;
    import com.futurescale.sa.view.popup.request.PopupRequest;

    import org.puremvc.as3.interfaces.INotification;
    import org.puremvc.as3.patterns.command.SimpleCommand;

    /**
     * Add, change or delete a Story.
     *
     * Popup the StoryPopup, and if the Story is
     * added or saved, persist it. If deleted, confirm,
     * then delete it.
     */
    public class ManageStoryCommand extends SimpleCommand
    {
        private var story:StoryVO;
        private var storyProxy:StoryProxy;

        override public function execute( note:INotification ):void
        {
            var storyStub:StoryVO = StoryVO( note.getBody() ); // Null if adding
            storyProxy = StoryProxy( facade.retrieveProxy( StoryProxy.NAME ) );
            if ( storyStub    ) story = storyProxy.loadStory( storyStub );

            // Request the popup
            var request:PopupRequest =
                new PopupRequest( handleEditPopupNote, this );
            request.data.story = story;
            sendNotification( PopupRequest.STORY_POPUP, request );
        }

        /**
         * Handle the popup actions.
         */
        private function handleEditPopupNote( actionNote:INotification ):void
        {
            var event:PopupActionEvent = PopupActionEvent( actionNote.getBody() );
            story = StoryVO( event.data );
            switch ( actionNote.getName() )
            {
                case PopupActionEvent.ADD:
                    storyProxy.addStory( story );
```

```
                    break;

            case PopupActionEvent.SAVE:
                storyProxy.saveStory( story );
                break;

            case PopupActionEvent.DELETE:
                var confirm:PopupRequest =
                    new PopupRequest( handleConfirmPopupNote, this );
                confirm.data.promptText = "Delete Story?";
                sendNotification( PopupRequest.CONFIRMATION_POPUP, confirm );
                break;

            case PopupActionEvent.CANCEL:
                break;
        }
    }

    /**
     * Handle the ConfirmationPopup actions.
     */
    private function handleConfirmPopupNote( actionNote:INotification ):void
    {
        var event:PopupActionEvent = PopupActionEvent( actionNote.getBody() );
        switch ( actionNote.getName() )
        {
            case PopupActionEvent.OK:
                storyProxy.deleteStory(story);
                break;

            case PopupActionEvent.CANCEL:
                break;
        }
    }
}
}
```

Deferred Instantiation

A less complicated but similar problem to pop ups is the case where declared components will sometimes have their instantiation deferred by Flex.

For example, imagine you have an accounting application with separate sections. You have complex View Components for Accounts Receivable, Accounts Payable, General Ledger, etc. In the MXML for your main application, you have declared a component called AppSections, which is based on the Flex Halo TabNavigator class. AppSections has declared as its children one of each of these custom accounting section View Components. You want to mediate the AppSections component so that other actors can send it Notifications to change the section displayed progammatically if need be. And you also want to mediate each of its children, which represent complex subsystems and likely warrant their own Mediators.

The problem with this is that by default, the `TabNavigator` (and the `Accordion` and `ViewStack` components) will only create the first child that is to be displayed at startup. It will *defer instantiation* of the other children until you navigate to them. This is done to optimize startup time. In the case of a complex system like our hypothetical accounting application, those hidden views could definitely take some time to create, making the app seem sluggish to launch. And we all know how important first impressions can be. So the app comes up quickly, and there is a small lag the first time you visit one of the complex children as it is created, but after that, it remains in the display list and switching to it is fast. There is a `creationPolicy` attribute that can be set to indicate you wish all the subcomponents to be built instead of just the first one. And if the children are simple, you might just want to set that property to `"all"` and mediate the children in the simple way we have done in the `PrepareViewCommand`. But if you need deferred instantiation to speed up your initial render time, you need a different mediation strategy.

In that situation, we could not mediate all the children of that `TabNavigator` at startup, since they would not exist. We could mediate the first one, but then we would have to listen for the others to be created and mediate them later.

The Application Sections TabNavigator

Class

AppSections.mxml

Code

```
<?xml version="1.0" encoding="utf-8"?>
<!-- APPLICATION SECTIONS -->
<mx:TabNavigator  xmlns:mx="http://www.adobe.com/2006/mxml"
                  xmlns:view="com.mycompany.myapp.view.components.*"
                  selectedIndex="{currentSection}">
    <mx:Script>
        <![CDATA[

            import com.mycompany.myapp.view.event.AppEvent;

            public static const AR_SECTION:Number = 0;
            public static const AP_SECTION:Number = 1;
            public static const GL_SECTION:Number = 2;

            [Bindable] public var currentSection:Number = AR_SECTION;

            private function sendEvent( type:String ):void
            {
                dispatchEvent( new AppEvent( type ) );
            }

        ]]>
    </mx:Script>
```

```
<!-- ACCOUNTS RECEIVABLE SECTION -->
<view:AcctRcv   id="acctRcv"/><!-- will be created automatically -->

<!-- ACCOUNTS PAYABLE SECTION -->
<view:AcctPay   id="acctPay"
                creationComplete="sendEvent( AppEvent.ACCT_PAY_CREATED )"/>

 <!-- GENERAL LEDGER SECTION -->
<view:GenLedger id="genLedger"
                creationComplete="sendEvent( AppEvent.GEN_LEDGER_CREATED )"/>

</mx:TabNavigator>
```

The Application Sections Mediator

Class

AppSectionsMediator.as

Code

```
package com.mycompany.myapp.view.mediator
{
    import com.mycompany.myapp.view.component.AppSections;
    import com.mycompany.myapp.view.event.AppEvent;

    import org.puremvc.as3.interfaces.INotification;
    import org.puremvc.as3.patterns.mediator.Mediator;

    public class AppSectionsMediator extends Mediator
    {
        public static const NAME:String = 'AppSectionsMediator';

        public function AppSectionsMediator( viewComponent:AppSections )
        {
            super( NAME, viewComponent );
        }

        protected function get appSections():AppSections
        {
            return viewComponent as AppSections;
        }

        override public function onRegister():void
        {
            // Mediate the first child which already exists by default
            facade.registerMediator( new AcctRcvMediator( appSections.acctRcv ) );

            // Listen for other children to be created
            appSections.addEventListener( AppEvent.ACCT_PAY_CREATED,
                                          onAPCreated  );
            appSections.addEventListener( AppEvent.GEN_LEDGER_CREATED,
                                          onGLCreated );
```

```
        }

        override public function listNotificationInterests():Array
        {
            return [ AppConstants.SHOW_ACCT_RCV,
                    AppConstants.SHOW_ACCT_PAY,
                    AppConstants.SHOW_GEN_LEDGER ];
        }

        override public function handleNotification( note:INotification ):void
        {
            // handle inbound requests to show different components
            switch ( note.getName() )
            {
                case AppConstants.SHOW_ACCT_RCV:
                    appSections.currentSection = AppSections.AR_SECTION;
                    break;

                case AppConstants.SHOW_ACCT_PAY:
                    appSections.currentSection = AppSections.AP_SECTION;
                    break;

                case AppConstants.SHOW_GEN_LEDGER:
                    appSections.currentSection = AppSections.GL_SECTION;
                    break;
            }
        }

        // Mediate AcctPay component when it is created
        protected function onAPCreated( event:AppEvent ):void
        {
            var apm:AcctRcvMediator =
                new AcctPayMediator( appSections.acctPay );
            facade.registerMediator( apm );
        }

        // Mediate GenLedger component when it is created
        protected function onGLCreated( event:Event ):void
        {
            var glm:GenLedgerMediator =
                new GenLedgerMediator( appSections.genLedger );
            facade.registerMediator( glm );
        }
    }
}
```

Dynamically Adding View Components

This is similar to Deferred Instantiation, only in this case, Flex is not in charge of instantiating the component and adding it to the display list, we are. We may or may not want to mediate that component, but we want it to be added on demand as our business logic dictates.

Consider a simple game where you have defined a GameBoard component based on the Flex Spark Group class, which is an absolute positioning container (i.e. child layout according to x and y properties). You have a couple of View Components you want to add to the GameBoard: a Player component and a Fixture component. Your Player may have a number of attributes like health, tools, etc. and fixtures might be bags of money, trees, or perhaps bombs that yield points, prevent movement, or kill you when you run into them. These configurations are persistable so that you can save a game.

Consequently you have created Value Objects called PlayerConfigVO and FixtureCon figVO to initialize a new Player or Fixture component before it is placed on the Game Board. These VOs will be retrieved or programmatically created and sent to the Game BoardMediator by Notification. For this example, we will assume that we only add the Player if it does not already exist, and when we do, it is to be mediated and placed in the center of the GameBoard. Fixtures are to simply be added to a random location on the GameBoard with no mediation (perhaps their events will be handled by the Game board itself or the GameBoardMediator eventually).

The implementation of the View Components and the configuration VOs are not of consequence to us in this example. We are only interested in how the GameBoard and GameBoardMediator work to allow us to have components added dynamically to the display list, with or without mediation.

The Game Board

Class

GameBoard.mxml

Code

```
<?xml version="1.0" encoding="utf-8"?>
<s:Group xmlns:fx="http://ns.adobe.com/mxml/2009"
        xmlns:s="library://ns.adobe.com/flex/spark"
        xmlns:mx="library://ns.adobe.com/flex/mx">

    <fx:Script>
        <![CDATA[

            // Add a Player component to the center of the gameboard
            public function addPlayerToBoard( player:Player ):void
            {
                player.x = this.width/2;
                player.y = this.height/2;
                addElement( player );
            }

            // Add a Fixture component to a random location on the gameboard
            public function addFixtureToBoard( fixture:Fixture ):void
            {
```

```
                    fixture.x = Math.random() * this.width;
                    fixture.y = Math.random() * this.height;
                    addElement( fixture );
                }

        </fx:Script>

    </s:Group>
```

The Game Board Mediator

Class

GameBoardMediator.as

Code

```
package com.me.myapp.view.mediator
{
    import com.mycompany.myapp.view.component.GameBoard;
    import com.mycompany.myapp.view.component.Player;
    import com.mycompany.myapp.view.component.Fixture;
    import com.mycompany.myapp.model.vo.PlayerConfigVO;
    import com.mycompany.myapp.model.vo.FixtureConfigVO;
    import com.mycompany.myapp.view.event.AppEvent;

    import org.puremvc.as3.interfaces.INotification;
    import org.puremvc.as3.patterns.mediator.Mediator;

    public class GameBoardMediator extends Mediator
    {
        public static const NAME:String = 'GameBoardMediator';

        public function GameBoardMediator( viewComponent:GameBoard )
        {
            super( NAME, viewComponent );
        }

        protected function get gameBoard():GameBoard
        {
            return viewComponent as GameBoard;
        }

        override public function listNotificationInterests():Array
        {
            return [ AppConstants.ADD_PLAYER,
                     AppConstants.ADD_FIXTURE ];
        }

        override public function handleNotification( note:INotification ):void
        {
            // handle inbound requests to add different components
            switch (note.getName())
            {
```

```
                    case AppConstants.ADD_PLAYER:
                        var pConfig:PlayerConfigVO = PlayerConfigVO( note.getBody() );
                        addPlayer( pConfig );
                        break;

                    case AppConstants.ADD_FIXTURE:
                        var fConfig:FixtureConfigVO = FixtureConfigVO( note.getBody() );
                        addFixture( fConfig );
                        break;
                }
            }

            // Add a mediated Player component to the Gameboard
            protected function addPlayer( playerConfig:PlayerConfigVO ):void
            {
                // Only add Player if it does not already exist
                if ( ! facade.hasMediator( PlayerMediator.NAME ) ) {
                    var player:Player = new Player( playerConfig );
                    var pm:PlayerMediator = new PlayerMediator( player );
                    facade.registerMediator( pm );
                    gameBoard.addPlayerToBoard( player );
                }
            }

            // Add an unmediated Fixture component to the Gameboard
            protected function addFixture( fixtureConfig:FixtureConfigVO ):void
            {
                var fixture:Fixture = new Fixture( fixtureConfig );
                gameBoard.addFixtureToBoard( fixture );
            }
        }
    }
```

Flex Mobile Mediation Strategy

Flex Mobile presents a radically different paradigm for the way the view hierarchy is constructed (and destroyed), so the normal approaches to mediation that we use on the desktop and web no longer fit. But fear not, PureMVC is infinitely adaptable, we just need a different strategy that takes into account the strange new View Component life cycle. In this section, I will contrast the normal Flex component life cycle and mediation strategy against that of Flex Mobile. Then I will describe a very common application premise with four Views, and finally show you all the important bits of the hypothetical application in code.

Typical Flex or AIR Mediation

Normally, in a Flex (browser) or AIR (desktop) app, you would have an Application or WindowedApplication declaring an initial hierarchy, which you mediate once created.

Whenever you want to add a View Component to an Application or WindowedApplication, you call addChild() on the app, passing in the View Component instance to be added. That call is best made by the app itself inside a `public` method, which can be called by a `Mediator`.

We handle the app's `applicationComplete` event by passing a reference to the app into an `ApplicationFacade.startup()` method. There, it is sent off in a `Notification` to a `StartupCommand` that mediates the application and any other top-level components on the display list that need mediation. `Mediators` can further mediate the top-level children of their View Components.

When View Components have their creation deferred (e.g. children of a `ViewStack` not being created until navigated to), their `Mediators` should listen for `Event.ADDED` and mediate the target of the `Event` in the event handler (e.g. a `Mediator` for a `ViewStack` component would dynamically mediate the children of the `ViewStack` as they are created).

At any time, you might want to dynamically create a View Component and add it to the display list with mediation. You just create it, register a `Mediator` for it, and send it off in a note that is responded to by an `ApplicationMediator`, who takes the component from the note and passes it to the application where it is added as a child. If the new View Component is to be added farther down the display list, then some other `Media tor` might handle the note instead of the `ApplicationMediator`, but the premise is the same.

`Mediators` are usually long-lived in a web or desktop app, remaining present throughout runtime since View Components are rarely destroyed. An exception is when Flex View States are employed, since View Components are created and destroyed when states change. From a life cycle perspective, Flex View States are remarkably similar to Flex Mobile `Views`.

Flex Mobile Mediation

The Spark `ViewNavigator` component is essentially a stack that `Views` are pushed onto or popped off of. A `ViewNavigatorApplication` is a top-level application optimized for mobile devices that uses a `ViewNavigator` as the primary container. You add your app's functionality to a series of `Views` that the user navigates between.

A major departure from `Application` or `WindowedApplication` is that you do not create a `View` before pushing it onto the `ViewNavigator`, you actually pass in the class name and the `ViewNavigator` creates it for you. That means you cannot use the approach of creating a component, mediating it, and then sending it off in a `Notification` to be added to the display list by some `Mediator`.

A `ViewNavigatorApplication` can have a `firstView` specified, which it will create automatically; you may mediate it at startup. All other `Views` are created only when pushed or popped back to. All `Views` are destroyed when they are popped off the `ViewNaviga tor`, or when another `View` is popped onto the `ViewNavigator` on top of them, except...

There is a destructionPolicy="never" attribute that you can declare on a View. However, this only means that the View will stay in memory when something is pushed on top of it in the ViewNavigator. When you pop a View with destructionPolicy="never", it is actually destroyed. So, "never" *actually* means "never destroy this View when something is pushed on top of it."

When you push a View onto the ViewNavigator, you can also supply an arbitrary Object as data to be passed to the View when it is created. It will appear in the data property of the View. Also, ViewNavigator has a property called context, which is an arbitrary Object. It is read-only and is passed as an optional argument to ViewNavigator.pushView() when pushing a new View. In the example, we will use it as a value that tells us what View we are on without having to refer to the active View and check its type.

In Flex Mobile, you need to dynamically mediate your Views, which are created and destroyed all the time. Your Mediators should only live as long as the components they mediate. Thus, your ApplicationMediator will be the only long-lived Mediator of the app, while the rest will be transient.

You may also need to manage when you push a View onto the ViewNavigator, and when you pop back to one. You could always just push a new View, each time you want to return to a particular screen, but sometimes you want a View to stay in memory until you come back to it. This means you also need to consider which Views are important to set destructionPolicy="never" on.

A Flex Mobile Example

Let's consider an application where you can log in, view a list of your Things, maintain your Things, or see a screen with information like what version of the app you are running, how much free space your mobile device has, and how much space your Things are currently taking up.

You have a LoginView as your app's firstView. Once logged in, you move to a List View, where you can see a list of your Things. From there, you can either log out (taking you back to the LoginView), see information about the app in an InfoView, or edit one of your Things in the FormView.

The ListView might take a while to render, especially once you have a lot of Things. You will want to set destructionPolicy="never" on it so that it does not get destroyed when you push an InfoView or FormView on top of it. When you pop back to the List View from the InfoView or FormView, the same mediated ListView will be shown. However, when you log out, the ListView will be popped off the ViewNavigator and destroyed, which makes sense because if you log in as someone else you do not want the previous list in memory anyway. Also, to demonstrate the ability to pass data to a View when pushing it, the InfoView will take an InfoVO. We will assume that the other Views get their data from their Mediators in the usual way.

All this begins with the application, which needs to expose some methods for showing the different Views. It will encapsulate all the push/pop logic, so the ApplicationMedia tor does not need to know anything other than what method to call to show a given View. Also, we want to mediate the initial LoginView component, which the app will create, so we need a method for getting a reference to the active View from the application.

Here are the important actors and their roles, in order of appearance in the startup process:

The IMyMobileApp Interface
> An interface showing the methods this application should implement (not required, but a good example of how to implement a contract between a Mediator and its View Component, helping the component encapsulate its implementation, and allowing the component to be swapped for another one that implements the same interface)

The MyMobileApp Application
> Based on ViewNavigatorApplication; creates the initial LoginView instance, starts up PureMVC, and implements the IMyMobileApp interface

The Application Facade
> Based on Facade; implements getInstance() and startup() methods

The Startup Command
> Prepare the Controller, Model, and View—in that order

The Application Mediator
> Listen to the application for Event.ADDED (sending any Views off in a MEDIATE_VIEW note), show interest in notes to change Views (calling the appropriate methods on the app in response), and mediate the app's firstView

The Mediate View Command
> Create and register the appropriate Mediator for the View, removing any registered instance of the Mediator first

The List View
> A typical View, except it needs destructionPolicy="never"

Now some code:

The IMyMobileApp Interface

```
package com.mycompany.myapp.view
{
    import com.mycompany.myapp.model.vo.InfoVO;

    import flash.events.IEventDispatcher;

    import spark.components.View;

    public interface IMyMobileApp extends IEventDispatcher
```

```
    {
        function getActiveView():View;
        function showLoginView():void;
        function showListView():void;
        function showInfoView( infoVO:InfoVO ):void;
        function showFormView():void;
    }
}
```

The MyMobileApp Application

```
<?xml version="1.0" encoding="utf-8"?>
<!-- FLEX MOBILE APPLICATION-->
<s:ViewNavigatorApplication
    firstView="com.mycompany.myapp.view.component.LoginView"
    implements="com.mycompany.myapp.view.IMyMobileApp"
    applicationComplete="facade.startup(this)"
    xmlns:s="library://ns.adobe.com/flex/spark"
    xmlns:fx="http://ns.adobe.com/mxml/2009">

    <fx:Script>
    <![CDATA[
    import com.mycompany.myapp.ApplicationFacade;
    import com.mycompany.myapp.model.vo.InfoVO;
    import com.mycompany.myapp.view.component.InfoView;
    import com.mycompany.myapp.view.component.ListView;
    import com.mycompany.myapp.view.component.LoginView;
    import com.mycompany.myapp.view.component.FormView;

    import spark.components.View;

    // RETRIEVE FACADE
    private var facade:ApplicationFacade = ApplicationFacade.getInstance();

    // READ ONLY CONTEXT
    private function get context():String
    {
        // if there is no context, then we are on the LoginView,
        // set by firstView (we can't set a context for firstView)
        return ( navigator.context ) ? String( navigator.context ) : LOGIN;
    }

    // CONTEXT VALUES
    private static const LOGIN:String = "LoginView";
    private static const LIST:String  = "ListView";
    private static const FORM:String  = "FormView";
    private static const INFO:String  = "InfoView";

    //----------------------------------------------------------
    // Below methods satisfy IMyMobileApp interface
    //----------------------------------------------------------

    // GET THE ACTIVE VIEW
    public function getActiveView():View
    {
```

```
        // Since the LoginView is specified as the 'firstView'
        // we need to mediate it in the traditional way, which means
        // we need to expose the active view
        return navigator.activeView;
    }

    // SHOW THE LOGIN VIEW
    public function showLoginView( ):void
    {
        // Only return to LoginView if we're not already on it
        if ( context != LOGIN ) navigator.popToFirstView();
    }

    // SHOW THE LIST VIEW
    public function showListView( ):void
    {
        // Only act if we're not already on the ListView
        if ( context != LIST )
        {
            // If returning (from Info or Form views), just pop
            // otherwise push a new ListView
            var returning:Boolean = ( context == INFO || context == FORM );
            if ( returning ) {
                navigator.popView();
            } else {
                navigator.pushView( ListView,  null, LIST );
            }
        }
    }

    // SHOW THE FORM VIEW
    public function showFormView(  ):void
    {
        // Only push a FormView if we're not already on it
        if ( context != FORM )
            navigator.pushView( FormView, null, FORM );
    }

    // SHOW THE INFO VIEW (PASSING IN INFO VO)
    public function showInfoView( infoVO:InfoVO ):void
    {
        // Only push an InfoView if we're not already on it
        if ( context != INFO )
            navigator.pushView( InfoView, infoVO, INFO );
    }
</fx:Script>

</s:ViewNavigatorApplication>
```

The Application Facade

```
package com.mycompany.myapp
{
    import com.mycompany.myapp.controller.command.StartupCommand;
    import com.mycompany.myapp.controller.constants.AppConstants;
```

```
    import com.mycompany.myapp.view.IMyMobileApp;

    public class ApplicationFacade
    {

        public static function getInstance() : ApplicationFacade
        {
            if ( instance == null ) {
                instance = new ApplicationFacade();
            }
            return ApplicationFacade( instance );
        }

        public function startup( app:IMyMobileApp ):void
        {
            registerCommand( AppConstants.STARTUP, StartupCommand );
            sendNotification( ViewerConstants.STARTUP, app );
        }
    }
}
```

The Startup Command

```
package com.mycompany.myapp.controller.command
{
    import com.mycompany.myapp.model.proxy.InfoProxy;
    import com.mycompany.myapp.model.proxy.ThingProxy;
    import com.mycompany.myapp.view.IMyMobileApp;
    import com.mycompany.myapp.view.mediator.ApplicationMediator;

    import org.puremvc.as3.interfaces.INotification;
    import org.puremvc.as3.patterns.command.SimpleCommand;

    public class StartupCommand extends SimpleCommand
    {
        override public function execute( note : INotification ) : void
        {
            // Prepare the Controller
            facade.registerCommand( AppConstants.MEDIATE_VIEW, MediateViewCommand );

            // Prepare the Model
            facade.registerProxy( new ThingProxy( ) );
            facade.registerProxy( new InfoProxy( ) );

            // Prepare the View
            var app:IMyMobileApp = IMobileApp( note.getBody() );
            facade.registerMediator( new ApplicationMediator( app ) );
        }
    }
}
```

The Application Mediator

```
package com.mycompany.myapp.view.mediator
{
```

```
import com.mycompany.myapp.controller.constants.AppConstants;
import com.mycompany.myapp.view.IMyMobileApp;
import com.mycompany.myapp.model.vo.InfoVO;

import flash.events.Event;

import org.puremvc.as3.interfaces.INotification;
import org.puremvc.as3.patterns.mediator.Mediator;

import spark.components.View;

public class ApplicationMediator extends Mediator
{
    public static const NAME:String = "ApplicationMediator";

    // CONSTRUCTOR - HANDLE COMPONENT BY ITS INTERFACE
    public function ApplicationMediator( app:IMyMobileApp )
    {
        super( NAME, app );
    }

    // CALLED AT REGISTRATION - LIST NOTIFICATION INTERESTS
    override public function listNotificationInterests():Array
    {
        return [ AppConstants.SHOW_LOGIN,
                 AppConstants.SHOW_LIST,
                 AppConstants.SHOW_FORM,
                 AppConstants.SHOW_INFO,
               ];
    }

    // CALLED AT REGISTRATION - LISTEN FOR EVENTS, MEDIATE FIRST VIEW
    override public function onRegister():void
    {
        // Listen for Views to be created
        app.addEventListener( Event.ADDED, handleAdded );


        // Mediate the firstView
        sendNotification( AppConstants.MEDIATE_VIEW, app.getActiveView() );
    }

    // HANDLE NOTIFICATIONS TO CHANGE VIEWS
    override public function handleNotification( note:INotification ):void
    {
        switch ( note.getName() )
        {
            case AppConstants.SHOW_LOGIN:
                app.showLoginView();
                break;

            case AppConstants.SHOW_LIST:
                app.showListView();
                break;
```

```
                    case AppConstants.SHOW_FORM:
                        app.showFormView();
                        break;

                    case AppConstants.SHOW_INFO:
                        app.showInfoView( InfoVO( note.getBody() ) );
                        break;
                }
            }

            // HANDLE ADDED EVENTS
            private function handleAdded( event:Event ):void
            {
                // Only act on Views
                if ( event.target is View ) {
                    sendNotification( AppConstants.MEDIATE_VIEW, event.target );
                }
            }

            // CAST THE VIEW COMPONENT TO THE PROPER TYPE
            private function get app():IMyMobileApp
            {
                return viewComponent as IMyMobileApp;
            }
        }
    }
```

The Mediate View Command

```
package com.mycompany.myapp.controller.command
{
    import com.mycompany.myapp.view.component.InfoView;
    import com.mycompany.myapp.view.component.ListView;
    import com.mycompany.myapp.view.component.LoginView;
    import com.mycompany.myapp.view.component.FormView;
    import com.mycompany.myapp.view.mediator.InfoViewMediator;
    import com.mycompany.myapp.view.mediator.ListViewMediator;
    import com.mycompany.myapp.view.mediator.LoginViewMediator;
    import com.mycompany.myapp.view.mediator.FormViewMediator;

    import org.puremvc.as3.interfaces.INotification;
    import org.puremvc.as3.interfaces.IMediator;
    import org.puremvc.as3.patterns.command.SimpleCommand;

    import spark.components.View;

    public class MediateViewCommand extends SimpleCommand
    {
        /**
         * Each View is destroyed once it is moved away from,
         * thus Mediators must also be transient. Any existing
         * Mediator is removed, and a new one registered
         * along with the new View. Any additional Mediators
         * associated with the children of these Views should be
         * registered and removed in the onRegister() and onRemove()
```

```
    * methods of the View's Mediator.
    */
    override public function execute( note:INotification ):void
    {
        var view:View = View( note.getBody() );
        var mediator:IMediator;
        switch ( view.className )
        {
            case "LoginView":
                facade.removeMediator( LoginViewMediator.NAME );
                mediator = new LoginViewMediator( view as LoginView );
                break;

            case "ListView":
                facade.removeMediator( ListViewMediator.NAME );
                mediator = new ListViewMediator( view as ListView );
                break;

            case "InfoView":
                facade.removeMediator( InfoViewMediator.NAME );
                mediator = new InfoViewMediator( view as InfoView );
                break;

            case "FormView":
                facade.removeMediator( FormViewMediator.NAME );
                mediator = new FormViewMediator( view as FormView );
                break;
        }
        if (mediator) facade.registerMediator( mediator );
    }
}
```

The List View

```
<?xml version="1.0" encoding="utf-8"?>
<!-- LIST VIEW -->
<s:View xmlns:s="library://ns.adobe.com/flex/spark"
    xmlns:fx="http://ns.adobe.com/mxml/2009"
    destructionPolicy="never">

    <!-- LIST STUFF HAPPENS HERE -->

</s:View>
```

CHAPTER 10

Onward

If you are an experienced PureMVC developer, you will now have less to explain to your coworkers who are not; just loan them the book (or show them where to buy it). If you are just starting out, then hopefully this book has given you an adequate understanding of what the PureMVC development process is like and the important points in the mindset for mastering it. As you seek to expand your skill with PureMVC, here are a few more tidbits to help you along your way.

Using a Debugger with PureMVC

Here is a short overview of the benefits of PureMVC from a debugging perspective. If you have never used your IDE's debugger, it's really simple, and I will show the basic steps here. If you are seasoned at debugging, I am sure you will appreciate the benefits of PureMVC's underlying organization of your application as soon as you set your first breakpoint and inspect the variables. As you may know, often, when setting breakpoints in your application, you cannot see stuff that the class you have breakpointed does not have a reference to, so while you can tell the state of your breakpointed class, it is hard to know what is going on elsewhere without setting breakpoints all over the place like roadblocks on Christmas Eve.

In PureMVC, setting a breakpoint on any executing line of any `Mediator`, `Command`, or `Proxy` gives you a reference to the `Facade`, which in turn gives you references to the `Model`, `View`, and `Controller`. They, in turn, give you references to all your `Proxy` and `Mediator` instances and `Command` registrations. And of course your `Proxys` and `Mediators` give you access to your services, VOs, and View Components. You can just drill into any other part of your application and inspect the properties. The series of screenshots, from Figure 10-1 through Figure 10-7, offer a quick peek at the `StoryArchitect` application.

```
60
61                    case AppEvent.SELECT_DRAFT:
● 62    Line breakpoint: ApplySelectionCommand.as [line: 62]  tDraft( null );
63                        context.selectDraft( DraftVO( event.data ) );
64                        break;
65
```

Figure 10-1. Setting a Breakpoint

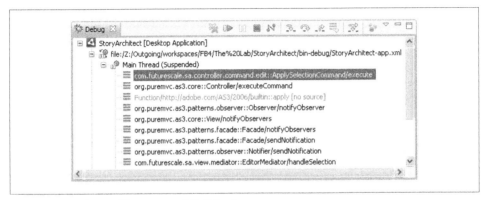

Figure 10-2. Launch the Debugger

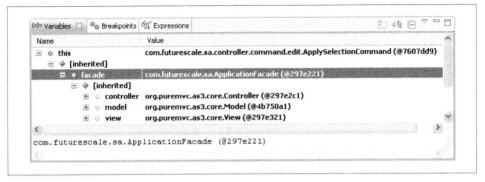

Figure 10-3. Debugger Transport and Call Stack

Figure 10-4. The Facade

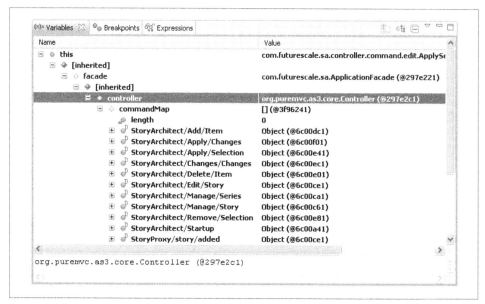

Figure 10-5. The Controller

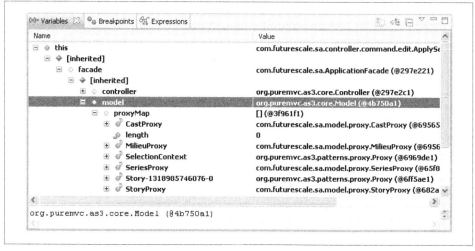

Figure 10-6. The Model

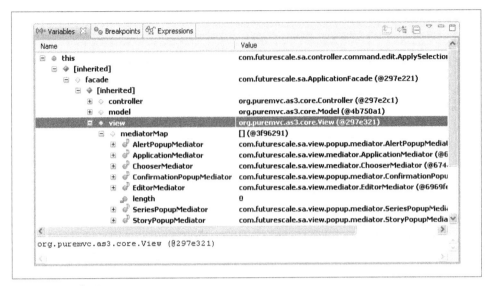

Figure 10-7. The View

PureMVC Utilities

One of the things about Open Source frameworks is that unless you clearly define and lock down the scope, the Creepy Feature Creature will have its way with the codebase, which will continue to grow features, which beget bugs, which beget bug fix releases with new features crammed in, ad infinitum. Developers then have to continuously upgrade to make sure their code still works and they have the latest and greatest capabilities. PureMVC was designed with the simple scope of achieving the MVC separation you can see visibly in the debugger above, and that you have hopefully seen the value of in this book. Additional features to handle common problems were to be added as a la cart utilities that you can take or leave as you choose.

You will find the Flex, Flash, and AIR utilities on the PureMVC website, under the Code section for AS3. Here are few of the really useful ones you might want to check out first:

- **AsyncCommand** (Flash/Flex/AIR)

  http://trac.puremvc.org/Utility_AS3_AsyncCommand

  By Duncan Hall (*duncan.hall@puremvc.org*)

  AsyncCommand and AsyncMacroCommand are similar to SimpleCommand and MacroCommand, but offer a solution to the problem of executing a series of Commands, each of which may need to complete one or more asynchronous operations before the next Command is executed. Standard and MultiCore versions are included.

- **Desktop Citizen** (AIR)

http://trac.puremvc.org/Utility_AS3_AIR_DesktopCitizen

By Cliff Hall (*cliff@puremvc.org*)

This utility provides the ability for PureMVC-based AIR applications to remember their window size, position, and window state (maximized, minimized, or normal) each time it is launched. It also provides a facility for requiring confirmation (or executing some shutdown process) before the application window closes.

- **Loadup** (Flash/Flex/AIR)

  http://trac.puremvc.org/Utility_AS3_Loadup

  By Philip Sexton (*philip.sexton@puremvc.org*)

  This utility offers a solution to the problem of how to manage the asynchronous loading of resources at any point during application runtime. It supports loading order dependencies, different media types, and is progress-aware. Standard and MultiCore versions are included.

- **State Machine** (Flash/Flex/AIR)

  http://trac.puremvc.org/Utility_AS3_StateMachine

  By Neil Manuell and Cliff Hall (*neil.manuell@puremvc.org*, *cliff@puremvc.org*)

  This utility provides a simple yet effective Finite State Machine (FSM) implementation, which allows the definition of discrete states, the valid transitions to other states available from any given state, and the actions that trigger the transitions. A mechanism is provided for defining the entire state machine in XML and having a fully populated StateMachine injected into the PureMVC app. Standard and MultiCore versions are included.

- **Undo** (Flash/Flex/AIR)

  http://trac.puremvc.org/Utility_AS3_Undo

  By Dragos Dascalita (*dragos.dascalita@puremvc.org*)

  `UndoableCommandBase` and `UndoableMacroCommandBase` are similar to `SimpleCommand` and `MacroCommand`, except they give you the ability to implement undo functionality in your application by maintaining a history of `IUndoableCommands` that have been executed. Currently only a Standard version is included.

Other Resources

A lot of people use PureMVC all over the world and a number have taken time to give back to the community in various ways. Their contributions come in the form of helpful discussions in the forums, ports of the framework to other programming languages, ports of the Best Practices document to other written languages, demos, utilities, debugging tools, project templates, training courses, insightful blog posts, and more.

It would be impossible to list them all here, but here are some highlights:

- **The PureMVC Project Website**

http://puremvc.org

By Futurescale, Inc.

Go here first to explore the documentation, community, and code.

- **PureMVC Forums**

  Join here: *http://contact.futurescale.com*

  Read/Post here: *http://forums.puremvc.org*

  If you are interested in actively working with PureMVC, you should sign up for a forum account and acquaint yourself with the available material. For several years now, the community has hashed out the biggest issues that arise in day-to-day coding with PureMVC. Chances are a question you have probably has been answered there at some point. But if not, please join us and chime in with your thoughts.

  Unfortunately, relentless spambots have forced us to shutdown the ordinary forum sign up process and implement a robot-proof facility. Please enjoy another fun Flex/PureMVC experience when you join using the wizard at the URL shown above. Follow the path starting with *Request Access to Futurescale-operated Forums.*

- **Darkstar PureMVC Roamer**

  http://darkstar.puremvc.org

  By Futurescale, Inc.

  The PureMVC Universe is expanding; roam it with Darkstar. As it has grown in popularity, a lot of content has found its home on PureMVC website, but who wants to navigate through web page after web page to get to it? Discover the Code, Community, and Documentation resources of the PureMVC project in an interactive network node browser. Built with Flex and PureMVC Standard Version.

- **KapLab PureMVC Console**

  http://lab.kapit.fr/display/puremvcconsole

  By KapIT

  This professional tool helps Flex and AS3 application developers that use the PureMVC framework for AS3 (Standard or MultiCore) by providing them deep insights on what happens with all instances of the important framework actors: `Notification`, `Command`, `Mediator`, and `Proxy`.

- **PureMVC-Gen**

  https://github.com/gjastrab/puremvc-gen

  By Greg Jastrab

  PureMVCGen is a ruby gem that wraps an ANT-based code generation utility for generating PureMVC ActionScript code. Currently for PureMVC Standard Version only.

- **Piping the Machine: PureMVC MultiCore with Pipes and the Finite State Machine**

  http://bit.ly/xpeco

  By Joel Hooks

  A great introductory article on modular programming with PureMVC. It combines these key utilities in a simple application that really shows off the power and simplicity of MultiCore. Completed application and source code included.

- **Garbage Collection in a MultiCore Modular Pipes Application**

  http://bit.ly/tuG4QQ

  By Simon Bailey

  The result of a deep study into proper GC handling with modular, piped PureMVC apps. All the steps essential to ensuring that memory is freed when you dispose of a module. Completed app with source code included. App shows memory stats as you add and remove modules.

- **PureMVC TV**

  http://puremvc.tv

  By Futurescale, Inc.

  A series of presentations by the PureMVC project architect delivered in a custom slide show format with audio narration. Includes *Standard Version Overview*, *MultiCore Version Overview*, *StateMachine Utility Overview*, and *Getting in the Groove* (building a music player application in MultiCore with the StateMachine and Pipes Utilities).

About the Author

Cliff Hall is a Software Architect with over 25 years experience in the industry.

His career has run the gamut from writing games in machine language for Commodore 64 and Apple II to implementation of large-scale, object-oriented, enterprise applications.

In 1993, he created Synapse: The Multimedia Journal of the Eclectic—the first CD ROM–based digital magazine (or "digizine"), which delivered multimedia text, audio, video, animation, and interactive VR through an organic user interface nearly a year before the first web browsers appeared.

Also a musician, he has scored planetarium soundtracks and performed at diverse venues from Manhattan clubs to a festival in the Puerto Rican rainforest. His current recording project, *Sea of Arrows*, can be found at *http://seaofarrows.com*.

He is the owner of Futurescale, Inc., where he builds Rich Internet Applications for major corporations and cutting edge startups worldwide. He is the Architect of the Open Source PureMVC Framework.

Engage him to build your next application at *http://contact.futurescale.com*.

Get even more for your money.

Join the O'Reilly Community, and register the O'Reilly books you own. It's free, and you'll get:

- $4.99 ebook upgrade offer
- 40% upgrade offer on O'Reilly print books
- Membership discounts on books and events
- Free lifetime updates to ebooks and videos
- Multiple ebook formats, DRM FREE
- Participation in the O'Reilly community
- Newsletters
- Account management
- 100% Satisfaction Guarantee

Signing up is easy:

1. Go to: oreilly.com/go/register
2. Create an O'Reilly login.
3. Provide your address.
4. Register your books.

Note: English-language books only

To order books online:
oreilly.com/store

For questions about products or an order:
orders@oreilly.com

To sign up to get topic-specific email announcements and/or news about upcoming books, conferences, special offers, and new technologies:
elists@oreilly.com

For technical questions about book content:
booktech@oreilly.com

To submit new book proposals to our editors:
proposals@oreilly.com

O'Reilly books are available in multiple DRM-free ebook formats. For more information:
oreilly.com/ebooks

O'REILLY®

Spreading the knowledge of innovators   oreilly.com

The information you need, when and where you need it.

With Safari Books Online, you can:

Access the contents of thousands of technology and business books

- Quickly search over 7000 books and certification guides
- Download whole books or chapters in PDF format, at no extra cost, to print or read on the go
- Copy and paste code
- Save up to 35% on O'Reilly print books
- **New!** Access mobile-friendly books directly from cell phones and mobile devices

Stay up-to-date on emerging topics before the books are published

- Get on-demand access to evolving manuscripts.
- Interact directly with authors of upcoming books

Explore thousands of hours of video on technology and design topics

- Learn from expert video tutorials
- Watch and replay recorded conference sessions

Lightning Source UK Ltd.
Milton Keynes UK
UKOW05f1053210915

258994UK00001B/48/P